Rav Dovber Pinson

THE JEWISH
BOOK OF

Life *after* Life

HEAVEN REINCARNATION N.D.E. SOULS AFTERLIFE

Rav Dovber Pinson

THE AFTERLIFE JOURNEY · THE AFTERLIFE · SOULS · THE AFTERLIFE EXPERIENCE · NEAR DEATH · REINCARNATION · HEAVEN · RESURRECTION · HEAVEN & HELL

THE JEWISH
BOOK OF
Life *after* Life

IYYUN PUBLISHING

Published by IYYUN Publishing
650 Sackett Street
Brooklyn, NY 11217

http:/www.iyyun.com

Iyyun Publishing books may be purchased for educational, business or sales promotional use. For information please contact: contact@IYYUN.com

Cover and Book Design: Rochie Pinson
Cover and Interior Illustrations: Rochie Pinson

pb ISBN 978-0-9914720-0-0

Pinson, DovBer 1971-
The Jewish Book of Life After Life
1.Judaism 2. Spirituality 3. Philosophy

This book was made possible by
the generous support of the

Nagel Jewish Academy

In honor and loving memory of

SHALOM DOVBER ע"ה

בן יבלח"ט
ר' מרדכי משולם

CONTENTS

OPENING..1

CHAPTER 1
Here & Now...11

CHAPTER 2
Who Are We?...19

CHAPTER 3
Consciousness..31

CHAPTER 4
Immortality...69

CHAPTER 5
Near Death Experience...80

CHAPTER 6
Soul Leaving Body..121

CHAPTER 7
Reincarnation..131

CHAPTER 8
Individual Memory, Collective Memory.. 171

CHAPTER 9
Afterlife Journey...188

CHAPTER 10
Eternity & Corporeal Existence 217

CHAPTER 11
And Therefore...230

NOTE TO THE READER...240

ENDNOTES...243

OPENING

"There is no greater joy than the resolution of doubt" *(Teshuvas Ramah 5. Toras Haolah 1:4).* The opposite is equally true. When there is nagging doubt and crippling uncertainty there is little room for joy. All psychological pain stems from insecurity and separation, whereas all real joy comes from clarity and connection.

A fundamental aspect of the fear of death is a fear of the unknown. Part of the pain we experience when a loved one passes is founded on a crippling uncertainty of what happens next:

Where does the person go?

Where is their soul?

What has died and left us, and what still remains?

When a loved one leaves this world there is a dreadful void and a deep cave of unknown darkness surrounds us. It is a fearful place that we are forced to enter into by circumstance where no light seems to shine. We are left with a rip in the seam of our certainty, a gaping hole in our understanding of life.

The Torah acknowledges the pain of this loss and confusion and in response offers us a wealth of wisdom and insight into the journey of the soul after it leaves its body and enters into a new reality.

In exploring the great body of Torah wisdom regarding the soul that we have been gifted with, the intention is to illuminate the dreadful shadow of death and loss with the light of life, clarity and knowledge.

The life of the soul is indeed the true life. The body is a temporary vessel allowing us to live in this world and achieve our Tikkun, the ultimate potential and actualization of our life's purpose.

Normally, we think that we are a body and that we have a soul, when in truth, we are a soul and we have a body. Our soul begins its journey long before our body, and the journey continues forever after.

In exploring the life of the soul we must always remember that what is most essential is this very moment. Through a deep understanding and appreciation of the soul's life and journey we can begin to live more fully in the eternal now; where past, present and future all merge and align as one.

The Difficulty of Language

When beginning to explore a big topic such as this, an immediate challenge presents itself: how to describe the indescribable; how to contextualize in conventional language that which functions on another plane; how to speak, using physical language, about the world of spirit.

Verbal language, the most common mode in which humans interact and exchange ideas, is designed to describe concepts housed and operating within a four-dimensional time/space reality (i.e., existing in some region of space during some interval of time). This method of communication is sufficient when it is employed to transmit sensory-based knowledge. The difficulty arises when we use these very same earth-bound tools to portray the spiritual (i.e., that which is outside of space or time).

When we wish to communicate something related to what occurs in the afterlife we often attempt to describe the process by employing spatial or temporal metaphors. For instance, the soul ascends into space, in the after life of time. This kind of language then defines the way we think about these issues. Which leads one to ask, "Where does the soul go?" As if there is a place for it to go.

Many years ago when a crew of Russian cosmonauts first returned to earth after orbiting space they held a news conference. During the question and answer session a high-ranking Soviet official asked them, "Having circled the earth and gone into the heavens, have you found G-d?" When the response was in the negative, the following day's headlines in all of Moscow's leading newspapers read triumphantly: "Communism is right, there is no G-d." They assumed and wanted to portray to the masses that after having gone into space (i.e., the Heavens) and not having found any sign of a Supreme Being, their communist doctrine, that there was no G-d, had been vindicated once and for all (chas v'shalom/Heaven forbid).

Ask a child, or for that matter an adult who is spiritually immature, where G-d is present and he will instinctively point above. But as we grow and expand our perception we slowly realize that 'up there' is merely a metaphor, a manner of speaking, and that the Creator is not literally somewhere out-there in space. The same holds true with regard to the afterlife. We tend to use terms like the soul went… and is in…and many other dimensionally related terms, while in essence what we are trying to convey is the dynamics of a reality that is beyond any description or conventional language.

Despite this challenge, we too will use language in our own exploration. Yet we must keep in mind that when we speak of a 'soul' as being 'higher' or 'lower,' for instance, these terms are not to be taken literally or linearly.

We need to think in terms of inter-dimensional fields of consciousness or awareness, not separated or segregated by hierarchies of space or time. There is nothing after life because life never ends. Life moves from one level to the next, always going higher and then even higher — although the word higher is in itself misleading, for there is no space as we understand it in those realms.

Another language-related issue that often emerges when discussing matters of the spirit is the issue of confusing metaphor for reality. It may sound quite comical today, but serious medieval theologians debated about how many angels were able to dance on the head of a needle. This is a clear case of mistaking the menu for the meal, and the map for the actual terrain.

A qualified teacher, along with a degree of spiritual sensitivity and maturity on the part of the student, is needed in order to decipher the poetic metaphor from that which is intended to be taken at face value.

Often, a mystical or spiritual teaching is meant to be read as a metaphor; other times a more literal interpretation is in order. And yet, occasionally such a teaching may paradoxically transcend and include both perspectives at once.

Take, for example, the creation story. The Kabbalistic view of creation is such: Prior to creation the Ohr Ein Sof/Boundless Light was too overwhelming to allow anything other than itself to exist, and so it went through a Tzimtzum/Contraction of its infiniteness, thereby allowing space for the finite/other to emerge. In addition to describing the process of creation, this metaphor also teaches us that at times the infinite within us, the unbridled soul, needs to contract itself so that we can function properly as healthy, well-adjusted human beings in this world. Love that is overbearing does not allow for any other expression. Infinite passion and tireless yearning ceaselessly expressing itself may hinder our ability to go about our life and contribute to society in a civilized manner. Here, in the case of this Kabbalistic teaching about the process of creation, we have an example of a teaching that can be understood both as a metaphysical account of creation and as a practical lesson in our day-to-day life.

With respect to the afterlife, the clear divide between an actual description of an occurrence and its metaphorical understanding is even more obscured. Concepts such as rebirth and reincarnation are perfect examples of this ambiguity. The holy Zohar, the primary text of Kabbalah, teaches: When a person passes onward, their soul is forbidden to leave the body and is unable to be in the presence of the Creator or to enter a new body until its previous body has been buried. The soul is unable to reemerge in another life-form until its former body is interred (*Zohar* 3, p. 88a).

On one level this teaching is simply relating information regarding what occurs immediately following death and providing a rationale for an immediate burial. On another level it is imparting a powerful existential message. It is suggesting that past experiences are not to be ignored and left unburied, so to speak. Rather, they need to be dealt with in order for one to fully move on. A negative/death experience must be buried and put to rest in order for one to move on with their life in a conscious and compassionate manner.

Reincarnation/transmigration communicates the idea to us that there are many paths and phases in life. Perhaps our challenges, and even our mission, may change throughout our soul's journey. And yet we can only move forward if we fully move on from our previous path/incarnation.

Still, sometimes a cigar really is just a cigar and the teachings are meant quite literally. The soul really does reincarnate and sparks of the soul do in fact journey on into new forms of life. The trouble, however, is that we are immersed in physical reality and so we tend to use three-dimensional imagery, symbols and language to describe experiences that are purely spiritual in nature. As we embark on this journey together, let us keep this in mind. Otherwise we may become completely lost in semantics and bogged down in details that distract us from the bigger picture.

Why Learn About the Afterlife?

The desire to know and explore what will occur in the afterlife stems from an innate human curiosity, much like the curiosity that landed man on the moon. More importantly, this inquiry arises from a deep desire to see life work out. For many of us it is quite frightening to think that evil people just get away with what they do and that good people are never compensated. When people observe the righteous suffering and the 'bad guys' prospering, one of the ways to come to terms with this cognitive dissonance is to say, "Just wait until they get to the next world, to the afterlife, then they will get what is coming to them."

For many people, the entire concept of immortality and the perpetual survival of self is a psychological cushion intended to help them make sense of a world that, at times, seems awfully unfair and unjust. Even though a belief may be comforting, believing in something does not make it real, although, it does of course make it real to the person who believes in it.

And so, in the face of such pressing existential questions we turn to the Torah for guidance. We turn to Sinai, the lowly mountain in the desolate wilderness covered in the clouds of glory, from which the Divine voice made itself known in the world. In addition to the Torah itself, we also turn to the spiritual teachers of our past and of our present generation, living masters who dedicated their lives to translating the word of G-d into the life of man.

Regarding the unknowable cosmic future, the time of redemption, the great twelfth-century philosopher and legalist, the Rambam writes, "Pertaining to all these issues and related things (referring to the arrival of the Moshiach), no one knows how it will occur until it actually occurs... Therefore, one need not ponder these issues, and should not consider them as fundamental, for they do not bring reverence for nor love of the Creator" *(Hilchos Melachim, 12:2)*.

Ideally this kind of philosophic detachment should be one's default approach to such matters of distant past or future events, but not everyone is that mature and ready to admit the limits of their own knowledge. Many people find that it is precisely these kinds of issues, and the intimate knowledge of their intricate details, that help them cultivate awe or love for their Creator, and by extension a deeper appreciation for life itself. For many, the contemplation of just such unknowable events and outcomes actually inspires them to become better people in the present moment. For instance, in the context of considering the afterlife, one may be motivated to weigh their every thought, word or action more carefully and consciously because of the knowledge of just how far reaching the effects of their behaviors and states of mind can be. In this regard we can see that these teachings can play a positive and functional role in a person's developmental path of character refinement.

No two people are alike and no two people are motivated or inspired by the same tune or idea. Broadly speaking, there are some people who find that the notion of their mortality is precisely what empowers them and provides them with perspective. Having some sort of defined and limited lease on life gives them more focus and meaning in their life today. For these people, the awareness—or fear—of death enriches their life. The very suggestion that all things come to an end forces them to develop themselves more definitively and appropriately. The parameter of the frame, so to speak, gives them a proper structure to work within. Otherwise, life feels much like attempting to sketch out a coherent image on an endless canvas. They fear that if it were not for the feeling of finitude there would simply be too much to accomplish. And often, creativity is best served within a defined paradigm and framework.

On the other hand, there are those for whom the knowledge that there is more to life than what the eye can see, both now and in the future, allows them to operate with less fear. They are then able to approach life with greater love and a more profound sense of harmony. For such people, the idea of an afterlife is both empowering and liberating.

In general, it appears that while modern man is advancing with leaps and bounds in many areas of life, such as how to enhance life performance and even extend it, in regards to the existential fear of death, man is becoming ever more immature and regressive.

Since the so-called 'death of god,' what has emerged in its stead is the 'birth of death.' What we have now is a modern mind that is devastatingly plagued by an overwhelming fear of death and old age.

The converse is also true: With the birth of G-d in one's awareness — individually or culturally — there is a corresponding 'death of death.' The more Hashem is alive and present within one's life, the less room there is for fear and anxiety.

Ironically, when people stop believing in Hashem(whatever that means), they do not necessarily believe in nothing; rather they often begin to believe in anything. This anything often includes all types of strange ideas that foster even greater fears and more invasive anxieties.

Our intention in discussing the afterlife is not to make a person feel morbid, downcast or dispirited. On the contrary, the sages of the Talmud suggest that one embark upon the path of Teshuvah/self-transformation and reintegration a day before death. But the obvious question arises: How is one to know when that will be? To which the Sages reply: "Let man do Teshuvah today lest he die tomorrow" (*Shabbos*, 153a). Since, Mors Certa, Hora Incerta/death is certain, but the time when it will occur is uncertain, we should do Teshuvah today and every moment. The question, however, remains: why say "a day before death," and not phrase it this way, "Do Teshuvah now because perhaps you will die today?"

One of the ways to solve this is by understanding that the sages had no intention of telling a person to think of their death as being imminent or looming. All that would accomplish is to create more anxiety and further apprehension. So, to paraphrase, they said, 'Sure you will live today, but think about tomorrow. And if you really think of it deeply, you may want to reorganize your life today.' Thinking of life and its fickle nature may provide us with the proper perspective regarding what is most important in our life right now (*Maor Vashemesh*, Parshas Vayigash).

The mind becomes wonderfully sharp and clear when the prospect of death is seen as a real and inevitable conclusion to life. Remember, what seems foolish in the light of death is essentially foolish at all times. And so, although the conversation is about tomorrow, regarding today there is still much more energy to be spent and life to be lived. Every moment is a precious gift. The present is truly a present. Let us try to honor it and live this way.

Now we will move to deeply explore who we are and what happens on our journey into the Afterlife.

Note:

In order that we may come to a fuller understanding of the following teachings concerning the afterlife contained in this book, we will begin with a substantial introduction to the nature and makeup of the soul as it is explained in the traditional sources throughout the ages. This background knowledge will enable the reader to make more meaning out of the sometimes cryptic and mind-bending teachings related to the soul's life after life. Chapters 1-3 therefore deal primarily with these foundational teachings concerning the soul and the relationship between this life and the next.

CHAPTER 1
Here & Now

Sanctification of Time

*I*nherently and by its very nature the discussion of the afterlife is fraught with difficulties. Other than the obstacle of trying to give language to and describe the ineffable, the trouble with engaging the mind with thoughts of an "after-life" is that it may cause the mind to forget the primacy of life in the present. Perhaps it is for this reason that traditional Torah texts often do not deal with the hereafter in an overt way.

Yet, scattered throughout the vast body of Torah wisdom one can, through extensive research and elastic interpretation, construct a comprehensive outlook on the afterlife journey, which is precisely the intention of this book. In general, this kind of information is more encrypted than apparent, more obscured than evident. The ambiguous tone of much of this material tells us that the fundamental priority of Torah is life in this world and not the next; the goal is to achieve connection, intention and inspiration in this moment and not to be fixated on some far-off future or remote past.

An excellent illustration of this is found in the very first Mitzvah we were given at the time of the Exodus. The common misconception is that the first Mitzvah heard was the first of the Ten Commandments, but that is not quite true. The first directive received by Klal Yisrael as they were about to be liberated physically, mentally and spiritually is that they should count and sanctify time. "This month shall be for you the beginning of the months…" (*Shemos*, 12:2). In other words: Witness the rebirth of the moon and consecrate that time as Rosh Chodesh/the New Month. Count the months, calculate time and establish the first day of each month as a significant and noteworthy occasion.

Though scientifically speaking it has been proven that time and space are not absolutes (i.e., there is no definite space or continuous flow of time), still, in the Newtonian universe in which we functionally reside, time and space appear as fundamentals. What defines properties within a four-dimensional universe is that they are located within a certain region of three-dimensional space (i.e., left/right, front/back, up/down), while at the same time they are also positioned within a particular wavelength of time.

Life as we know it exists in a spatial and temporal state of affairs. This is precisely the first liberating concept the nation of Israel needed to know on its journey towards freedom, autonomy and ultimate responsibility: It is of the utmost importance to sanctify time. It is this very act that allows one to recognize and celebrate the holidays and Shabbos. Additionally, it is also necessary to sanctify space in order to have three-dimensional objects with which to perform Mitzvos in the physical world.

This paradigm stands in stark contrast to that of their 'masters,' the Egyptians. The Egyptians were a death- and after-life obsessed civilization, dedicating much of their energy to preparations for, and in anticipation of, the hereafter. The first collective Mitzvah was thus to sanctify the seemingly mundane time of daily life.

Ultimate freedom is gained by achieving a mastery over all elements of creation, time included. As such, spiritual life and growth is never about asceticism or detachment and always about involvement and transformation. With full mastery comes the power to hallow the seemingly mundane and to transform the ordinary passage of time into a sacred rhythm of seasonal story, song and celebration.

The Purpose is in the Now

It seems that the mind is always on one excursion or another, either back into the past or forward into the future. The last place the mind wants to settle is in the present. Worry, anxiety, regret and guilt are some of the more pronounced emotions found within the human psyche. Evidently, those who worry about what will be think too much about the future, while those who suffer from regret and resentment are paralyzed by the past.

Whenever our minds are turned toward the past or future, we lose our connection to the time in which life is truly unfolding, the now. Life is best served when it is lived in the present moment. Overall, where we were in the past - even a past life - or who we will be in a future life is not as relevant as where we are at in this very instant.

What will occur in the future afterlife may not be, at least for some people, of great value to their understanding of the life they lead today. When our lives are meaningful in the present, we do not need to look into the future or back into the past for validation or confirmation.

As Rebbe Yochanan Ben Zakai, the illustrious Talmudic sage, was laying on his deathbed, he began weeping bitter tears and declared: "In the afterlife there are two paths upon which my soul can journey, one is the path leading to heaven, the other to hell. I do not know on which of these two paths I will be guided" (*Berachos*, 28b).

This poignant existential doubt punctuating the end of a saintly life is unquestionably a mark of profound humility. Still, what is interesting in this anecdote is that this noble sage never found this existentialist dilemma of any importance until he was at the end of life. While in the midst of living a meaningful life dedicated to learning, teaching and perpetuating goodness, he did not give the afterlife any thought. He had no desire to be absent from the present by peering into the future and getting lost there.

In another moving tale, the great teacher and founder of the eighteenth-century Chassidic movement, the Baal Shem Tov, relinquished his portion of the afterlife, and was only too happy to do so.

The story goes like this:
Once, on the day before Pesach/Passover a woman who was having difficulty conceiving a child came to visit the Baal Shem Tov and brought him many of the necessary provisions for the Holiday. Being in a joyous and heightened mood, the Baal Shem offered her a blessing to give birth to a healthy beautiful boy that very year. Since this woman was genetically unable to bear children, it was decreed that although the blessing would be fulfilled, the Baal Shem Tov would lose his share in the World to Come for having troubled Heaven, as it were, in such a

manner. When the Baal Shem got wind of the decree he became quite joyous. Now, he said, he would be able to serve his Creator with a complete heart, without any ulterior motives or thoughts of future compensation or rewards (Notzar Chesed, Chap. 4, Os 22).

The Future in the Present

Notwithstanding the aforementioned thoughts, a conversation is required to explain many of the esoteric teachings regarding the soul's journey and the afterlife. This is due to the fact that for many people the notion of an afterlife empowers them to be more conscious, compassionate and sympathetic individuals in real time, today. Torah, by definition, means both wisdom as it caters to the mind and the intellect as well as experience, as the word Torah itself comes from the root word Hora'ah, which implies a kind of life lesson (*Nesivos Olam*, Nosiv Ha'Emuna, Chap. 2. *Tifferes Yisrael*, Chap. 9). Therefore, the wisdom of Torah incorporates the totality of one's being, including both mind and heart, trickling down into one's actions. Torah knowledge is not simply designed to enlighten or entertain the mind, offering more information to grasp; rather, it is meant to inspire a complete reorientation of self and all aspects of one's life. Its teachings climax when the mind is educated, the heart is inspired and the actions are aligned.

As a result, a persuasive and quite compelling motive to explore the afterlife is that its wisdom may be harnessed as a productive tool in navigating one's day-to-day life. Not as mere brain-games entertainment, but rather as a form of life-altering knowledge. The realization that actions taken within a three-dimensional universe can exert influence on more subtle planes of existence, and that events in the present can have consequences and repercussions throughout all of eternity, can empower a person to be more thoughtful and intentional with their behavior in the present moment.

Part of the discourse of life necessitates that we at least include mortality, even if not necessarily the afterlife, into any real existential discussion. Death is a part of life as much as its culmination. To speak of life while ignoring mortality is incomplete. Death is an inseparable element of life, as important as living life itself. While for some the conversation concludes with mortality, others find that conclusion unsatisfactory. For some, to live life fully and to learn how to navigate their way demands a degree of understanding as to what will happen in the future. This knowledge allows them in their present state to be less fearful and more open, less ridden by anxiety and more attuned to love and embracing the moment.

There are those who are more philosophically inclined and suggest that faith is a derivative of fear. This position posits that, ultimately, religion is developed as a collective response to humanity's fear of death. As one skeptic put it succinctly, religion is a necessary invention to "create happy endings to miserable lives." Yet, what these thinkers do not know or care to realize is that the Torah does not explicitly refer to an afterlife. Undoubtedly, the belief in the afterlife is part of the oral tradition as it is encoded throughout the Torah. Yet as far as the written Torah is concerned, the afterlife is not blatantly mentioned, as it is not the essential point.

One of the many reasons offered for this notable omission is that the main objective of Torah is life in the present moment, as opposed to some theoretical past or future. The Torah's aspiration is to imbue us all with a consciousness beyond fear so that we can approach life with love, openness and harmony, making it all the more possible that we will be able to shift our awareness in order to see creation as Hashem views creation: "And G-d saw all that had been created and behold it was very good" (*Bereishis*, 1:31). Through a gradual, experiential process of inculcating oneself with the teachings of the Torah, a radical worldview comes into focus. If the world once seemed cruel, unfriendly or indifferent, a thread of warm light begins to seep in, instilling reality with goodness, optimism and positive affirmation, bringing with it a sense of purpose, meaning and ultimate destiny.

Life in this realm of existence is indeed beautiful! All we need to do is open our eyes. Once when Rebbe Eliezer was quite ill and distraught, Rebbe Yochanan came to pay him a visit. Finding Rebbe Eliezer sitting in darkness and weeping he asked, "Why are you crying? Is it because you have not sufficiently innovated in the realm of Torah? Don't you know what we have learned? 'All are equal, those who have attained more and those who have attained less, so long as their hearts were directed towards Heaven.' Is it because you lack material sustenance? I am sure you understand that not all people possess both tables of wisdom and prosperity. So why is it that you are crying?" "I lament", Rebbe Eliezer responded in an existential fashion, "for all the beauty that will one day be swallowed up in the dust of the earth" (*Berachos*, 5b).

The awareness that life, at its core, is beautiful in its original state of creation, and needs to be celebrated as such, is also applicable to the future and the afterlife. According to the Torah all of existence is rooted in Divine goodness and consequently all is good, every moment, whether in this life or the next. Just as we are encouraged to participate with openness and joy in the life we have now, part of this positive admission is functioning fearlessly and deeply understanding that what will be in the future is also good. An eloquent way to phrase this perspective is found in the final words of the nineteenth century Chassidic Rebbe, Rebbe Yisrael Yitzchak of Alexander; "It was good, it is good, and it will be good."

A world of infinite goodness can be appreciated even while being embodied within physical form. When a human being lives life fully and is entirely in sync with the goodness and divine spark within, the outer world will reflect the inner and he will experience a world bathed in light and positivity. The future transcendent existence merges with the present and transforms life today into the most beautiful of experiences. Adjusting to such a paradigm can afford one the power to behold, as a poet once described, "a world in a grain of sand, and heaven in a wild flower;" as we will all come to see, "Earth crammed with heaven, And every common bush afire with G-d."

CHAPTER 2
Who Are We?

The Body as Self

Who are we? And what constitutes our beingness?
This is the most essential of all existential issues.

To begin to discover who we are, let us start by examining that which is the most apparent and most manifest, our body. In truth, to many people the physical aspect of self is a primary component of their self-evaluation and sense of value. The more beautiful their bodies appear, the more confident they are and vice versa.

But what is the body?

In its widest definition, the body can be viewed as a collection of cells working in harmony to form a larger unit we call the "body." Simply put, the body is nothing more than a grand total of some 150 pounds of protoplasm that we can see, feel, touch and maneuver as we desire.

But can this be the real you? Towards which body part can you point and accurately say that if you lose that physical property you will become less of who you are now? Say a person loses a limb, a hand or foot for example. Does that person in any way become 'less' of who they were prior to the injury? Certainly not. So what makes up the real you? If you are not defined by your arms, legs, toes or fingers then why assume that you are the sum total of these individual fragments?

For argument's sake, one can still insist that indeed we are the sum total of all the parts of the body. Individually, the body is seen as an assemblage of loose parts, but as one cohesive unit it become a "you" or an "I". To counter this line of reasoning we ought to contemplate the fact that the substance of every human's body, even a healthy and robust one, is constantly being replaced and regenerated. At a sub-nuclear level the elements that make up our atoms, the quarks and gluons, are perpetually being annihilated and recreated. So we are in fact never the same body as even a moment ago.

As odd as it may seem, ninety-eight percent of the atoms in your body were not there a year ago. Your skin, for instance, is renewed every month; your stomach lining, every four days; and the surface cells that actually come into contact with food, every five minutes.

Being that the body is ceaselessly being regenerated, it would seem peculiar to acquire a sense of identity and selfhood from that which is in constant flux. Thus the identification of the self with the body alone is apparently ruled out. The body, material as it is, is ephemeral by its very nature. Even the brain, the storage house of all experiences and knowledge, is in a state of continual flux. As such, the challenge then becomes to discover that which is lasting, permanent and unchangeable. To find that which exists as the background and also the thread that runs through all of life, the 'thing' or 'self' that experiences all of the various changes and vicissitudes of life. What is that which was "you" at age 8 and is still "you" right now?

Additionally, based on the fact that we can feel and are aware of the sensations of our body, we arrive at the greatest confirmation that we are, in fact, not our body. For that which can be felt is not, by definition, the feeler. As that which can be observed is not, by definition, the observer. We cannot be that which we are conscious of. When observing some object or thinking of it, you cannot be that object as you are separate from it. If you think about your body it means that something separate from your body is doing that thinking. Now that we have established that our bodies are merely a part of us, who are we?

The Essential Self

In the quest for self-discovery the challenge becomes to locate and identify the experiencer and the feeler, as opposed to just the experience or the feeling. And what is that which experiences and feels? The soul.

Our soul is the unchanging aspect of self that registers all of the changes we go through, the continuous element that observes that which is discontinuous, the uninfluenced essence that informs the influenced. As the body's cells are constantly being modified, so are our emotions, thoughts and actions, but the "I" that resides within, the essential self, remains the same.

The I within is eternal.

Everything else comes and goes, but our 'I', the uncorrupted awareness of being alive, when not overly-identified with anything such as the body, mind or heart, is always the same, never shifting and never modified.

Soul is who and what we are. It is not the part of us that is temporal or spatial, nor is it entirely subjective or dependent upon external stimuli. It is the deeper 'I' that is independent of environmental influences or physical identities. It is the internal I, the I that was there when you were young and said "I am young," the I that was there when you grew a bit older and said "I am middle-aged," and the I that is there when you will say "I am old." This is the perennial I, the soul. The soul is the deeper inner Self which incorporates all levels of beingness, including the small surface i of selfhood. It is the ultimate reality and the true I of existence.

From time immemorial, man, in his search for 'self,' has come to describe that unchangeable divine property in various terms ranging from the soul, the psyche, the light, to the more modern terms such as the force, our center or ground of being or life energy; and yet for the most part they all describe, or wish to describe, the same underlying pulsating reality.

The soul, as we tend to call it, is a unique spiritual manifestation with a distinct individual 'personality.' And it is through the lens of our 'individuated' soul energy that we come to experience life.

The path towards self-actualization and fulfillment is found in this discovery — the unearthing of and living in accordance with the 'infinite' spark of the Divine that is made distinctly present in our own finite lives. The fullness of the I of the world, the infinite, is revealed beautifully in the individual finite I-ness of self.

Essentially, our soul is not something we possess. It is, in fact, who we are.

It does not belong to us, it is us.

The soul is the higher self. It is the self of our limitless potential, the part of us that stands above ego, selfishness, aggression and resentment.

Our soul is the backdrop of our being, the light that illuminates and clarifies our thoughts, emotions, actions and, effectively, the whole of life.

The soul is the observer of life, the essence deep within that perceives life and witnesses it unfold. Certainly, the known cannot be the knower. If you know your thoughts than you cannot be your thoughts. If you know your passions, emotions and desires, you cannot be them either.

An important medieval philosophical/ethical text attributed to the twelve-century French Rishon, Rabbeinu Tam, states that: the soul is the knower of the known. In other words, the soul is the small voice beyond the mind that impels the conscious mind to think, feel or act.

Anyone who has ever dabbled in meditative techniques, or for that matter in the philosophy and mechanics of the mind, knows that the mind appears to have a mind of its own and that there are levels beyond levels within the mind itself. When a person tells himself to think a particular thought it is one level of mind telling the more surface level what to think. And yet, having this awareness tells us that there is still a deeper level of mind that experiences this consciousness. This mental exercise can literally extend itself to no end. At the deepest level, it is the essence of Self – the only I there is who governs and instructs the I of the ego or small self.

Take a moment and try to be aware of the wall in front of you. Now, be aware of that level of mind that is aware of the wall. Then go a little further and try to be aware of that which is aware of that which is aware. You can do this exercise ad infinitum until you reach a point where you realize that there is a part deep within that is, as some tend to call it, the absolute self or the pure witness. This can never truly be grasped because it is what grasps. It can never truly be understood because it is the understander. It cannot be known on an intellectual level, for it is the knower of knowledge.

In its highest, deepest and most pristine form the soul, or the higher self, is part of the divine I. It is part of that reality wherein the knower and the known are one and the same. This is what the Rambam describes as the level of Ultimate and Unconditional Beingness (*Hilchos Yesodei HaTorah*, 2:10). It is the aspect of reality where the experience and the experiencer, the observed and the observer are one and the same. This level of consciousness is rooted in a 'place' beyond duality, polarity, separation or contextualization.

Similar to the Creator who defies and transcends human logic, the soul embodies the paradoxical and its 'entity' is oxymoronic, at least to the human mind functioning as it does within a constricted reality. The soul is both infinite and finite in its properties and expression. As challenging as it may be to intellectually grasp this, the soul is simply a finite sliver of the infinite, a holographic particle of infinitude. Perhaps this conception violates our way of thinking, and it does so because the brain is basically a binary instrument. For the brain it is either up or down, left or right, 0 or 1, but never both at once. But this is only a limitation of the physical brain, which has difficulties navigating or interacting with a universe that allows for simultaneous and contradictory coexistence.

On a simple level this means that although each soul is rooted and sourced within genuine oneness, as it emerges, while it still sparkles with infinitude, it also becomes quite distinct, unique and defined as it descends to become embodied within the individual and particular human form.

The Particulars of Infinity

Pulsating within each of us is a Self that is uniquely us. Each person has distinctive, unmatched and unparalleled characteristics of soul personality. "In the afterlife," the celebrated Chassidic sage, Rebbe Zusha of Anipoli said, "I will not be asked, 'why were you not more like Moshe?' Rather, I will be asked, 'why were you not more like Zusha?' Why did you not reach your own full potential?"

Just as no two people are alike physically, so too spiritually. Everyone in his own way is exceptional and unique. Each soul demands to be expressed and experienced differently. Every human being has a unique spiritual vocation to be fulfilled that only that person can fulfill.

The individual and particular way that we each experience life is a result of the individuality of our soul. Not only do we see the world around us through the lenses of our own distinct soul, but the world around us is also affected and influenced by the uniqueness of our soul. Whoever and whatever a person connects with emotionally, intellectually or physically he indelibly imprints this 'personality' of soul upon those people, places and events. Every relationship we entertain becomes colored and imprinted — hopefully for the better — with our soul individuality.

Scientific exploration and advancement has come a long way. Today we have computers, which are essentially artificial intelligence machines that can solve mathematical riddles and win chess games against the best and brightest of human chess players. Yet for all that A.I. technology (artificial intelligence) can do it still lacks a human soul. A self-enclosed machine lacks the ability to go outside itself and judge itself. A.I. can perhaps know how to react and what to do in a certain situation, but it will never know why it reacts this way and not in another way. A.I is deficient of what some philosophers call "qualia," it is incapable of experiencing pleasure, desire, anxiety or hope. True, it can carry out brilliant arithmetic calculations and play a wicked game of chess. Even so, while it plays does it know anything of playfulness? Does it get excited by winning or agitated when losing? Does it worry about its next move or regret its previous ones?

Extending this idea a bit further we come to the realization that the various 'things' that demonstrate our humanity, primarily our emotions, are experienced by each of us differently. It is, in fact, quite wrong to assume that "all happy families are alike." Happiness and sadness, or for that matter the whole gamut of human emotions and feelings are unique, singular and felt by each of us in our very own distinct way.

It should be added that although the soul, at its core, is unchangeable as it is the element of permanence that runs throughout one's life, the manifestations of the soul are certainly not static or stagnant. The more dense levels of soul, those aspects that are more present as everyday consciousness, are continuously expanding in relation to our life experiences. The more externally oriented aspects of soul are in a perpetual state of flux and growth, as will be explained in more detail in future chapters.

Body & Soul

True, what defines us is our soul, and yet another valid truth is that we are psychosomatic beings, comprised of soul and body. Part of who we are is a reflection or a result of the body we possess. On some level we are who we are because or despite of the bodies we possess. Take, for example, short people. Some short people tend to be more introverted and timid because of their physical contour and some short people act quite the opposite and, instead exhibit characteristics of what is referred to as a Napoleon complex, they are aggressive, loud and domineering. Mentally speaking, the shaping of one's internal personality may be forged by physical appearance — heavy, thin, tall, short, black, white. How we perceive ourselves affects the way we project ourselves, for better or worse.

In all honesty, whether our personality is a result of our physical appearance, meaning that a facelift or the like will actually make us feel different or if alternatively, our physical presentation is a manifestation of our personality or soul, ultimately depends on us. It reflects whether we choose to live life from the inside-out or from the outside-in. People who choose to live from the inside-out will project their physical form as an accurate representation of their spiritual state — their body will reflect their soul.

By its very nature the body is a physical representation of the inner pattern of the soul that animates it. The question is whether we live in alignment with that level or not. When we do live from the inside-out and cultivate a healthy internal outlook the result will in fact be apparent in our physical posture.

All in all, the body is not a prison for the soul. The body, by its nature, is not an alien abode meant to oppress and stifle the spirit. Rather, "the bodies of the upright are holy" (*Zohar* 3, p. 70b). "The body is like the parchment upon which the Torah scroll is written" (Ritvah, *Moed Katan*, 25a. Ramban, *Torah's Ha'adam*, Inyan Keriah).

The Creator's infinite presence is to be found everywhere, from the sublime to the mundane, from the spiritual to the physical, even in as coarse a matter as corporeal existence. The body is, at least in its natural and original form, a physical expression of the spirit that animates it and gives it life.

Body and soul can and should be the best of friends. When the body and soul work in unison, when they are both engaged in positive acts and thoughts, then the body can be a vehicle through which one can experience freedom. When the converse occurs the body becomes a prison, an oppressive place instead of a liberatory one.

In the book, "The Jewish War," the historian Josephus recounts a personal anecdote. Josephus was a commander of the Jewish forces in the Galilee, before becoming the historian we know him to be. The story is that once as his forces were battling the Roman general Vespasian, later to become the Emperor, his battalion was being overrun and so he retreated with his remaining men to a cave. Realizing their predicament they urged him to commit suicide. To them it was better to die by their own hands than to be captured by the enemy.

Josephus was not very fond of this idea and so he addressed his fellow comrades: "Why are we so anxious to commit suicide? Why should we make those best of friends, the body and the soul, part company?" Although there is a measure of controversy regarding the integrity and reliability of Josephus' work, still there is much wisdom to be found in his books. Certainly there is more than a kernel of truth to this argument of his. Body and soul can indeed become the best of friends, all one needs to do is acknowledge their interdependent relationship.

To exist as a fully functioning human being is to be joined as one, including both body and soul. There is no body without a soul. When the soul departs the body is no longer animate. And there is no soul without a body. Without the body it is just pure spirit, not human (*Tanchumah*, Parshas Vayikra, Chap. 6).

Body and soul are likened to a blind and lame person combined as one entity (*Sanhedrin*, 91b). One sees but lacks the legs and arms to reach its heart's desires. The other can move and act but has no inkling of when and where to go. The soul empowers us to see but it is the body that actually gets us there. The body moves about but it is the indwelling spirit that directs the movement. Together in harmony they join and can become the best of friends.

As all good friendships demand, each partner is required to equally contribute to the relationship. As it is in every other area in life in order for the proper outcome to occur there needs to be correct internal balance. As much as the body needs to be appreciated for its value, it must not become an object of obsession or worship. Indulgence and involvement yes, but not overindulgence or inordinate preoccupation.

This position expands to all measure of the material world. Someone once came to the home of Rebbe DovBer, the saintly Maggid of Mezritch, to pay him a visit. To say the least, the Maggid's home was far from impeccably furnished. Perhaps a wobbly three-legged chair was all the Maggid had to offer the visitor. After some time spent discussing the issues at hand, the guest mustered the courage to ask the Maggid why he chose to live this way. Transposing the question, the Maggid asked the guest, "And where is your beautiful furniture?" "Well," he said, "now I am on the road and on the road you travel lightly. But at home it is a different story." Smiling gently the Maggid said, "You speak words of truth. We are all now on the road and on the road we travel only with what is most valuable and important. On the road, all the other 'things' of life are reduced to being insignificant and immaterial."

Genuine integration and wholeness is achieved when we come to view both the body and the soul in the light of their respective purposes. Spiritual equilibrium is attained when there is harmony and symmetry between the various aspects of our personality and being. This occurs when the physical body/self expresses the spiritual soul/Self, and when the body is seen not as a hindrance or shackle binding the spirit, but rather as a vehicle for the most powerful forms of soul expression.

The self is a beautiful synthesis of body and soul, ego and transcendence, finite matter and infinite spirit. A fully-realized selfhood can only be complete when we are fully aligned and able to create a perfect harmony between all aspects of our being, when we are fully present and our I-ness is effusively lived on all levels of our existence. When we achieve this, the 'perfect self' is expressed and we become fully aware of how our finite i is one with the infinite I of all reality.

CHAPTER 3
Consciousness

We will now go deeper into our exploration of the thematic nature of the soul. In the broadest sense the historical development of Jewish philosophy and thought can be broken down into three general eras: the Tanach, Talmudic, and post-Talmudic periods.

The Tanach period (Tanach is the acronym for Torah, Neviim/Prophets and Kesuvim/Writings) began some 3,300 years ago with the exodus from Egypt, and concluded some 2,500 years ago with the destruction of the first Beis Hamikdash in the year 586 BCE. That entire era was known as the age of the Neviim and the Kesuvim.

As prophecy came to a close the Talmudic age of the sages began to take shape starting with the period of the Ta'na'im/original teachers and continuing on through the Amara'im/interpreters. The era of Ta'na'im lasted for a period of about two centuries, coming to an end with the passing of Rebbe Yehudah HaNasi in the year 219. C.E. While the period of the Amora'im, and the era of the Talmudic sages as a whole, came to a close with the completion and publication of the Talmud some fifteen hundred years ago, in the year 500.C.E.

Following the conclusion and publication of the Talmud, the so-called 'modern' or post-Talmudic period began, ranging from medieval times to the present. In this period, of which we are a part, there appears to be two predominant trends of thought — the mystical/kabbalistic and the rational/philosophical.

Our intended aspiration in the context of this book is to demonstrate the nature of the soul according to the way it is represented in the traditional sources. As mentioned, earlier Tanach texts for the most part shy away from offering particular details regarding the nature of the soul, or of the afterlife in general for that matter. At most, Tanach may drop a coded hint or symbolic allusion that would later be extrapolated and fully articulated by the sages of the Talmud and Medrash. Due to this developmental nature of the ideas communicated by and contained within the canon, our journey towards discovering the nature of Self and Soul will begin with the Talmudic sources; from there we will venture onward until the modern period is reached.

Ego & Transcendence

Recognizing the apparent existential conflict and duality that exists within the human heart, the Talmudic sages named what they saw as the two competing internal forces: The Yetzer Tov/good inclination and the Yetzer Ha'ra/evil inclination (*Berachos*, 61a).

According to our Sages' model, the human psyche has a noble and good inclination with a proclivity towards performing positive and life-affirming actions; this inclination is driven towards transcendence. At the same time, a person also has an ego-driven inclination, a force that desires and craves survival on the level of the physical. This inclination is fixated on the preservation and protection of the ego, the sense of individual self or personal I-ness.

To simplify, we can say that the former inclination is the transcendent "inner-oriented" self, while the latter is the egoic "outer-oriented" perception of self; the former is selfless, altruistic and other-oriented, while the latter is self-centered as it seeks to satisfy its own appetites and aggrandizement.

Yetzer is from the Hebrew root word Yatzar, meaning to form or to construct. We are a being who is in a constant state of becoming, constantly shaped and influenced by the choices we make — intellectually, emotionally and actively. The choice of whether we approach life from a transcendent or egocentric gestalt is entirely in our own hands; as such, our Yetzer is our own Yatzar. Meaning that we are in no small part responsible for the being we have become. We are co-creators in partnership with the ultimate Creator of the form and function of our life.

In the beginning of Bereishis, as Hashem is creating the universe, it says: "G-d observed creation...and behold it was very good." According to the ancient Rebbes of the Medrash, the words 'very good' refer to the "evil inclination." "For were it not for our Yetzer nothing would compel us to build a home, enter a relationship, have children, or do business" (*Medrash Rabba Bereishis* 9:7). The ego gives the human being certain essential powers and drives necessary for survival and self-preservation. In this context we can see that the ego-based inclination is not purely negative, in fact, it is quite important and valuable as it guarantees physical security and survival.

In fact, it is quite normal and adaptive to be self-centered up to a certain point. According to the Rebbe's comment concerning the necessity of the Yetzer Ha'ra, self-centeredness itself can be the initial incentive to participate and partake in any number of physical activities, even ones that have positive repercussions beyond their initial satisfaction, such as raising children.

Creativity is a good example of the ego's involvement in the initial stages of the process, and yet this kind of ego-drive can only get the person to the drawingboard, but no further. An artist once shared his personal method of painting. "What first arouses me in the morning and gets me into the studio," he writes, "is my ego." The ego tells him, 'today you are going to make a wonderful painting.' But slowly, as he sits in front of his canvas he realizes that the ego itself is unable to paint. It can get him to the studio and even put the brush in his hands, but it cannot actually create a work of art. While his ego attempts to paint, the critic within keeps on telling his ego that the painting is going nowhere. Finally, when his ego is completely humbled into submission and collapses, the still small voice within him surfaces and inspires him to paint.

The ultimate objective is not to completely surrender or relinquish one's ego, but rather to include and embrace it within a more transcendent and noble context; in effect, to render it less opaque and make it more transparent to the light of the soul. Through this process one is attempting to harmoniously integrate the surface self with the deeper Self so that one's external state expresses one's inner reality. True, the Ra/negativity of the Yetzer/inclination needs to be purged and uprooted, but the actual drive and vitality itself ought to be harnessed and utilized towards a positive and constructive purpose. Without the Yetzer, the I of self (including positive ambition, passion and the general drive of life) would come to a standstill. This Yetzer/urge is the "yeast in the dough," which raises us beyond our current state, ensuring that we strive to reach or even exceed our dormant potential (*Berachos*, 17a).

One illuminating Talmudic tale specifically illustrates this point. Once, a group of sages converged and decided that it was time to permanently remove the Yetzer/Eros from the world. Moving heaven and earth, their request was granted. They finally had within their grasp the most elusive, powerful and salacious of all animalistic desires and energies, the libido. After three days life seemed calmer and yet the zest and vitality of life was missing, so much so that they were not even able to find a freshly laid egg. Simply put, their life was now void of passion and thus static, flat and dreadfully bland. Contemplating their predicament they had no other choice but to allow the Yetzer to once again roam freely (*Yumah*, 69b). The message this tale wants to convey is quite clear: these so-called animalistic passions, desires and drives are not negative per se. It is only when their energy is focused in the wrong direction that they become detrimental and spiritually/morally harmful.

A name often used for this level of beingness is 'the animal soul.' Animal in that it acts, or better yet reacts, instinctively and reflexively similar to the rest of the zoological kingdom. What this soul seeks is the survival, perpetuation and aggrandizement of itself. It is the innate impulse for self-ishness that ultimately ensures the survival of the species, so to speak. This impulse is similar to what today is known as the Id, a self-serving, amoral and ethically impartial instinct.

Herein lies the ultimate internal challenge: the harnessing and piloting of this neutral inclination in the correct direction, ensuring that the ego is on the road to greater spiritual awareness and activity and not the opposite. When this does not occur and one sheepishly capitulates to the ego, the laws of inertia dictate that uncontrolled selfishness inevitably leads to innocuous vice and perhaps even to evil itself. The ego and anyone else in its immediate vicinity can survive simultaneously, but the moment the ego feels threatened, whether real or imaginary, it will attack.

The drive to get married or to go out and make a living is positive. The trouble arises when these drives are not properly balanced with the transcendent Yetzer. When people are one-dimensionally self-centered their relationships with others become vampiric and abusive, their business dealings become exploitative. So what begins as a neutral drive can end up as a source of negative and destructive behavior. As such, it is man who exaggerates these amoral inclinations, passions and necessities for survival into 'evil.' In this framework, the word Yetzer Ha'ra does not imply an 'evil' inclination, for it is not intrinsic within its nature to gravitate towards negativity. Rather, it is an inclination that can easily transform, when left unchecked, into an evil and dehumanizing force (*Tanchumah*, Bereishis, Chap. 7).

Ego Unchecked

Many psychiatrists and criminologists studying some of the shadier characters of society conclude that there is a common disposition found in many people and that is that they lack the capacity to be empathetic. They are unable to understand in their mind or feel in their heart the pain of another human being. What this means is that they cannot see themselves in another. And then there are those criminals who are naturally quite empathetic, they know very well the pain they cause. In this case the troubling thing is that they revel in causing others pain. What they are missing is compassion, the desire to not cause another person to suffer.

The most telling truth of this hypothesis is that all these emotional states, the deficiency of empathy or compassion, originate from an excessive dose of self-centeredness, which is aptly called narcissism. Individuals who spew anger and hate feel god-like and truly believe that they have the power and the right to decide whose life is dispensable and expendable and whose is not; whose life is worth saving, whose life is insignificant, and in the bigger scheme of things, whose life is simply just collateral. These inhumane people are so entangled and intoxicated with themselves that they cannot see past their own 'four cubits,' so to speak. There is no valid 'other' and every relationship is of an I relating to an it, an object to be used and perhaps even abused.

While the preoccupation with one's sense of self generally manifests as narcissism or hubris, it can also show up as a total lack of self-esteem and self-worth. In addition, it can be argued that narcissism is in fact a sign of a person who despises himself and thinks little of himself; his demands to be noticed are nothing but psychological defenses of a deeper existential lack. In any event, whether this self-centeredness expresses itself in exaggerated self-esteem or a complete lack thereof, or whether narcissism is rooted in self-love or self-loathing, essentially all these expressions are exhibitions of a person who is totally preoccupied with his sense of self and ego.

Clearly the above-mentioned construct of narcissism is an extreme example of self-centeredness. And yet the root of this behavior is not purely negative, but as noted earlier, it is the ego, which is biologically adaptive and physically beneficial. A minor form of narcissism is something that all human beings are born into.

The Course of Human Development

Young infants are notably selfish - if that word can be applied without any moral connotations; they think the world revolves around them and that everyone is there to serve them. They cry when they are hungry, they do not stop crying until they are fed, and they just go to sleep whenever they are tired. In fact, for the first few months of life there are no distinctions or separations, everyone and everything appears to be part of an all-encompassing extension of themselves.

The next stage is what is called 'Separation Individuation,' where infants come to realize their state of existential separateness, and as the child grows older and matures he comes to the realization that there are in fact other people with their own wants, needs and desires. At some point, the child learns sympathy and empathy, becoming capable of placing themselves in another person's shoes, as it were, and feeling another's predicament.

Looking at human development from this perspective, the life of a healthy individual can be seen as a perpetual decline in egocentrism and self-orientation, as well as a simultaneous and continuous incline of sensitivity and awareness of others. One's initial feelings are almost completely egotistic and selfish, and then, as one grows older, both physically and mentally, they become more selfless and transcendentally oriented.

We can surmise, from this developmental viewpoint as put forth by the Sages, that while the Yetzer Ha'ra - which is the egoic self-serving instinct - fully inhabits the body at birth (*Sanhedrin*, 91b. See however, *Tehillim* 58:4, *Rashi* ad loc), the Yetzer Tov - the good, transcendent inclination begins to develop at conception although it does not become fully absorbed and integrated within the body until the time of mental maturity. Traditionally, maturity is seen to begin for girls at the age of twelve and for boys at the age of thirteen. Intellectual and mental maturity, which includes the ability to value others and to discern and dispense proper judgment in meaningful decision-making, comes together with, and is the result of the transcendent element of soul coming more clearly into focus.

Once this transcendence begins to settle in, the life of a healthy and well-integrated person becomes a balancing act between these two forces. Self-centered action is necessary to get one out of bed in the morning to take care of oneself and their dependents, while the transcendent soul ensures that one's self-involvement does not come at the expense of other people.

Conversely, unidirectional transcendence, which results in a total surrendering of the "I" of self is also not considered a virtue, much less a spiritual state of existence. Rather it is considered more akin to a psychological breakdown. Ultimately, the outer i of self and the inner I of self need to be properly balanced against each other, and only then can the fullness of who we are be fully expressed.

Part of the Weltanschauung of the Yetzer Ha'ra is that it perceives reality as fragmented events and objects unrelated to each other and unhinged from their Source. Antithetically, the Yetzer Tov's outlook is unitive and all encompassing; it is able to sense the oneness of the Creator that permeates all of creation and all reality within the diversity of this seemingly splintered universe (*Akeidas Yitzchak*, Parshas Naso, Sha'ar 73).

The 17th century scientific revolution brought about the rise of atomism which views the world as consisting of fragmented particles, with each unit isolated in time and space. This construct inevitably spilled over into philosophy. When Locke asserted that the social whole is an illusion and the rights and needs of the individual were primary, all he was doing was taking the scientific hypothesis of his time to its logical conclusion as applied to social philosophy.

Years later, some spoke of the human being as an amorphous entity isolated within the impenetrable boundaries of the ego and concluded that people could never know each other in any real and intimate way. They went as far as to say that the commandment to "love thy neighbor as thyself" is the most impossible commandment ever written.

These sentiments are true if we take the human being to be nothing more than the ego, but certainly that is not the whole of us. Ego, and its attendant sense of separate individuality, is but our 'lower' surface-self. The soul is our transcendent aspect, our higher Self. There are those who unearthed the lowest nature within man, and did so unflinchingly and brilliantly. Conversely, we have the choice to unveil the higher levels of self and make them shine in all of their brilliance.

Let us return back to the ego for a moment. Being that the perspective of the 'self-centered' inclination is limited and confined it therefore informs the person to seek that which is rewarding in the moment. Effectively, it inspires the person to pursue only realities that can be immediately perceived and tangibly felt. In contrast to this impulse there is the deeper self, the transcendent soul that beholds the entire picture beyond what is right in front of its eyes in any given moment. As the transcendent aspect of self looks into the past, becomes aware of the present and envisions the future, it forces a person to take a deeper look at their life in order to take all of life and reality into consideration.

True, acting out a selfish urge may be satisfying in the moment, but ultimately it may prove to be counterproductive and detrimental. In the words of the sages, the lure of the Yetzer Ha'ra may be "sweet in the beginning, but will be bitter in the end" (*Medrash Rabbah*, Vayikra 16:8).

In general, selfishness breeds contempt for anyone who stands in the way of one's goals. It creates an inability to relate to other people as anything other than utilitarian cogs in the wheels of one's own desires. Eventually, it can even give rise to loneliness, and perhaps in the end, may be the source of apathy and despair.

The Illusion of Separateness

Here we have it — two forces — one pulling upwards, the other keeping us grounded, both battling for control of our consciousness. Yet, as extraordinary as it may sound, the truth is that this inner strife is, in large measure, an illusory form of imaginary combat; a kind of shadowboxing.

The Zohar - the book of illumination teaches that this egotistical inclination is in fact a divine messenger veiled in a mask of obscurity. It is sent to challenge us in our commitment to Hashem, to Torah, to Mitzvos, to goodness, to others, and to our higher Self (*Zohar* 2, p. 163a). The ego, which is the illusory sense of separate self and individuality, is but the surface reality. Practically speaking this means that rather than characterizing the ego as an existing adversary to struggle with, one may begin to realize that there is nothing other than the true Self, the I of all reality. Anything that exists outside the prism of connection to the true Self of the Creator is but a camouflage.

Transgressions and all negative activity lend credence to the ego and allow it to flourish as a separate and independent force. Conversely, transcending the pull of ego shows that the sense of separate and distinct individuality is but an illusion, in which case the inner 'battle' is then won without the need for a fight.

Evil, even in its most pronounced form, is like a shadow, a mirage or a phantom that has no energy of its own. Evil should not be engaged as an autonomous seductive force. There is only one truth, one reality. As a result one should not wrestle with internal negativity, for the more one fights it, the more one perpetuates its existence. The only way to rid oneself of a shadow is to open the floodlights and illuminate the empty space. Light up the void in which the darkness functions and it will no longer be a source of anxiety or ignorance.

Darkness and evil are the antithesis of the only real existence, which is called 'light.' Beyond being a romantic and idyllic image, this idea holds up rationally and psychologically. Many who lack empathy and perpetuate destructively negative behavior suffer from symptoms of rejection or neglect. Those who spew anger and hate are generally projecting their feelings of being unloved upon others. At the inner core man is good and decent. When people appear to behave contrary to this fundamental reality that is because they are reacting to stress, pain and a deprivation of the most basic human necessities such as security, love and self–esteem.

Illuminating Darkness

Older people who show tendencies toward this type of behavior were, for the most part without making generalizations or sweeping assumptions, rejected, unloved or unappreciated as children. Adults who lack empathy and compassion were once children who did not receive empathy and compassion themselves.

A child who suffers extreme neglect or cruelty in the hands of someone they think loves and cares for them will inevitably feel unworthy of love or concern. These self-degrading feelings can grow to such measures of self-contempt and loathing that, in the child's mind, the only way to survive is to become indifferent to others' evaluations and then, by extension, to others' feelings. If these sentiments are never countered with love and compassion from other people the child may completely shut out the external world. Just as they felt they were acted towards indifferently, they too will also become indifferent to others.

People who suffer from a low self–esteem, those who think they are unworthy, also believe that all people around them are similarly unworthy. Just as a person who is loved can love, those who were not loved have difficulty loving, and they transfer their experience of being despised and abused to the despising and abuse of others.

Certainly this perspective is not intended as an excuse for a lack of healthy relationships, nor is this interpretation meant as a rationalization or justification for such negative behavior. Though these arguments may be valid, still, it is the person himself, assuming he is a sane human being, who makes the final decisions on how to conduct himself. It is deleterious and counterproductive to live life in a state wherein one is constantly giving ultimate causality over to external circumstances out of their control (such as upbringing, environment and so on) to explain one's behavior or emotions.

Yet, if we do desire to help these emotionally crippled human beings, the best way would be to give them what they always needed, to show them love and compassion, and communicate to them that they do indeed matter. Give them the 'basic trust,' as some have called it, to help them build a healthy and well-balanced self-esteem. Within standards and a sense of commitment, teach them that they are loved - Hashem loves them unconditionally - and that they are cherished and valued. Shed light on their darkness and watch their negativity dissipate.

Pre-personal vs. Transpersonal

Earlier it was explained that children are naturally self-conscious before they become conscious and aware of others. Being, however, that mankind is a hybrid of ego and transcendence, the idea of sympathy and emotional identification can also be found within young infants. On the one hand infants epitomize selfishness, thinking and acting as if the world is but an appendage of the self. While on the other hand they also display remarkable signs of advanced empathy.

Researchers who have studied the development of young infants have observed that babies tend to cry in response to the crying of other babies, a fact which Rashi already states a thousand years earlier. (*Rashi*, Sotah, 12a) They weep in response to a human cry more than to any other, which shows that their weeping is not merely a response to the noise of crying babies. Rather, they cry as a demonstration of empathy with the other crying baby.

It should be pointed out that these emotions of the infant are not transpersonal (i.e., beyond the self), as before there can be a 'trans-personal' awareness there needs to be a personal identity. Before someone can be conscious of others they need to be conscious of themselves.

In other words, identity must be ascertained before it can be transcended.

It is more likely that infants are unconscious of both themselves and others and thus identify others as being merely part of themselves. Recall that the first Yetzer to thoroughly enter the body is the ego-centered one, the one who sustains and reinforces the self, and it is only later on once a person has developed a level of self-consciousness (thirteen for boys, twelve for girls) that the transcendent dimensions of soul enter the body. Genuine transcendence of self is demonstrated when a mature and self-conscious individual shows empathy. To be mature and empathetic is to be transpersonal, moving beyond the small/separate self in order to enter into the more expansive space of the divine Self, and thus to identify oneself with another.

As such, we are not the Noble Savage; nor are we Natural Brute who would destroy all of life if only society would allow us, as the cynics counter. Rather, we possess both tendencies; we have a dual nature, one being deeper than the other. The objective is to refine and integrate the ego, the more surface nature, within the greater context of the transcendent self.

Beyond the balancing and reorienting of the ego it is also important to make sure that the source and foundation of our choices are based on the Yetzer Tov – the transcendent drive. When one's organizing principles are purely survival based, their behavior follows the ego. Life is then interpreted as an extension of, and in service of, the small i, and therefore there will be always friction and tension between the separate I of selfhood, and the rest of the world. Life on this particular wavelength is full of petty competitiveness and unnecessary drama. Life in an I-centered monologue is thus limited to one's I becoming more significant — via power, money or prestige — than everyone else's I.

In this state of neediness and dependency there is no attainable satisfaction as nothing is ever enough. Conversely, when one's ground of being is the Yetzer Tov — the G-dly, transcendent self — the actions one performs are bound up with the Infinite power of the universe. This serves and empowers not only the individual who taps into the vast resources of the soul, but has a positive cosmic consequence for all of creation, of which we are each a co-creator. Living transcendently empowers all of reality to be more positive, sympathetic, open and giving.

The Philosophers & the Soul

Up until this point we have explored the soul purely from Talmudic-era sources. We will now move into the post-Talmudic perspective.

There is a fundamental disagreement between the founding fathers of Western philosophy (Plato and his disciple Aristotle) regarding the nature of the soul. Plato theorized that the soul has a separate and distinct existence from the body, implying that the soul is an independent form that exists prior to the body and lives on long after the physical form has decomposed. On the other hand, his student Aristotle conjectured that body and soul are united as matter and form. The soul is the form and the body is the matter. Together as one unit they comprise a complete human being.

This essential schism can be detected throughout the entire body of philosophical literature. Some ardently agree with Aristotle, while those who adhere to Plato's position, vehemently disagree. The dualists declared: "I know that I have a mind. I know that I have a body. And I know that the two are utterly distinct."

The daulists envisioned a fundamental separation between mind and matter, between res cogitas/a thinking thing, and res extensa/an extended thing, between mental substance and material substance. Forced to find a point of interaction between the soul and body-machine he postulated that it is the pineal gland situated in the middle of the brain (actually located at the triangle point between the two eyes and the forehead) that brings these two aspects of the self into communion. This, he believed, was the gateway or interface between the physical body and the nonphysical mind/soul.

On the other hand, the monists believed that within the universe — mankind included — there cannot be two principles. According to them, mind/soul and body are, in effect, attributes of the very same substance.

Interestingly, there is a passage in the Zohar that says that many of the Greek pre-Aristotelian ideas are similar to that of the Torah's (*Zohar* 2, p. 236). This is certainly true in the case of the soul. For the most part, the soul, as interpreted in the Platonic definition of soul, is more akin to the post-Talmudic/Torah sources although with some minor and major variances as will be explored below. Also, it is important to point out that unlike Plato, who viewed the body as a prison cell for the soul, the Torah reaveals to us that the body is a potentially holy vessel, with which the soul joins at birth, giving us the opportunity to consciously and creatively direct the body with its animating presence.

A relatively widespread theory is that there is actually no dependent or particular soul and each soul is just a part of the whole. From this perspective everything in the world is interdependent and there is no such thing as an isolated core individual. The personal soul is simply an extension of everything else that makes up the All. This is not consistent with the truth as revealed by the Torah, which views each soul as being distinctly unique, with leads to each person having a unique mission and purpose, as will be explained shortly.

Three Levels of Soul:
The Natural Soul, the Living Soul, The Rational Soul

Classical Jewish philosophy speaks of three aspects of the soul. The lowest soul or dimension of soul is called Nefesh Tivis/natural soul, otherwise called Nefesh Tzomachas/vegetative soul — the raw bio-energy that impels physical expansion and growth. This soul-type is one that is found in all of animate reality, whether in a blade of grass or in a mighty beast. It is a sort of Nefesh Hazana/nutritive energy assisting and securing sustenance for the life-form. It is the energy responsible for the vital functions of the body: blood circulation, breathing, growing and remaining healthy.

A step deeper is the Nefesh Chiyunis/living soul, sometimes called the Nefesh Behamis/animal soul or Nefesh Margeshes/sensitive soul — the dynamic energy that does not just grow upwards while staying in one place like a plant, but also roams outwards, far and wide. This soul impels one to move about and distance oneself from the root of one's generative origin. It is a soul energy that human beings share with the entire zoological kingdom, as it represents the animal within.

The deepest and highest soulular expression is referred to as Nefesh Maskeles/rational soul, the power of reasoning. This is the objective property within the self, the inner voice that seeks honesty and truth, thus it also craves for more than what is offered in one's immediate surroundings and seeks transcendence. Because this soul affords man the notion of genuine freedom it is also this soul that allows a person to distance himself from his own nature and from his center of being, as freedom by definition works both ways.

Though each of the above levels of soul has dominant features (for example the animal within is instinctively reflexive and emotional, and the rational aspect is primarily objective, proactive and intellectual), nevertheless, each of these souls is in themselves complete. In other words, each one of these souls embody in a holographic and inter-inclusive way, the entire array of personality traits, ranging from the innermost desires up until the power to materialize actions. Essentially they each contain the four main components that constitute a soul, which are:

Ratzon - Will / Seichel - Intellect / Midos - Emotion / Ma'ase - Action

The difference, however, is that on the level of the vegetative soul, all elements, dimensions and traits are animated by the desire to secure existence and make sure the person is physically healthy and developing. When a human being operates on this level of soul all his capacities are directed towards physical growth and expansion. All his instincts, feelings, emotions and intellectual capabilities are focused on acquiring more food and getting more sleep, securing and sustaining a healthy body, much like a tree that bends towards the sunlight to make sure it receives the proper nourishment.

One who functions on a higher/deeper dimension of soul seeks more than simple physical growth; he also strives to preserve his stature and status, much like animals do in their own kingdom. His instincts, emotions and intelligence are all garnered to help him climb the so-called ladder of 'success,' which is predicated upon the social law that whoever has more 'things' and more 'territory' wins.

Beyond this, we also have the power to operate from the place of our rational soul, making sure that our objectivity and desire for inner truth and spiritual growth overrides our baser instincts, urges and lusts.

With the power of the rational soul we can go beyond our own biological immediacy and mechanical necessity and experience a transcendence of pure self-centeredness, becoming sensitized to the 'others' in our midst. Empathy, compassion, sympathy and all other relational feelings are manifestations of this soul, the soul that allows a person to experience more than just him or herself.

A major contention between the various early Torah-grounded philosophers who discuss the three souls is whether they are three separate and unrelated souls (*Mekor Chayim*, Sha'ar 5, Chap. 20. *Even Haezer*, Koheles 7; 3. *Toras HaNefesh* Chap. 4), or three manifestations of one singular force (*Shemonah Perakim*, Chap. 1. *Sha'ar HaShamaim*, Maamor 11. Meiri, *Pesicha Beis HaBechira*, p. 15. *Derashos HaRan*, Derush 3. *Shivilei Emunah*, Nosiv 6. *Magen Avos*, Part 2:4, *Akeidas Yitzchak*, Bereishis. Sha'ar 6. Rebbe Yosef Ibn Tzadik, *Ha'olam Hakatan* pg 37).

The Zohar (1, p. 206a) and the later Kabbalists (*Pardes Rimonim*, 24:11) speak of the soul as one unit with multiple layers. On the deepest level there is only unity, absolute oneness — and the soul, which is rooted in the unity of the Creator, certainly reflects this unity.

Interestingly, there are, even amongst those who argue in favor of three distinct souls, those who maintain that these souls are all interconnected and powerfully linked. The soul in its most pristine state begins as a 'pure thought' and gradually evolves or devolves into the shape, form and coloring of the human configuration, eventually enclosing itself within the human body and enlivening it.

At its most dense individuated level the soul is interrelated and interfaced with the more refined parts of the body, such as the circulation of the blood, and through them vitalizes and gives life to the human body (*Kuzari*, Maamor 2:26). It is thus the part of soul that is considered the physical aspect of the spiritual, which unites with the most spiritual aspect of the physical, the literal life-force of the body, which is the blood.

As a whole, the vegetative and animalistic souls are much like the earlier mentioned Yetzer Ha'ra, the self-oriented and survival-based instincts of the ego. Impulsive, impetuous and involuntary behaviors are by-products of operating on these levels of consciousness. On the other hand, well thought-out, intentional and deliberate conduct is a reflection of one who is performing on the level of the 'rational soul.' The discerning soul is what galvanizes, enables and empowers the individual to rise above their immediate predicaments and consciously act as he or she so chooses.

Form and substance, Tzurah and Chomer, is another way to divide these elements of soul. Chomer/substance is the actual physical configuration of the body and its spiritual life force, the energy that enters the body at conception and slowly dissolves at death. Tzurah/form is the intellectual cognitive soul that lives on even after the substance of the body is no longer existent.

Tzurah is the level of soul that offers man the power to elect freely. It is the creative aspect of personality. The rational element of the soul allows a person to become a creator of his own limited perspective and transcend his genetics, environment and past perspectives in order to be more than just a machine reacting out of mere instinct and habit.

When we live life on this level we will find that our behavior is proactive and not reactive, we will feel empowered knowing that we are the ones who choose life. Ultimately, we are not enslaved to what life has to offer, whether it is experienced as good or bad, for we have the power to conceptualize, articulate and interpret reality however we desire.

Intellect, so to speak, lets the 'fly out of the box.' Intellect affords a person the opportunity and vision to see life from a deeper vantage point, a perspective not limited and restricted to the immediate moment. It offers man the openness and clarity to sense that there is more to life than what the physical eye encounters and it invites and evokes deeper, and then even deeper, exploration.

Beyond Duality

The mind creates distinctions. No matter how profound an understanding of the soul is, when that understanding is articulated in the language of philosophy, duality and separateness reign supreme. Yet, the Mekublim/ the Kabbalists take us beyond this paradigm (*Bereishis* 2:7 Ramban and Rabbeinu Bachya, ad loc). Unlike the philosophers who speak of the soul as a superior intelligence created by its creator and thus possessing an existence of its own separated from its Source, the mystics view the soul as a part of the Divine, a direct emanation of the Emanator (*Shefa Tal*, Hakdamah. Yavatz, Avos 1:17, 3:19. *Pardes Rimonim*, Sha'ar 32:1. *Ohr Ne'erav* 1:3. *Maamor HaNefesh* 3:8. Shalah, *Ohr Chadash*, p. 23. *Chesed LeAvraham* 2:44. *Tanya*, Chap. 2). The idea that we are created in a divine image is not simply seen as an abstraction or an allusion of sorts, but is taken quite literally. Deep within the heart of man there is a spark of the Infinite, an aspect of his personality that is not part of creation, but is rather an actual part of the Creator. This spark is thus a divine property that links a finite human being to the awesome power of the Infinite.

Whereas the intellectual element of soul has the ability to lead us to the door and point us in the right direction so to speak, the Divine soul actually takes us through the door. With the rational soul we can contemplate, ponder and perhaps even understand the oneness of the Creator, still it is only with the Divine soul that we are able to actually open that door and walk through it, so as to actually experience and sense the incredible truth of infinite oneness.

Finally finding the home of his beloved he knocks at the door and the voice from within asks, "Who is there?" And he answers, "It is I, your beloved." But the voice says, "This home cannot contain us both." And the door remained closed. Disgruntled and disheartened he runs deep into the forest. Alone in solitude he prays, meditates and engages in all sorts of spiritual practices. After a full year has passed he decides to return. Once again he knocks on the door and the voice from within gently says, "Who is there?" And he says, "It is thyself." And the door was opened.

This transcendent element of self gives us the ability to ascend into higher/ inner spiritual realms of reality, linking heaven and earth and allowing us to transcend our very own physical limitations. What's more, not only does the soul show us the door and illuminate the path, it inspires entry and advance. More than access, the soul actually prods us in such a direction. Just as a candle flickers and leaps upwards, the soul, which is the candle of Hashem, yearns to return to its Source. Beyond the subconscious there is a deeper sub-subconscious, so to speak, which is the yearning of the soul to reconnect with Hashem, it's Source of life.

Parenthetically, the alleged 'death wish' can perhaps be understood, at least in this light, as a distorted and unrectified manifestation of the soul's deep longing to be rejoined with its Source.

Five Expressions of Soul

In addition to the three levels or types of soul that we explored earlier, there is another five-tiered model of the human soul expounded by the Kabbalists. This five-tiered model does not negate the usefulness of the previous three-fold model. In fact, it builds upon it, using the three aspects of soul already covered as the foundation for the next two levels of soul that are added in this new model.

*NOTE: It should be said at this point that due to the extremely long and roundabout history of Kabbalah, revealed as it has been in different places and in different times, there are often numerous models available to explain the same idea or phenomena. These models should not be seen as mutually exclusive. More appropriately, they can be understood as different tools or keys that one has at their disposal to be used when necessary. The three-fold model of soul will at times be more appropriate or fruitful for the interpretation or understanding of a specific teaching or ritual practice, but sometimes the five-tiered model will yield greater, more relevant results. Do not be confused by the presentation of multiple models for the same thing, they are not meant to negate each other, but to function in a complementary fashion.

According to an ancient teaching the human soul is bequeathed with five names (*Medrash Rabbah*, Bereishis, 14:9). Each name represents various grades and dimensions of consciousness. Nefesh is the so-called lowest representation of the soul's energy, it is the part most bound up with the world of physical action; it is a functional consciousness. Ruach is an emotional awareness and state of consciousness. Neshamah is the cognitive and intellectual dimension of the soul. Chaya is the will, a transcendental consciousness. And Yechidah is a state beyond self-consciousness, where the soul is one with the All Inclusive Source of all life.

Originating from the Source of all reality the soul extends into the inner depths of the human being. The soul is likened to a beam of light. In its most pristine state the soul is in total harmony and oneness with the source of all light. Traveling 'downwards,' metaphorically speaking, the soul becomes less intense and brilliant until it manifests as the energy and life force of an apparently autonomous and independent entity. In truth, this apparent autonomy and independence is but an illusion, for there is in fact no completely autonomous entity independent of its Source and Creator. Yet this is how existence appears from our finite perspective.

These five levels of soul represent various degrees of awareness and means of relationship between the self and the external world. Employing the image of an ocean as a metaphor for the soul, the body of the ocean would be like the source of all souls, the All-Inclusive Oneness, with the more individualized elements of soul being likened to the individual waves (*Magid Devarav Le'yaakov*, Likutei Amorim, 53, p. 22. *Yosher Divrei Emes*, Shavuos). When looking at a wave from the perspective of the ocean, one can see that the wave is always part of the oceanic whole. However, for someone looking from a distance and seeing only the tip of the wave, each wave appears as an independent entity. The closer the wave is to the ocean the more apparent it is that it is indeed an aspect of the ocean from whence it came. Conversely, the further removed it is from its source, the more detached and autonomous it appears/feels.

In the higher reaches the soul is very much one with its Root. Gradually, as it devolves and descends its innate connectedness becomes less and less apparent. As the soul proceeds downward it sets into motion the process of particularization until the soul becomes the life force of an individual person. Yet, it must be pointed out that the emerging individualized soul is not merely a product of a spiritually unsophisticated awareness, rather it is a veritable reality just as any other reality, and its perspective is genuine on its own level.

There is a unique signature to each soul, a distinct personality, through which the person who carries that soul comes to experience and impact life. This state of soul individuality, the crest of the wave so to speak, beyond retaining its distinctive form during this life while vested within a physical body, also maintains its existence as a unique spiritual force in the afterlife. It never becomes part of the whole by losing its individuality, rather, after death the finite becomes enfolded within the infinite without losing its integrity, as the following chapters will illustrate.

Nefesh:

Nefesh is the energy of the physical, the ethereal of the material, the soul of matter, and the element that is the least conscious of its Source. Nefesh is related to bodily awareness, the world of doing, and everything connected to physical pleasure or sport.

The human instinct for survival is a coarse representation of this dimension of soul. Nefesh enables the body to persevere, organizing the cells and transforming them into a coherent whole that can sustain itself. There is a force that some theoretical scientists refer to as a morphic field, which is a type of energy-field that encircles each organism and prods it towards advancement and more intricate measures of complexity and diversity. This energy is analogous to Nefesh, the spirit that moves physical existence along its own path and towards its own development and growth.

Ruach:

Ruach is already a more refined and less materially related spirit — it is the world of emotions and feelings. A craving for self-expression is a manifestation of Ruach. Love, passion, and what is generally referred to as spirituality is connected with Ruach. Being moved by a work of art, a symphony of music or a beautiful person or object, are all associated with the soul dimension of Ruach.

Both Nefesh and to some degree Ruach are influenced by the body they come to inhabit. Their original brilliance can become somewhat obscured and clouded by the activities engaged in and perpetuated by the body. If such is the case, in the afterlife they may need to undergo a refurbishing and cleansing so that they can shine once again and regain their full transparent luster and awareness. Conversely, the deeper reaches of the soul remain pristine and pure, they are essentially unaffected by material or physical actions or concerns. Still, even these levels of soul need to wait until the lower properties are cleansed so that the soul as a whole can rejoin and become one with the Source above, as will be explored.

Neshamah:

Neshamah is an intellectual awareness, much like the rational soul that is discussed in philosophical texts. Neshamah is the power that allows us to be a creator in our own right, to choose and co-create our life by crafting the contexts within which our life occurs. Therefore, by taking an active role in forming and refining the perspectives that generate our psychic responses to the content or stimulus that we experience throughout our life, we can collaborate with the Creator, so to speak, in the creation of what is then experienced as "our life." Neshamah is the real I, the human in the being, the interior, deeper and realer self that makes those ultimate choices that determine our lives and shape our character.

Neshamah is the cognitive faculty of the human being, represented by the linear sequential manner of processing knowledge. Language is a derivative of this way of thinking. The linguistic mind, the ability to form comprehensive ideas and formulate communicative constructs, is a by-product of Neshamah.

In the book of Bereishis, when speaking about the creation of mankind, the Torah says, "Hashem blew into Adam's nostrils a Nishmas Chayim/a breath of life." The phrase Neshamah implies, according to many ancient commentaries, the spirit of speech (*Targum Onkulos* 2:7). It was at this particular juncture in the process of humanity's creation, the point at which humanity received the power of speech, that Adam became a full-fledged human being. The human is therefore ultimately defined by his G-dlike ability to articulate and express his thoughts, dreams and feelings to others. This fundamental impulse, of one human being sharing himself with another human being, is in fact the basis of society and culture. Civilization itself begins to form as a common language takes hold, transforming a loose-knit group of individuals into a cohesive unit, with shared elements of history, purpose and identity as communicated through myth, narrative, poetry, philosophy and law.

Collectively, the Nefesh, Ruach and Neshamah (known by their acronym, Naran) comprise normative human consciousness; in other words, they constitute the conscious levels we primarily operate on as humans. Mapped onto the Kabbalistic model of the ten Sefiros, the channels through which divine energy flows into creation, Nefesh is connected with Malchus/kingship and power, Ruach is associated with Tiferes/the arena of beauty and emotion, and Neshamah is linked with Binah/the intellect (R. Shimon Ben Tzemach Duran, *Magen Avos* 3, p. 35. The Ramak, *Pardes Rimonim*, Sha'ar 31:1). It is no coincidence that within our mundane universe — which is but a reflection of the ultimate spiritual realm — Power, Beauty and Brilliance are the greatest and, to some extent, the most formidable forces that inspire and impact the world.

Living in integrity and harmony with these amazing tools and talents gives us the opportunity to climb the ladder of 'inclusive transcendence,' wherein we are able to both incorporate and move beyond our definitions and limitations as we seek greater unity with the Creator and with all of Creation. By building on a strong foundation of vital energy we are then able to mobilize and focus our emotional and intellectual capacities in order to live a more spiritual, sensitive, transcendent and G-dly life.

In a world gone astray, however, a world that is disconnected and alienated from its Source, power translates as brute force, beauty becomes the source of blind devotion and intelligence is revered no matter where it leads. But it must be stated clearly: Power is not synonymous with force.

Genuine power is a derivative of whole-system existential integrity. That is, when one is in total alignment with their own gifts and unique purpose as well as with the supreme power of the universe, then, and only then, are they in their true power. Being powerful means that one is strong enough to allow another person to exist and express himself. Force, on the other hand, is ultimately an expression of a state of powerlessness. Force is an indication of lack and need. A powerless individual feels the need to control others through force. Life for the powerless is a continuous quest to dominate others.

Similarly, unrectified beauty emerges when aesthetics become an object of devotion in and of themselves, rather than a means of serving the greater purpose of evoking admiration and even a sense of awe for the ultimate Creator.

And lastly, intellect or rationality, when it is not situated within its proper spiritual or ethical context, becomes a truth unto itself, inviting one to follow its reasoning all the way to its logical conclusion, no matter what that conclusion may be, or where it may lead.

Chaya & Yechidah:

Beyond Nefesh, Ruach and Neshamah (which comprise one's normative consciousness), there are deeper, higher, more expansive states of soul that, for the most part, envelop and encircle the human being. These are the aspects of soul that transcend the individual personality of the person.
The first outer level is called Makif Ha'karov/the immediate surrounding, which is otherwise referred to as Chaya. The deeper level is called Makif Ha'rachok/a distant, far removed surrounding referred to as Yechidah (*Pri Eitz Chayim* 1, *Sha'ar Ha'akudim*, Sha'ar 6:5. *Sha'ar Pinimiyus V'Chitzoniyus*, Derush 10. *Derush Pinimi Umakif*, Derush 1). These levels are not limited, defined or bound by the doings or non-doings of the body. Although these two Makifim (plural for Makif) exist within all of us and access to them is always available, because they are higher arching dimensions of soul, they are not, for most people, the normal wavelengths of everyday consciousness.

Principally, Nefesh, Ruach and Neshamah unfold and reveal themselves in a linear progression. Meaning that the older and more mature one becomes, the higher the level of soul that is able to express itself (*Sha'ar HaGilgulim*, Hakdamah 3). There is an ascending hierarchy to these three levels of soul that does not allow the attainment of one level before perfection of the previous one has been achieved. Still, since life as a whole, whether it is physical, mental or spiritual, does not always follow a straight line, occasionally a person can leap ahead and skip to expanded states of soul, only to go back to the earlier ones at a later time, with a deeper appreciation or maturation. At peak moments a person may exist fully integrated with the truth of Yechidah, only to later plunge back into the realm of Nefesh in order to continue their path of gradual development. But, again, the general trajectory is that first Nefesh unfolds, then Ruach, and then Neshamah.

As mentioned, the Makif Ha'karov/immediate surrounding is also referred to as Chaya. Chaya is literally translated as 'life,' as the Chaya is the life energy of the human being as a whole. This is not to be confused with Nefesh, which we have also described as a sort of 'life energy.' Life energy on the level of Nefesh is confined to the vital animating energy of the body. Chaya is this same kind of vital energy, but in the realm of the whole being. This is expressed as the attribute of Ratzon/Will.

Will is acknowledged as one of the most formidable forces of the universe. Will is the propelling drive, the power that transforms potential into actual and mere dreams into reality. Not coincidently, as a reflection of this meta-physical truth, many secular western thinkers have speculated that will is the prevailing and predominant force of the universe, not only within the microcosmic image of mankind, but of the entire cosmos.

In the domain of will there are many forms and expressions, ranging from will emanating from the ego, to will rooted within the most transcendent part of the self. The will to go buy the latest gadget or the newest car is a relatively superficial expression of will. A deeper, more profound manifestation of the will would be the innate drive to live and to self-preserve. This inner will for life itself is manifest in the will to eat, sleep and procreate, or to hang on to life at any cost even when one is no longer conscious. More powerful still is the will to be at one with one's deepest self, expressed as the natural longing to be free and unhinged from all humanly defined contradictions or constrictions.

The innermost will and volition of the human being is to be in sync with the deepest will of creation — the will of the Creator. The Creator's will is the underlying foundation of all reality and all worlds. To be aligned with this will is to be in complete harmony and synchronicity with the deepest truth and purpose of all creation.

Intuition is another expression of Chaya. Whereas Neshamah is the cognitive and logically based aspect of the intellect, Chaya is more subtle and sensitive. Chaya is the intuitive aspect of consciousness, which is somewhat closer to the essence of our being (*Nefesh HaChayim*, Sha'ar 2:17).

Makif Rachok/the farther removed enveloping energy is also known as Yechidah/unique oneness. It is the part of our soul that is rooted and unified within the absolute oneness of the Creator. It is the apex of our soul's potential and the pure transcendental part of our being. It is a deep place within us that is utterly beyond duality, polarity, splinteredness or fragmentation.

Although Yechidah is linked with the ineffable and cannot be quantified or contextualized, what can be said is that it is the part of the self that remains consistent throughout all of life. Accordingly, Yechidah cannot ever truly be understood for it is the understander; it cannot be observed for it is the observer; and it cannot be experienced for it is the experiencer.

From another perspective, one could say that Chaya is, in fact, the Infinite part of the self — the observer, the experiencer, the emptiness upon which the fullness of life is superimposed. In that sense, Yechidah is then understood as the ultimate "context" that simultaneously contains the finite and the infinite, the fullness and the emptiness, including them all within a singular frame.

On the level of Nefesh-Ruach-Neshamah every person is unique and distinct with a particular purpose and soul mission. On the level of Chaya, the backdrop of life, there is only oneness. From the perspective of Yechidah, unity and multiplicity, everything and no-thing, unity and infinity are included and integrated into a whole larger than the sum of its parts.

Nefesh-Ruach-Neshamah is the finite self.

Chaya is the Infinite Self.

Yechidah is beyond and inclusive of both the infinite and the finite.

Yechidah is our fullest reality, comprised of our potential prior to birth, the details and experiences of our lives lived out to their fullest, and our Infinite, unchanging observing self.

To live in a state of Yechidah is to live life in perfect symmetrical harmony with the creator and creation. Interpersonally this means to be able to see another human being for who they truly are by being able to move beyond all the trivial prejudices and biases by observing their core. Rebbe Schneur Zalman of Liadi, the illustrious eighteenth century Chassidic Rebbe known affectionately as the Alter Rebbe, once acknowledged that when he looks at someone else he sees them as they exist in Adam Kadmon/ the Primordial Man. That is, he was able to observe people the way they actually are in pristine potential and rooted within their primordial source.

Adam Kadmon:

Adam Kadmon/the Primordial Human is the cumulative context that contains all five levels of the soul as one, including all of reality from Infinity to finitude, as well as Ayin/emptiness/no-thing-ness and Yesh/some-thingness/observable existence.

The word Adam, translated as human, comes from the word domeh (as in the "likeness" or "in the image"), and is also rooted in the word dimyon/ imagination. Kadmon means primary or primordial. Thus Adam Kadmon is primordial likeness or primordial image.

Adam Kadmon represents the world of Divine desire and will. The original desire and primordial will of all creation is the desire and will of the

Infinite, Unified Creator to create and enter into a relationship with an apparently finite "other."

Adam Kadmon is the way reality exists in the perfect "imagination" of the Creator. It is the way we, and all of reality, exist in the perfect imagination of the dream of the Infinite One. In that reality, we are all our perfect selves.
Perfection is the way we exist within Adam Kadmon. In the Divine imagination the Creator envisions and imagines us living out our utmost physical/emotional/mental/and spiritual potential.

A metaphor of this idea would be of a person having a strong desire to build a beautiful home. When he closes his eyes he sees in his imagination the perfect home. But then there is the actual process of buying the materials, gathering the equipment and the arduous labor of constructing the home. Adam Kadmon is the way the home exists within the imagination and desire of the Creator. Then there is the actual process of creation from Infinity all the way down to dense matter and physical form, eventually culminating in this world here and now. This is the house that we live in.

Adam Kadmon is the world of our perfect selves, albeit in potential.

We are all rooted in this level of the primordial likeness of the Creator.

Perhaps, at times, some people's actions do not reflect this basic truth. They are at that moment not living up to their highest physical, emotional, mental or spiritual potential. And yet, as observers, we are always presented with a choice — we can either choose to look at the externals, or we can look deeper in order to see others as they exist within Adam Kadmon, in their perfect and noble potential.

Observing people in the image of their potential and believing in people because of their primordial root actually helps them reveal this potential and root. This is what was by the above statement that the Alter Rebbe saw every person as they exist within Adam Kadmon. He saw them simultaneously as they were and as they were meant to be.

The more we believe in people, the more those people believe in themselves.

All five rungs of the soul are interwoven with each other. All aspects of the self are one, constituting a singular totality of beingness. One way to understand the emergence of the individualized aspects of soul that we have outlined thus far is by comparing them to the act of human creation, most notably birth. The higher reaches of the soul would be equated with the umbilical cord, still very much connected with the mother's womb, the source of the child's creation. The more particularized elements of the soul would be similar to the actual fetus itself. Although it is somewhat separate and independent it is still connected via the cord with its source. In fact, the fetus's very existence and nourishment is dependent on the mother. The deepest level of soul, Yechidah, would be the child's potential in the mind of the parent, the way the creator/parent and their creation/children are still connected in the co-creation of the same reality, even after the child is born.

Yechidah is the inner space where Infinite and finite merge, where they are undistinguishable and one. And yet, while the Nefesh — or as the philosophers have phrased it, the vegetative — is the furthest removed from its source, it is still part of the link, connected to the source of all life.

Integrating all levels of Beingness

The soul-wave we operate on is in accordance to the way we choose to live our life. Generally we ascend from one rung to the next, expanding and climbing further. Yet, occasionally life does not follow strict order and we have the ability to quantum leap and skip levels, only to fall back to the earlier developmental stages later on. We can live for moments on the level of Yechidah, only later to plunge back into the realm of Nefesh; we can live from the level of Chaya and then return to a strictly vegetative level of awareness. Fundamentally, it is our choice whether we live from the place of the surface self, the less sparkling levels of soul, or from the higher more expansive and brilliant levels of our soul.

By our very nature we are essentially hybrids, admixtures of various aspects, ranging from the more sublime and transcendental to the more material and bodily. A genuine sense of wholeness and integration is achieved when there is a cohesion and uniformity between all multifarious aspects that comprise our beingness. Having been given a body we are obliged — morally to our bodies and spiritually to our deeper selves — to take care of our physical, mental and emotional welfare, and to see that they all work in unison with the innermost purpose and design of creation.

For some two and a half years the celebrated Talmudic sages from the house of Shamai and the house of Hillel debated the weighty existentialist question: To be or not to be? The question as they phrased it was: "Was it better for man to have been created or not to have been created?" At the end, the conclusion was: "It would have been better for humanity to not have been created, but now that we have been created let us reflect carefully upon our actions" (*Eiruvin*, 13b). As conscious creations we must reflect upon and differentiate the good, benevolent and constructive actions from their opposite, and then to contemplate the qualitative nature of the good actions themselves.

On the surface it appears that both schools are in favor of an approach to life that is free of attachment. Practically, this means that it is better to disengage from physicality than to become involved. We need to be only as much as we are forced to. In this paradigm, asceticism and detachment would be the most appropriate approaches to life. However, this is not quite consistent with either Sages' worldview.

Taking a deeper look at the wording of their argument it becomes clear that such a detached approach to life was never their intention. While the colloquial way to translate this passage of Talmud is whether it is 'better to be or not to be,' the word they actually use is noach, which means 'ease,' as in easier or more comfortable and less strenuous (*Nishmas Chayim*, Maamor 2:6). Clearly their dispute was not about what is 'better,' but rather about what would be easier and less exhausting for the person. Their summation is this: it would have been easier for the soul not to descend in order to inhabit the body. But they all agree that as far as purpose and life design goes, the objective is to integrate all elements of self — physical, mental and spiritual. True, to live a one-dimensional and one-sided life can be easier, as it is fraught with less difficulty and with far less challenges, but that is not where the ultimate existential intention of life lies.

The Torah comes to codify an integrated life style, aligning the human with the being, coordinating what would normally appear as divergent energies so that we can harmonize our ostensibly conflicted nature and act from a place of integrity and wholeness. The Torah does not teach the denial or the sacrifice of the animal aspect within, its quest is to meld the two — the animal with the angelic — so that each can serve the other in the greater context of growth and expansion of consciousness and compassion.

Spiritual immaturity expresses itself through the soul's yearning for exclusive transcendence to function on its own terms while ignoring its mission to fuse the divergent energies of self. As maturity rises one comes to the realization that the body is not a jailhouse for the soul, nor is the soul a contradiction to what the lower elements of the self desire. Once the soul becomes properly acclimated to the realities of the body, it wishes not to fight it, but recognizes that together they make a good, dynamic partnership. The natural transcendence of the soul becomes all-inclusive and gives focus to the needs of the body, while the body offers the more rarified parts of the self the opportunity to experience finitude. Ultimately, they both benefit, so much so that when it comes time for the soul to journey onwards, the soul does not want to leave. It actually does not want to part with its best friend, the body.

Our sages tell us that, "Against your will you are born…against your will you will die" (*Avos* 4:22). This seems like a contradictory statement. If it were against one's will to be born, that means that a person (soul) would rather not be alive, so why then would they say that, "against your will you will die" (The Rebbe Rashab, *Safer Hamaamorim* Ranat, p. 7–8). The deeper meaning is as follows: Before a soul descends into this world the soul observes the temptations and challenges of this world and does not wish to enter a body, as it were. But then the soul comes to live within a body and realizes the amazing abilities and opportunities the body and the physical world present it with, including the wonderful transformations that can occur only while alive within a body, and thus, "against your will you will die," the soul wishes to remain enclothed within the body for as long as it can.

CHAPTER 4
Immortality

Eternity not Extinction

The human being, out of all other living organisms, must live with the awareness of life's fleetingness. The irony is that while man is acutely aware of his finitude, he eagerly desires to attain infinitude and immortality, whether physically, mentally or spiritually. The quest for the fountain of life has been around since the very dawn of civilization. Magical potions and methods to attain eternal life have existed sice time immemorial. Perhaps because of this dreaded awareness so much of life's energy is spent warring against it and trying desperately to reverse the natural sequence of events.

Yet, immortality and the survival of the self do exist on various levels. There are those who contend that immortality is always present; for there is no one to pass-on, as there is no distinct person to die. The real self is part of the whole and what occurs at death is merely a fusion of the illusory self with the real self, which is the totality of creation. From this perspective, the question of what will happen in the afterlife is then considered trivial. In fact no one was ever born, and therefore no one will ever die.

To phrase this a bit more candidly, from this perspective the ultimate goal of life is to disappear, to merge with the infinite wisdom and goodness of the universe and shed all sense of selfhood. The latter part of such an equation (i.e., to "shed all sense of selfhood") is in stark contrast and is diametrically opposed to the way the Torah views life and its purpose.

The Torah teaches that there is a so-called individual distinctive soul and the objective in life is to live out our individuation to our maximum spiritual potential. The goal is not to lose our unique place within the universe, but rather to find our deepest self and to sense its oneness within the Infinite One. For this reason in the afterlife our souls do not become extinct or disappear, rather they experience individual immortality, living on as a self-contained finite 'entity' within the greater existence of the infinite 'everything.'

Eternity, not extinction, is the ultimate. What eventually expires is the ego, the sense of separate individuality, but not individuality itself. True, the ego disappears, but the individual soul is not a product of the ego. What is false and fleeting is the imposter of the ego, not our uniqueness. The individuality of the soul is rooted in being an eternal portion of the Divine, a finite manifestation of the infinite, and as such, when one is liberated from the ego, and the ego expires, the spiritual self does not cease.

Death, Birth, Life

Immortality and eternity are experienced on multiple levels, from the more apparent experience in which the soul lives on, to the more esoteric aspect, which is the preservation of the physical. At this point, some of these expressions of immortality will now be explored.

To some degree every death births life. The circle of life is an endless transformation from one form to another. Nature is continually creating and destroying, building and demolishing in one perpetual rhythmic motion. Every fall and demise on one side gives rise to life on the other side.

Even as we eat, we ingest and then eject what is not usable for the body and the excrement becomes the life and stimulus for further creations. Generally, life feeds on death. For one living organism to survive it must consume another form of life.

As a whole, nature is continually changing and putting on different coats. As the physical form slowly joins the earth it becomes the soil upon which new life grows. Flora becomes the nourishment for insects and then another more forceful creature lives off the insect, which in turn can become the food for man, and the circle continues. Minerals become plants, plants become animals, animals to man, and man in turn returns to the earth.

The cycle of life necessitates individual deaths so that life as a whole can survive. Death on one side births new life on the other. From this perspective, a certain degree of immortality exists as part of the ecosystem of the entire reality of existence, mankind included.

Collective Immortality

On a more anthropocentric level the idea of eternity means to be immortal in the context of history. Even if we suppose that the individual passes on, the nation, the collective never dies (*Temurah*, 15b). The individual person may die but the whole always survives. The human being, though no longer in existence (on a physical level) lingers on in the continuity of collective mankind, historically living on in the continuity of people. The human race continues, although the individual does not.

There are two types of eternities: One is referred to as Kayamim B'ish/ eternity in form, such as the planetary system including the sun, moon, stars, galaxies and their greater sense of celestial permanence. And there is Kayomim B'min/eternity of a species, such as the collective immortality of mankind (*Yerushalmi*, Berachos 1:1). B'Min means that although the personality passes away, humankind marches on.

In other words, individual man survives by continuing to be part of the entire human race that lives on, a kind of social immortality. The B'min immortality is expressed elegantly in Homer's Iliad: "As is the generation of leaves, so is that of humanity. The wind scatters the leaves on the ground, but the live timber burgeons with leaves again in the season of spring returning. So one generation of men will grow while another dies." It is not the individual that lives onward, but rather the collective. An indication of this primary condition of eternity is our reproductive system, which reflects our innate capacity to give birth to offspring and thus experience immortality vicariously.

More specifically, every living being is a continuation of his or her parents, grandparents and great grandparents, all the way back to the first human being. Our lives are an extension of the lives of our parents and they in turn of their parents. Our bodies, to some measure, are not only our bodies per se but a conglomerate of all the bodies/genetics of all of our ancestors.

Life is not lived alone and nothing occurs in a vacuum. We are like twigs in a great tree, distinct and unique but sourced in one root. Still, for all its value in the strict sense of the term, this is not individual immortality.

Individual Immortality

On a more personal note, individual memory survives, and that also occurs on many different levels. Most superficial memory survival is through the actions of other people. When another living being does something in honor or in memory of someone that has passed away, the memory of that person lives on. Giving charity in honor of a beloved's memory (Rabbeinu Bachya, *Devarim*, Chap. 21:8), or studying Torah in honor of a beloved's memory (*Yevamos* 122a, Rashi), are some of the actions that are referred to in the Medrash as appropriate. Also, there is mention of building a monument as a physical lasting memorial (*Yerushalmi Shekalim* 2:5). The monument serves as a tangible reminder of that person and his or her achievements.

Today it has become popular to light a candle in honor of the deceased. Although there is no apparent early source for this, still it has been widely accepted and is brought down as a custom that is relevant and worthwhile to carry out. So much so that according to Rabbeinu Bachya, the early fourteenth century commentator/mystic, "The soul is delighted for the lighting of candles...she expands and manifests from the pleasure she receives from the light."

A deeper and more profound measure of self-perpetuation is achieved through our own actions on behalf of the deceased. By creating something that is everlasting and immortal, something that extends far beyond our physical reach, we attain a degree of imperishability. Parenthetically, every person has the capacity to live in a state of immortality even while in the strictures and parameters of finitude. Every action has permanent significance. It is limitless both in potential and in effect. How much more so is this true when it comes to actions that are inherently eternal and everlasting? When a person brings about correct actions and lives in synchronicity with The Eternal (i.e., G-d), a measure of eternal life is attained here on earth.

Beyond eternity through actions, there is immortality through influence, creative immortality, where one passes on but leaves an impression and lasting legacy and teachings for others to follow. "A righteous and learned person's words are his memory," our sages say (Yerushalmi Shekalim 2:5). In one cryptic and mysterious passage in the Talmud, the sages suggest that recounting a departed person's teachings causes the lips of the deceased person to murmur in the grave (Yevamos, 97a. Sanhedrin, 90b). The teachings that originate from one in the grave, resonate within the hearts of the living, and are then echoed back into the lips of the one who spoke them first.

Biological immortality is a more concrete form of immortality. Genetically, one's genes are passed on to one's offspring, and then in turn to their children. In this way there is a continuous genetic transmission. Children are the way a mortal man overcomes death and mortality (see; Taanis, 5a. Baba Basra, 116a). When Adam and Chava/Eve were first faced with their mortality, she conceived and gave birth and they called their child Kayin/Cain because they had "acquired a man to G-d" (Bereishis 4:2). By affirming that this child will be "to G-d" after their death, they are confirming that he will, in effect, stand in their place. Through this, they are overcoming their mortality (Ramban, ad loc). This is especially the case when a person's progeny chooses to follow the same path as he himself had chosen. Then, not only is it a genetic/physical continuation but also a mental/spiritual one.

Bodily Immortality

Death is only something that the shell, the cocoon experiences. But even the shell in reality does not perish; even the physical matter of the body does not truly expire. What happens is that the physical form transforms from one substance to another. The elements that comprise the body are restored to their original source and then continue existing in these other forms. Death in this context is simply a rearrangement. The elements that made up the body now return to the root that birthed it (*Zohar* 1, p. 122b). Yet, physical immortality goes beyond the above-mentioned. There is a part of man that never does rearrange into other forms and remains humanlike at its core for all eternity, and that is the Luz bone.

There is a small bone in the body, perhaps too minuscule and infinitesimal to be detected, which never perishes. There are some opinions that recognize this bone as existing at the base of the spine, while others believe it to be on the back of the skull (HaAruch, Erech Luz. Avodas Hakodesh 2:40. Likutei Torah, Nach, Shoftim). This parcel of bone is indestructible, neither water nor fire can detroy this bone (Medrash Rabbah, Bereishis 28:3). The luz does not succumb to the ravages of worms or any other natural putrefaction, for it is truly everlasting.

The preservation of this bone has real value in that it is precisely through this small bone that the resurrection of the body will occur. As such, the resurrection of the body is not a new creation, but rather a revival, a reanimation of the luz bone, and from there the rebirth will expand to the entire body (*Zohar* 2, p. 28b. *Siddur Beis Yaakov*, Melava Malka, p. 206).

We know, however, that every rule has an exception. While for the most part bodies laid to rest decompose, and do so rapidly, there are certain abnormal cases where that does not occur, and they in fact survive for a longer period of time than usual (*Medrash Tehilim*, Chap. 119:9. *Shabbos* 152b. *Baba Basra*, 17a, Rashi, ad loc). Ordinarily, the course of life is as follows: A soul descends to inhabit a human form. Throughout life, body and soul labor in unison. When the time comes for body and soul to part ways, the soul soars upwards while the body merges with the denser elements of creation. The exception from this rule is for those who have worked tirelessly to incorporate the body within their spiritual journey and have succeeded in transforming the body into a prolocutor for the soul. For those who have fully embraced the body and created a deep sense of unity within their beingness, some form of bodily immortality will be experienced. In a manner of speaking, the entire body is transformed into the luz bone (*Maor Vashemesh*, Parshas Vayechi. *Medrash Talpiyos*, Os Yud), and thus is preserved for a far longer period of time than is usual.

Interestingly, the same holds true for a particularly evil person as well. The polar opposite of the great and holy human being is the 'great' ungodly, diabolical and evil person. They both have extreme focus. Their genius is pulling together the various forces within themselves to reach their greatness. For one person the greatness manifests in goodness, for the other in devastating evil. Being so utterly one-dimensional, completely neglecting the soul and identifying solely with materiality (i.e., power, money and appetite), their bodies assume some form of unity and cohesion. In which case, even after the person is no longer alive the body will continue to 'hold together' and preserve for a period of time, decomposing at a much slower pace (*Safer Chassidim*, Chap. 143).

One of the ways such an individual can attain Gan Eden/paradise, a state of transcendence and purity, is through slowly weaning himself off of his dependencies and attachments with the bodily realm of existence. One who has been fixedly preoccupied with physicality at the expense of the spirit, engrossed with immediate self-gratification to the detriment of others, their soul's detoxification and disengagement is achieved by having an awareness of the lifeless body, and gradually, as it decomposes, recognizing its transient, ephemeral and fickle nature.

Personal Immortality

Up until this juncture we have explored the mostly corporeal oriented aspects of immortality; now let us explore some more personal aspects of immortality. Just as the whole of the universe can never be lost (the notion of extinction and total annihilation is scientifically and logically impossible, as matter cannot fall out of the universe, and energy, which is a condensed form of matter, is continually being recycled), the same is true of the human being. Just as the amount of energy in the universe never changes, certainly this is true of the energy of the human being.

A something cannot become a nothing, and some-one cannot become a no-one. What is left to be explored is the various degrees of immortality experienced by the divergent energies of the soul, or souls.

Earlier, the Talmudic, philosophical and mystical views regarding the nature of the soul were mentioned and we observed that to some degree, at least on the lower levels of soul, they are all portraying the same reality in different terms, each anchored in their own particular genre or level. Overall, there are fundamentally two classifications of souls: there is the ego/vegetative/animal, on the one hand; and the good/rational/transcendent on the other. The first set is physically oriented, its principle function is to service the body, to persevere and sustain physical existence. This is the aspect of the soul that needs the body. While the second set, the good/rational/transcendent part of the soul allows us to climb upwards and reach that which is beyond and deep within us; this soul exists independent of physical form (Rambam *Hilchos Teshuvah* 8:3).

Being that the ego/vegetative/animal souls are all at the service of the body, when the body passes on so does this level of soul. However, just as the body ceases to exist in its distinct form but continues to survive as part of something else in a recycled form, the same is true with regard to this aspect of soul. These particularized lower elements of the soul, when properly integrated during life will in death reappear transformed as a seat of the Divine chariot (*Likkutei Torah*, Shelach, p. 40). This is more a form of collective and non-personal energetic immortality, rather than an individualized one.

Absolute eternity, both in shape and form, existing as it does prior to the body's creation and perpetuating long after its demise, can only be experienced through that part of the soul that is beyond physical/temporal/spatial limitations. Immortal are the nonlocal aspects of consciousness; those which are not confined to the nervous system and are more than the sum of the material brain or body. Only the rational soul, which was given 'from heaven,' or the Divine soul, which is itself 'a part of heaven,' can truly experience immortality (although this Divine spark is also subdivided holographically into the lower, more dense ego and survival-based aspects of the soul, as well as the more transcendent aspects, permeating the whole of the person). Only that which emanates from an ethereal and celestial realm that precluded physical reality, can supersede the laws of nature and live on for all eternity.

The manner in which this soul experiences immortality is in its own idiosyncratic construct, as a particularized existence and as an individualized soul residing within Gan Eden, or in another incarnation, as will be explained later on. The soul is a spark of the Infinite, an eternal portion of the Divine. It is infinite at its core, and thus after the demise of its physical representation the soul returns to its Source and merges with the Oneness of the Creator. The only difference is that now, after living on a physical plane, the soul has become all the more comprehensive, collecting years worth of human experiences.

Prior to the soul descending, its infinitude was very much one-dimensional — infinite in expression and experience, but unconnected to and precluding anything of the finite. Now its infinitude includes both infinite and finite. It is infinite in its potential and core, but finite in many of its experiences and memory. This is a personal measure of immortality, where personal consciousness and identity lives on.

CHAPTER 5
Near-Death Experience

Defining the Near Death Experience

"The beginning of wisdom", a wise philosopher once noted, "is the defining of terms." A near-death experience is defined as an event in which an individual has clinically died and somehow survives to tell the tale of what they encountered on the threshold of life and death.

It is important to understand that these experiences are near death, not after death experiences. By definition death means a point of no return. Those who went through these experiences were in the process of dying, but they did not technically die. What precisely constitutes death and what exactly are the criteria for declaring a person dead are questions that are greatly debated.

Nowadays, in most modern societies an electro-encephalo-graph or EEG, an instrument that amplifies and records even the minutest of the brain's electrical activity, is used to monitor and identify the point of death. Death is established when the machine shows a flat line. Yet, as is evidenced by a case wherein someone who was declared clinically dead and was later revived and resuscitated, it is clear that this quantifiable measurement of brain activity does not completely define the point of death; for in deed the body was not completely lifeless to the point of no return. In fact, some people, when they experience hypothermia, which is a dramatic lowering of the body temperature, can sometimes show no sign of brainwave activity, until later on when they are warmed back up to a more normal functioning temperature.

While the actual phrase 'near-death experience,' otherwise referred to as NDE, is a relatively modern term, the phenomenon itself has been reported throughout the ages. Reports of such experiences date back thousands of years. There are cave paintings found in Europe, such as in France and Spain that seem to depict scenes of the afterlife. These images appear strikingly similar to the modern day documented cases of NDE. The earliest western and secular description of a near-death experience is found in Plato's "The Republic". A story is told of a Greek soldier by the name of Er who was declared dead, when in fact he was not. In the narrative Er is killed and just as he is about to be cremated, he awakens and tells a story of leaving his body and traveling with others to an otherworldly reality where he was to be judged.

In the modern era, this occurrence and the reporting of these types of events is quite wide spread. According to some recent reputable polls in the United States alone an estimated thirteen million people have reported that they have gone through some kind of near-death experience. Near-death experiences appear to have no relationship with one's religious affiliation or lack thereof. The frequency of these experiences is proportionately the same across cultures, occurring independent of whether one is devout, spiritual, agnostic, atheistic or materialist. Age, race, gender or social status also seems to make no difference in a person's susceptibility to such experiences.

Many who report experiencing a near-death experience describe similar encounters. There are numerous ways of how to divide these experiences. To serve our immediate purpose and to make the issue more comprehensible the encounter will be divided into ten progressive stages.

Ten Stages of the Near Death Experience

At first the individual may experience a sense of not being amongst the living. Oddly, the person may even overhear other people pronouncing them dead.

Stage two is when the person enters a state of extreme tranquility and peace accompanied by the absence of any pain or anguish.

In stage three a person may begin to hear an uncomfortable noise, occasionally described as a buzzing or hissing type of sound.

In the fourth stage an awareness of the process of separation and divestment from the body arises. Consciousness seems to separate from the body and appears to acquire the ability to perceive one's surroundings without the mediation of the senses. Yet, although their consciousness lacks a physical form, the person still feels, implicitly or explicitly, as if they are within a kind of phantom body. There is in fact, at this point, still some form of 'body,' albeit not one that is corporeal or physical. Some describe this body as an energy field, a type of cloud, a form of light or a swirl of colors. The body they assume is felt to be comprised of something less dense than physical matter; it is one that can go through rocks and travel instanta- neously to great distances. Being in this 'body' the person has an expanded awareness of everything around and within them, yet it appears that no one else is able to notice them.

At the fifth stage one senses the self passing through a dark passageway, a tunnel of sorts.

At stage six he encounters ethereal 'entities' that upon deeper reflection seem quite familiar to him. At times they are family members or previous- ly deceased friends. It appears that they have come to help the soul. An- gelic figures also may make an appearance at this point. All these 'entities' appear to be enveloped in a kind of glowing radiant light.

Soon thereafter, in the seventh stage, a person may experience an encoun- ter with a Being of Light, which one understands to be G-d. This light is one that emanates powerful and unconditional vibrations of infinite love.

At some point, often in the eighth stage of the above-mentioned order, the person experiences a total life review, resulting in a profound sense of self-evaluation. This is not a total recall of all the details of life in a sys- tematic and orderly fashion. Rather, one experiences a sort of panoramic and instantaneous review of their life. Additionally, even the emotions and feelings associated with a particular moment being recalled are relived and re-experienced. It is a passionate and experiential recollection of life.

Following this stage of recollection and evaluation, one's experience shifts subtly away from the life as it was lived out and experienced within the confines of space and time. The ninth stage is then characterized by a strong sense of timelessness and even spacelessness. The notion of compression or restriction has no bearing on the experience. There is, at this stage, a kind of free-floating feeling, which follows the reliving of one's narrative.

Ultimately, in the tenth stage the person comes upon a type of barrier, a door, a bridge, or something similar, which apparently separates life in this world from life in the next.

This is the overall picture and process of a near-death experience that has been described and depicted by countless people throughout the ages and across the globe. To be sure, not every person that reports going through a near-death experience encounters all of these stages and certainly not in the same sequential order. Some experience one or two of the events, and others more. It is not a rigid model per se, but more like a general template. It also appears that how deep into the experience a person travels depends on whether the person experienced clinical death, and if so, for how long. The longer one was assumed to be dead, the deeper and further they seem to travel.

Within this general subject matter there is something that is called 'Empathic Near-Death Experience,' where a person who is close to someone who is nearing death senses a separation from their own body and of accompanying their loved one's soul on the journey into the afterlife. For some people this manifests as an experience of becoming aware of the all-embracing and loving light. While others speak of sensing the presence of deceased relatives or friends who come to greet the soul who is drifting away.

The Interconnectedness of all Realities

Before these possibilities are explored it is important to keep in mind that while simple speculation is for the most part meaningless, except as a purely mental exercise, there are many who find that exploring these issues is quite intriguing, inspiring and even comforting. In times of deep mourning many people find that the knowledge of what occurs to their beloved's soul is valuable information and suitably soothing.

From a finite perspective of reality, physicality and spirituality operate on completely different planes of existence and the divide or chasm between the two worlds is irreconcilable and completely uncrossable. While there is much validity to this assumption, no living being, no matter their expertise or genius, can truly approximate what the afterlife is really like. Even the greatest amongst the Prophets, Moshe, declined to offer details regarding what awaits man in the hereafter (*Sifri*, Devarim 356). Yet, it is also true that creation was originally patterned in a way that the divide can be traversed and the partition can be crossed, albeit for a short period of time.

All reality is a unified whole. All universes are interlinked and interlaced. What begins as a lively spirit can, through the process of creation, eventually manifest as seemingly inert matter. Reification is merely a culmination of a process that begins as pure Divine energy, which then becomes three-dimensional concretized objects. Upper/inner realties and lower/external realties are all seamlessly interwoven and symbiotically interconnected.

Revelation is a means by which the Transcendent becomes available to the immanent. Torah, which was given at Sinai, is revelation par excellence. Through Torah we are empowered to pierce the veil, lift the screen and take a peek into a reality that is both far beyond and deep within us. The transmission of Divine wisdom is present and accessible for all. Throughout history there were, and always are, those highly sensitive and spiritual individuals who are able to tap into realms of existence that are beyond the immediate. Quite frankly, the echo of Sinai has never ceased; it is only man who has distanced and alienated himself to a point where he is no longer able to hear The Voice. Some evolved and extraordinary souls, and occasionally some ordinary souls in extraordinary moments, are able to relive Sinai — hearing, seeing and being receptive to the deeper truths that are otherwise unnoticed and undetectable.

Dreams are another, though more obscure, mode of acquiring transcendent insight, particularly with regard to the soul's journey in the afterlife. Death and sleep are closely related and aligned with each other. Ancient Greek philosophers referred to sleep as death's sister. The sages of the Talmud teach that sleep is one sixtieth of death (*Berachos*, 57b). Sleep is a mini form of death. While the person is asleep major aspects of their soul depart the body and may roam into deeper/higher dimensions of reality (*Medrash Rabbah*, Bereishis, 14:9). During these nocturnal journeys it is possible for the higher levels of the soul to inform the lower ones that remain earthbound of alternate realities.

Whether the dreamer will register enough to be consciously or subconsciously aware of the wisdom depends on the spiritual development of the dreamer, how integrated they are with the various aspects of self. As for those who are more existentially integrated (whose external expressions of self - thought, speech and action - are harmoniously aligned with the inner most desires of their soul), such people will indeed have a conscious awareness of the prophetic teachings brought down in their dreams. Others may have a more intuitive awareness, which can be less clear to them, though still meaningful.

Collective and individual revelations at Sinai and throughout the ages, whether through prophecy, Ruach Hakodesh/Divine intuition, inspired dreams, or the like, are the foundations and the sources of the Torah's view on the afterlife. According to this view this body of knowledge is not mere folklore or hyperbole, suggestions or speculation, but rather these are teachings that have been verified by the direct experience of the transmitters, only to be later transcribed and documented as written testimony. From this perspective, we are dealing with a body of wisdom that is sourced in the Torah and based upon prophetic and inspired experiences of individuals in alternate states of consciousness and expanded modes of knowing. Based on this understanding of the nature of our material we can now continue our exploration of near-death experiences and the afterlife.

The Ten Stages in Traditional Torah Sources

Incidences wherein one returns to life from 'death' are found sprinkled throughout Torah. There are a number of descriptions in the written Torah and later in the Talmud that recount tales of 'resurrection' (*Melachim* 1, 17:22. *Melachim* 2, 4:35. *Baba Basra*, 10b. *Kesuvos*, 77b). In these events prophets and sages performed the impossible in resurrecting those who have passed on. While there is the possibility to interpret these incidences as cases of resuscitation as opposed to resurrection, reviving as opposed to rebirthing, traditionally many of these events were indeed viewed as resurrections.

Beyond resurrection there are also recordings of people in Torah (both written and oral) who have encountered what can be referred to as near–death experiences. In one Talmudic story a sage was so deathly ill that his soul departed from his body, though he did not actually 'die.' Later on when he resumed consciousness he recounted what he saw. He spoke of an inverted universe, where everything appears to be the opposite of the way reality seems to be here on earth. Humble people were placed on pedestals, while those who are normally considered superior in our society were seated below. At which point he heard a Heavenly voice declare: "Honorable is one who enters these realms of existence with Torah wisdom at his disposal" (*Baba Basra*, 10b).

Rebbe Yosi was once paying a visit to his sick neighbor when he heard a voice proclaiming: "A soul has come in front of me prior to its destined time, woe to those neighbors in his village who have not done anything to help him." Sensing the truth of the message, Rebbe Yosi hurried and placed the juice of a dried fig on the sick man's lips and slowly the man was nurtured back to life. Upon his recovery he told Rebbe Yosi that his soul had in fact left his body and was brought before the throne of the King. "I would have stayed there," he told Rebbe Yosi, "but the master of the universe desired that you be given the opportunity to have the merit of restoring my health" (*Zohar* 2, p. 61a–61b).

Stage One:
Being Aware of Death

Once the soul leaves the body it experiences a tremendously heightened measure of awareness, both of itself as well as of everything else that is going on in relation to its lifeless body. Even if the near-death experience is not an indication of an after life, there is still a peculiar phenomenon that is scientifically troubling to explain.

One would expect that consciousness would begin to slow and shut down as the physical brain increasingly deadens and unravels, amazingly, however, the precise opposite occurs. Reality appears to become more real, perception more vivid, and there is a total expansiveness of consciousness. On a metaphysical level this can be understood as a result of the soul unhinging itself from the constriction of the material brain. Once the soul leaves the body the expansion of awareness is no longer filtered through the ego or the sensory functions, hence awareness is completely lucid and transparent.

Everything that is spoken of in front of the lifeless body the soul perceives. The soul, in a sense, watches and surveys what transpires from a distance, as if viewing another person's body. Even after burial, for the first three days the soul hovers over the body and observes (*Shabbos*, 152b. *Yerushalmi Moed Katan* 3:5. *Ma'avar Yavak* 2:7, p. 206).

Stage Two: Peacefulness

In the second stage, as the person realizes that he or she is no longer among the living and a sense of peacefulness and painlessness sets in.

Even if up until the point of death they may have been experiencing fear or apprehension, the moment they sense the soul leaving the body there is a complete absence of any type of anxiety, fright or panic. Death is like removing a strand of hair from a cup of milk. Such is the way the Talmud describes the process of the soul of the righteous leaving the body (Berachos, 8a). Yet, this is not always the case. Occasionally, the process of the soul exiting the body is similar to trying to pull a tangled rope through a narrow opening or withdrawing embedded thistles from a sheep's wool (Medrash Tehilim 11:6). This depends on the level of spiritual integration the person is at in the moment of death.

Later on we will discuss why some people (although optimistically speaking, few in number) experience fear and anguish while their soul is wrestling itself out of its physical form. For the most part, the transition from one life to the next is smooth, painless and utterly peaceful.

Stage Three:
Sounds

In the next stage many report hearing an uncomfortable hissing sound. Undoubtedly, however, this noise, as it is explained, has no physical property or resonance, otherwise everyone else would also hear it. Pleasant acoustic sounds and harmonious music appear to universally represent a sense of cosmic order. Conversely, acoustic dissonance and disharmony symbolizes an atmosphere of chaos and agony.

While a direct and explicit explanation is not found within the sources, the Talmud does mention sounds that the soul generates when leaving the body, as well as speaks of the cosmic noise created by the movement of the celestial spheres (*Yumah*, 20b. *Medrash Beis HaMedrash*, Perek Gehenom). The hissing we are speaking of may be somewhat related to this cosmic sound. And ultimately, whether it is heard as pleasant or annoying depends on the spiritual stature of the individual.

Stage Four:
Guf Dak - The Mental Body Double

As the physical body lies lifeless, the person undergoing the near-death experience may feel that he is assuming another form, a more refined translucent non-material type of 'body.' Every human being possesses both a Guf Gas/dense body and a Guf Dak/ethereal body (*Avodas Hakodesh*, 2:26. *Nishmas Chayim*, 1:13). The Guf Gas formation that we inhabit in this realm of existence is physical in shape and form. The Guf Dak is a more distilled and transparent version of the physical body. This Guf Dak is the body's prototype, the prefiguration that existed as primordial form prior to the emergence of our physical bodies. The Guf Dak can also be understood as a distinct, 'spiritualized' luminous configuration, which parallels the opaque physical form and holds together consciousness and body.

There are numerous names for the Guf Dak. At various times it is referred to as the Chaluka D'rabanan/garment of the sages (*Zohar* 1, p. 66a. *Shaarei Kedushah* 1:1), as a Malbush/garb (Seforno, *Kavanas HaTorah*), a Tzelem/shadow, otherwise known as the aura (*Nishmas Chayim*, 1:13), or simply as Ruach/ spirit (*Abarbanel*).

A person's relationship with his energy-body or his 'angelic-like' double, so to speak, is symbiotic and reciprocal. It is the means through which the body expands and develops (*Sefer Ha'emunos*, 6:4), and conversely it is also sustained throughout life by the person's very own behavior and mindset (*Beis Elokim*, Sha'ar Hayesodos, Chap. 53).

Everything a person thinks, feels or does has multi-layered and multi-di-mensional effects. A mental manifestation or projected image is exuded and fashioned through every action a person does or does not do. Positive vibrations emit positivity, while negative thoughts or actions generate fur-ther negativity. Mitzvos create a refined ethereal form while transgressions produce a negatively charged energy. The nature of the 'afterlife body' that the soul assumes is a direct reflection of their performance here on earth. These outer behavioral projections become a person's 'spiritual' body in the afterlife. Often, when people who have encountered the near-death expe-rience speak of an ethereal body that is perfect, without pain or paralysis, it can be assumed that the 'creator' of this body was a good person. Once the soul divests itself of corporeality it enters this insubstantial form and journeys on with this 'body' in the initial stages of the afterlife.

Guf Dak has no coarse representation and is therefore barely discernible. There are those who suggest that this body is a particle/wave-like energy system that has not yet been detected by any quantifiable measurement. Some have even given this energy field a name; some call it 'psitrons,' while others call it, 'theta agents.' But of course, since they have not yet been seen, just calling them a name does not make them any more real than if they were nameless. Either way, Guf Dak is a 'life-form' that is, for the most part, undetectable to the physical eye. And yet, sometimes people do get a glimpse of that reality, and occasionally even more than a glimpse.

After his passing, Rebbe Yehudah would appear every Friday evening in this ethereal life-form and recite the Kiddush over a cup of wine for his family (*Kesuvos*, 104a). According to some, he came in the form of his Guf Dak (*Rabbeinu Bachya*, Bereishis 49:33. *Sheivet HaMusar*, Chap. 35). Souls that become apparent in four-dimensional reality need to conform somewhat to the rules of this reality and so they enter a type of 'body' so that they can interact with physical human beings.

Many, apparently sane, individuals have reported sensing the presence of someone who has previously passed on. Even more, some even speak of 'seeing' a presence of someone who is no longer amongst the living. While the definition of 'seeing' is difficult to define, it appears as if the apparition possesses a human form. Occasionally, it seems as if the 'dead person' is suspended over a gathering, or even over his own funeral. Some of these phenomena, though not all, can be scientifically explained and substantiated. Yet, alternatively, it may also be a case in which a soul - or in some instances an angelic figure - descends and enwraps itself within a Guf Dak, within a Malbush, and becomes noticeable by those who experience a degree of heightened awareness. By embodying the Guf Dak, the soul of a departed person can become readily perceivable, so much so that their appearance seems as real to the observer as the floor they are standing upon.

Bodiless Energies

Inevitably this opens the door to discussing the general idea of ghosts, spirits, apparitions, phantoms and all the invisible entities or energies that many feel permeate our very own atmosphere. Those who profess a belief in the abovementioned speak of a sixth sense that resonates and picks up vibrations or traces of these forces. The way these 'entities' or energies are normatively experienced is by one sensing that something is there, an external or quasi-objective feeling or presence of sorts. Spirits are viewed as a residual resonance of the past being expressed in the present. Clearly these 'external' energies cannot be visually or empirically perceived, at least in the traditional way of seeing things, yet for those who claim to sense these realties they are as real as anything else. While the physical eye does not see the spirit, the 'third eye' does.

Years ago, prior to the modern revolution of science, any force that was quantifiably indiscernible but was still somehow felt was attributed to the world of spirits. This is one way modern man tries to explain away the idea of spirits, relegating them to a world of illusion or fantasy — the concept of something being a figment of one's imagination is another colloquial method of discounting these occurrences or apparitions. Accordingly a fair number of scientifically oriented individuals speak of apparitions as a type of illusion, a mental image originating in the mind that is projected as an external entity.

Illusory perception is indeed the way some authentic interpreters treat the classic tale in Neviim regarding necromancy. The book of Shmuel tells the story of the first king of Israel, Shaul and the witch. In the Tanach period, before a ruler engaged in battle, he would first ask the prophet whether he thought it was a good idea and the prophet in turn would enter a prophetic

state and seek divine guidance. When, following the demise of the prophet Shemuel, war with the Philistines appeared to be looming, Shaul tired
every possible method to procure divine counsel, but to no avail. When all
else failed, he felt he was left with no other option but to summon the soul
of the prophet by ways of witchcraft — even though it is against Torah law.
And that is exactly what he did. Disguising himself as a simple traveler he
left his palace and went to visit a witch.

During their encounter the witch apparently succeeded in her task and
Shaul was able to communicate with his departed master. While most traditional commentaries view this episode as a genuine exchange between a
deceased soul and a living one, there are some who interpret this incident
as a case of elaborate imagination and a piece of chicanery without a kernel
or trace of any validity (*Shmuel* 1, 28:14. Radak, Rashi and Ralbag, ad loc). According to those commentators, Shaul experienced an illusionary conversation
and perceived it as genuine. To put it simply, he was fooled.

Besides the workings of the imagination that may come into play, there is
also a rational explanation for the sighting of spirits, one that is not connected to the supernatural or paranormal. Any type of recording that is
done is achieved through imprinting an image or sound on a certain type
of medium that is receptive. For instance, a photograph is accomplished
when light activates certain chemicals to produce photochemical reactions.
The scene of the picture is transferred to the medium and is later reproduced on a sheet of paper. Perhaps, as some scientists suggest, the seeing of
'ghosts' is but a reproduction of an image that was long ago imprinted and
recorded in the fabric of a surface, much like a film, and when light shines
in a particular way on that surface the image reappears. The object appears
to exist but in reality is nothing more than a picture.

In a case where a photographic image is not feasible, the scientifically minded resort to the idea of illusionary perception as a valid explanation. From a spiritual perspective, these two, imagination and reality, are not necessarily mutually exclusive. Illusionary does not automatically mean that the thing one is hallucinating has no external property. An illusion can be an unclear or even lucid vision of something that does in fact actually exist. Some illusions are internally based and are purely a figment of the imagination. But there are some 'things' that may have an external reality, and yet the only way they can be perceived is not via the normative or rational ways of perceiving (i.e., the way the mind normally processes three-dimensional realities), but rather through the more imaginative faculties of human consciousness.

Souls, whether enclothed within a body or not, tend to sense each other's presence. The way consciousness feels this attraction is by sensing a 'presence,' something pulling or goading them towards a certain direction, thereby focusing their attention on a specific phenomenon within their immediate surroundings. The reason some people speak of sensing a lifeless soul within physical properties is because the soul, even when it leaves the state of corporality, is still connected and enclothed within a type of mass, a weightless translucent 'body,' and it is this 'body' that the living perceive.

Stage Five:
Passing a Tunnel

The tunnel is the next step in the near-death experience. A tunnel, or as others see it — a gate or bridge, is a symbolic image of transition. It is a metaphor for a state of passage, demonstrating the soul moving from one state of being into another. The tunnel itself is something like an intermediary stage connecting two very different fields of reality. There are sources that speak of the tunnel of Machpeilah/the burial site of Adam, Chava, the Patriarchs and most of the Matriarchs, as just such a liminal and transitional space (*Zohar* 1, 127a). After the soul passes from this world it journeys through the cave of Machpeilah en route to a higher realm of existence.

Stage Six:
Encountering Loved Ones

In the following stage one may encounter deceased family and friends as ethereal 'entities,' glowing in a radiant light. Angelic figures may also make their appearance in this stage. Esoteric Torah teachings speak of close relatives, friends and occasionally teachers who come to accompany the soul to the place of eternal rest (*Zohar* 1, p. 218b. Note: *Medrash Rabbah* Shemos, 52). They serve as a kind of guide to initiate the soul into the universe of bodiless consciousness.

Husbands and wives find each other here in the afterlife (*Zohar* 3, p. 167b. *Sha'ar Ta'amei HaMitzvos*, p. 5). And generally, families reunite and travel together to Gan Eden (*Kehilas Yaakov* 1, *Gan Eden* 8, p. 324). It goes without saying that there is immense spiritual excitement in heaven when souls realize that their beloved ones are about to rejoin them.

Our sages mention celebrated historical figures coming to greet souls who may have had a special connection with them. When the illustrious Talmudic sage Rebbe Yochanan Ben Zakai was about to pass on he said: "Prepare a seat for Chizkiah the King of Judah who has come to welcome me" (*Berachos*, 28b). According to other traditional texts, one of the people the soul perceives during the dying process is Adam, the primordial human being, the root of all souls and the genetic source of all mankind (*Zohar* 1, p. 57b. *Medrash Rabbah*, Bamidbar, 19:18). Interestingly, throughout the Torah in various incidences where it describes a person's passing, it says that the person has gone on or is gathered unto his ancestors, perhaps suggesting and alluding to this spiritual reunification.

Encountering Angelic Beings

Angelic beings or 'light entities' are another phenomenon that is often spoken of at this stage. The appearance of and reference to angels are found throughout the entire body of Torah. There are archangels and there are subangels, there are angels that were created in the beginning of time and there are angels that are continuously being brought into existence throughout time. There are angels that were created before man was created (Abarbanel, Bereishis 1:1. *Mifalos Elokim* 3:3–4), and there are angels that humans create (*Avos*, 4:11. Bartinora, ad loc. *Tomer Devorah* 1:2).

Angels are messengers and transmitters of energy (*Moreh Nevuchim*, 2:6. *Maam-or Haikkarim*, B'Ruchnim). An angel is a spiritual conduit, a qualitative reality that receives divine plenty from one realm and transmits it to another, and vice versa. Angels are the channels through which divine energy flows upwards and downwards, ascends and descends. Essentially, every force of creation is a kind of angel.

Being lodged in a four-dimensional universe, a world apprehended through the five constricting senses, man is unable to perceive that which operates on another wave-length or frequency. An angel may embody and project itself to a human being in a humanlike form, or for that matter assume a Malbush/an ethereal type of 'body,' so that a person can recognize and identify their presence. Yet these are only assumed forms and the true and inner essence of the angelic reality cannot be distinguished or detected by any physical instrument or operative system.

Angelic and physical realities function on two dissimilar wave-lengths, with polarized organizational principles and functional rules. While there are classic opinions that speak of angels as a refined version of fire (*Pirush on the Rambam*, Hilchos Teshuvah 8. *Meiras Einayim*, Parshas Re'eh, *Pardes Rimonim* 2:7), and there are those who confirm that angels are comprised of distilled fire and wind (Ramban, *Torah's Ha'adam*, Sha'ar Hagmul. *Sodei Razya*, Hilchos Malachim, p. 163. *Siddur Im Dach*, p. 275), there are yet others who speak of angels existing within any one of the four basic elements — fire, wind, water or earth (R. Mattisyohu Delecreta on *Shaarei Orah*, p. 100–101. *Pardes Rimonim* 24:11. *Kli Yakar*, Bereishis, 6:16). Nevertheless, the majority of opinions view angels as divested of all materiality (Rambam, *Hilchos Yesodei Hatorah* 2:3. *Safer HaNikud* 3:3). All are in agreement, however, that angelic properties (if they actually do have any) are radically different than anything experienced in a four-dimensional universe. For lack of anything better, the finest way to describe or picture the indescribable essence of an angel is as a pillar of light — light being the one property that is in fact physically detectable while at the same time physically ungraspable, it is both observable yet intangible.

After a person passes from this world the soul is welcomed and joined by angels (*Pesikta Rabti* 2:3). In fact, there are two or three angels that travel with us throughout life (*Pesikta Rabti* 44:8. *Hakdamah LeZohar*, p. 12b–13a. *Zohar 2*, p. 199a). They are what we generally call "guardian angels," the angels that walk with and beside us wherever we go. It is these spiritual manifestations that chronicle and retain the records of our life, including all our actions, thoughts, words and experiences (*Pesikta Rabti* 44:8. See also *Taanis*, 11A. *Tanna Divei Eliyahu Zuta* 1). Everything we do, think or feel creates an energy that assumes an objective reality, and that force itself is an accurate imprint of our life and actions. These angelic figures are replicated spiritual images of the totality of who we are, so much so that they are 'shaped' like us and even 'speak' in the same tonality and voice as ourselves (*Safer Chassidim*, 1161. *Ma'avar Yavak* 1:30).

A cosmic effect of every thought, action and experience is that it gives rise to an angelic energy. Physical/tangible actions influence physicality and inspire a material transformation of such energy, while the intention, the focus and the emotions involved in the act create a spiritual objective force, a pure angelic creation. The force that empowered the act becomes an entity unto itself, and that energy is then 'shaped' in the form of that action (*Sheim Me'Shemuel*, Shabbos Teshuvah). Angels that are brought into being through positive actions performed with complete mindfulness, fervor and passion, are 'perfected' energies, imbued with passion and purpose. While an angel created through half-hearted mindless actions are 'imperfect,' incomplete and disfigured.

The system is reciprocal. Positive actions inspire and create positive forces, while negative actions create negative vibrations. The completeness and wholesomeness of the angelic figure depends on the level of intellectual and emotional awareness and involvement of the person when they performed the action. Being fully present produces fully developed angels, while half-hearted actions create disfigured and disjointed ones.

Whereas light is a metaphor for an angel, it can also be a way to illustrate or allude to one's own higher self. As angels are identified with light, so are souls. "A candle of G-d is the soul of man," says the wise King Shlomo (*Mishlei* 20: 27). Encountering light may be the most accessible way to depict experiencing a revelation and manifestation of one's own higher/inner self. Every human being has an individual advocate above, an angelic force that guides him. The image of man below is a mirror reflection of that angelic image above. In other words, mans own inner image and that of his angel are one and the same (*Sodei Razya*, Hilchos Malachim. *Chachmas Hanefesh* , p. 382). To the person dying, radiant light is most often the metaphor employed to express what it feels like to experience the full articulation of soul, unhindered and unrestricted by the physical body.

Stage Seven:
Sensing the Light

Besides these ethereal light beings, one of the more prominent experiences of the near-death encounter is the sensing of the presence of an all embracing, loving and warming light, a radiant brightness that many identify with the Creator of all life.

A soul does not leave this plane of life until he sees the Divine presence (*Zohar* 3, p. 53a. 1, p. 98, 99a, p. 118b. *Medrash Rabbah Bamidbar* 14:2. *Pirkei De'rebbe Eliezer* 34. *Torahs Kohanim* 1). No soul departs from this world before the Shechinah/the divine feminine aspect of the glory of the Creator appears. And as a result of the deep longing to reunite with the Shechinah, the soul gently passes on and moves onward into the light.

Light is employed to capture the Imageless and Ineffable Creator (Devarim 4:24. *Mekor Chayim* 1:4). Categorically, the inner core and essence of the Creator cannot be contextualized nor quantified. No conventional language or poetic imagery can do justice to that which transcends all definitions. Yet, for lack of any better metaphor, divine emanation is referred to as Ohr/light, as in the Kabbalistic appellation, Ohr Ein Sof/the endless light. Universally, light is used as the image for enlightenment, wisdom and warmth. Seeing the great light has, historically, been one of the dominant ways human beings entrenched in dimensionality have described that which is beyond dimension. To those souls who feel at one with the light, the light is welcoming, emanating unconditional love and comfort. While to those souls who feel disconnected from their essence, the very same light appears threatening, overwhelming and blinding.

Stage Eight:
Panoramic Life Review

At a crucial point, often in the above sequence, the dying person experiences a total life review. At this point, a sort of panoramic view of one's entire life is revealed.

Nothing is ever lost. Everything is recorded. No experience, impression, emotion, thought, word or action ever vanishes completely. All of life is accurately transcribed and will one day be played back to us. Everything is "written down" (*Avos* 2:1. See also *Chagigah*, 5b. *Sotah*, 3b). When a soul passes into the next world all of his life is brought in front of him to be appraised and evaluated. There is a total life review (*Taanis* 11a. *Zohar* 2, p. 222a). Everything resurfaces to consciousness and there is an individual assessment of each thought, feeling or action, and of how they affected other people around them. Customarily in the life review everything appears at once, without a sequence or progression. The entire picture of life is on display as one image, as a single snapshot.

Speaking of the life review, one Medrashic source implies that the accompanying angels who travel along with man throughout life will be the ones to bear witness to man's behavior. Other sources speak of the soul bearing witness to its own evolution. And still other sources conclude that it is the limbs of the body that actually testify (*Taanis*, 11a. *Pesikta Rabti* 44:8. *Tanna Divei Eliyahu Zuta* 1).

Overall there are five witnesses that testify to the life one has lived, and they are: 1) his possessions, 2) his accompanying angels, 3) the limbs and bones of his body, 4) his soul, the backdrop of his story, 5) and the Creator (*Sodei Razya, Chachmas Hanefesh*, p. 1328–329). The essential point of all this is that all of our life (i.e., our thoughts, words, actions, feelings, thoughts, experiences and so forth) is imprinted on the very psyche of the human being. Either the encoding is in their surrounding aura, the angelic-like energy enveloping us (the Guf Dak), in the soul itself or even within our very limbs (i.e., the physical body). Nothing is ever lost in the universe (*Zohar* 2, p. 100b). This is the scientific principle of the conservation of energy. And one day, all of life (both energy and matter) will reappear and once again become manifest.

All of our memory is received, recorded and retained in a spiritual 'dropbox,' so to speak, and perhaps the material brain is nothing more than an antenna that beams and transmits our consciousness and memories to this 'virtual drive.' Everything is registered. The brain then selectively funnels through and allows only the critical information that it deems essential for our own existential survival to pass through to our conscious mind. Once, however, the soul is no longer restricted by the limiting apparatus of the mechanics of the brain (i.e., once the filtering device of the brain ceases to function and there is no ego identity to secure and uphold), the mind/soul, which by now has joined the 'mind of the Creator,' is completely expansive, open and transparent.

As the 'great limiter' of the ego is no more in control, there can be total recall and a unified measure of consciousness. In such a clear state, all of life becomes crystallized and one gets to observe and remember their entire life, the good as well as its opposite. Whether this viewing is a pleasant event or not depends on what is being shown, i.e., the contents of one's life.

In the course of experiencing a life review many report appearing in front of some form of board or judiciary body. Traditionally this is referred to as the Beis Din Shel Ma'alah/the Heavenly Tribunal (*Rosh Hashanah*, 8b). Once a soul leaves the body it must look deeply into the proverbial mirror of truth and face its own image. If negativity shows up in that mirror, a process of cleansing is in order. It is not 'revenge' or 'pay back', but rather an act of kindness so the soul can re-enter and join with its Source in Gan Eden (*Minchas Oni 2*, p. 355. *Maamorei Admur Hazoken*, Haketzarim, p. 451. *Minchas Yehudah*, Yechezkel, p. 168). Revenge is a negative act and one that is prohibited by the Torah. Certainly, the Giver of the Torah, the Creator of this spiritual principle and source of all of life, does not take revenge (*Beis Yaakov*, (Ishbitz) Vayikra, p. 4a).

At this point, the soul willingly desires to undergo the cleansing process, realizing that the procedure enables it to once again shine in its original brilliance. The light within can only merge with the 'light without' when there is a total level of integration and transparency—scrubbing off the 'dirt' of one's experiences accumulated throughout their life is the means to reach that ultimate goal.

Life and the hereafter is one seamless whole. What occurs in the afterlife is an extension of what occurred in life. Negativity in this life — whether by omission or commission, by act or by attitude — disconnects the doer from his inner self, and the effects, which are carried over into the next realm of existence, do not allow for a smooth soul reengagement or return to one's Source. The force that holds the soul from soaring upwards, the power that weighs the soul down from surging higher, is the gravitational pull of this negativity. It is our actions or inactions themselves that allow us to soar higher or sink lower, in this life and in the next.

According to tradition, the process of one's life-review follows as such: First comes Din/judgment, then comes Cheshbon/accounting (*Avos* 4:22). Though the order seems to be in reverse, typically there is an accounting and then a verdict follows, the wording is precise, full of both insight and intent. Following the journey through life one is shown a recording of an anonymous life. It is as if they are watching a film. They are then asked to pass judgment. Being as the ego and its attendant internal defense mechanism is fading, the judgment that is dispensed is objectively offered, with openness and fairness. Once judgment is given, the soul is informed that he was starring in the motion picture, which was, of course, the story of his very own life (*Likutei Maharan*, 113. *Bnei Yissachar*, Elul 2:4). The person himself gives the verdict. We are, essentially, our own judge (*Keser Shem Tov*, Hosofos, p. 26); albeit without knowing that we are also the one on trial.

The moral contained within this narrative or series of events is: "Judge every person favorably" (*Avos* 1:6). Train yourself to be less judgmental and that will serve you well, in the now as well as in your afterlife. If you are in the habit of being non-judgmental, and when you do pass judgment you do so favorably, in the afterlife you will appraise yourself sympathetically.

Overall, although the experiences reported are near-death experiences, not after death, and the traditional life review is primarily an 'after' death occurrence, even still, on the day of a person's passing they are granted a vision that is otherwise unavailable, and they are able to see their entire life pass in front of them (*Zohar* 1, p. 79a). And so, even in a near-death experience one may get a glimpse of their life in such a simultaneous panorama. Indeed, there is a life review both after death and before death, during the moments when a person is moving on from this world and into the next.

Righteous people are shown Gan Eden even before they pass on (*Medrash Rabbah*, Shemos 52:3) so they can pass from this world and move into the next with joy, peace and tranquility (The Alshich, *Ma'avar Yavak* 1:17. *Akeidas Yitzchak*, 22).

Stage Nine:
Beyond Time

Timelessness is felt throughout the near-death experience, everything appears to be occurring instantaneously. It is not everlastingness that is necessarily felt, but rather eternity, and there is a marked distinction between the two. Everlastingness is the sequence of time itself forever unfolding, eternity is outside the realm of time. The experience of eternity, as timelessness and spacelessness, is appreciated as a sense of operating in a universe that is entirely unrelated to time or space.

Stage Ten:
Asked to Return

Ultimately, a divider or gate of sorts is reached and the soul then returns to the body (if they are indeed experiencing a 'near-death' experience). In the initial stages, the deep yearning and longing to reunite takes hold and the soul desires to be lost in the light, at which point the radiance of this universe is displayed and the accomplishments that can be achieved via embodiment are revealed. The soul then gradually becomes manifest once again in the body.

In conclusion, although many of the issues raised and the texts explored were referring to the 'after-life' and the near–death experience is 'near' not 'after,' even still, as the righteous are about to depart this world their due spiritual reward is shown to them and the vision arouses great joy within them. The enchanting imagery appears specifically during the process of death (not only after) so that the soul can leave the body in a state of ease and a sense of pleasantness.

Arguments & Counterarguments
Supporting the Authenticity of the Experience:

What remains an open question, and perhaps one that can never be fully answered, is whether these reported near-death experiences are in fact genuine or not. But what is certain, is that there is a real possibility for an authentic experience.

As in every other facet of life there are several available avenues of interpretation. Some people adamantly view the near-death vision as proof for an afterlife, and yet others are more skeptical and hesitant to draw the same conclusions. Often, this more skeptical viewpoint is espoused by those who would also agree that the absence of evidence is not necessarily conclusive evidence of absence. The primary issue they take with the proposition is whether it is scientifically grounded or not.

To present a comprehensive overview of the subject it behooves us to give voice to both opinions, including the arguments and counterarguments, the supports and refutations.

A basic contention for the skeptical minded is that the description given for the near-death experience is fundamentally the same description that is offered by those who are 'hallucinating' due to an intake of narcotics or some other external stimulus. The argument is that the experience is purely a chemical reaction that causes such illusions, and is therefore not a vision that arises from some sort of bodiless consciousness. In a dying patient, it is the oxygen deprivation that gives rise to fantastical imagery, and not some spiritual out of body phenomenon.

Those who are more psychologically oriented may argue that the myriad of beautiful and delightful visions that appear to the mind are conjured up by the dying person himself as a self-protective mechanism to uphold and push aside the overwhelming fear of death. In effect, it is the person himself who produces the imagery of an afterlife so that he can tame his fear of absolute extinction.

We will now explore the counter-arguments for each of the ten stages of the near-death experience.

Stage One:

Earlier the near-death experience was divided into ten progressive stages, the first being the experience of hearing oneself declared dead. Yet, researchers speculate that even while people appear to be unconscious information still registers in the brain. To the extent that many people seem to recall what occurred around them even when they were, at the time, unconscious. While this may be true it does not explain the testimony, assuming they are trustworthy, of people who speak of knowing what was said and done in other rooms or for that matter when a blind man reports accurate details of his room's formation or color. In such cases the physical reception of the brain is an unlikely resource of information and the knowledge needs to be attributed to some other source.

Stage Two - Three:

A sense of peacefulness, tranquility and total serenity, which is the second stage, can be explained away rationally and scientifically without reverting to the supernatural. The body, we have come to learn, produces natural painkillers called endorphins, which are pumped into the bloodstream during a time of crisis. Endorphins are internally created morphine-like chemicals. Among their effects are pain reduction and feelings of euphoria. The body protects itself from danger. In moments of extreme pain it will naturally produce these painkillers so that it will feel less or even no pain at all.

Pain, generally speaking, is not a 'bad' thing, for it is the means by which the body informs the mind that danger looms, forcing the person to respond accordingly and find help. Too much pain however, as when the body is dying, can cause an overload to the brain and be counterproductive. For this reason the brain produces pleasant painkillers and gives the body a better chance to recover. These 'calming chemicals' are one way to explain why a dying person feels serenity and peacefulness.

There are those who speculate that the near–death experience is due to anoxia, which is a lack of oxygen to the brain, which would explain why the experience is similar to seizures of the temporal lobe. Others argue that it can be a result of hypoxia, an overabundance of oxygen, which would explain why the experiencer would feel quite peaceful and at ease. Yet, these rationalizations are somewhat flawed simply because many people, as research has shown, who have encountered the near-death experience are neither anoxic nor hypoxic.

Stage Four:

At some point the dying person senses himself separating from his body and viewing his body from above. Being survival-based, people will conjure up or imagine anything possible to help them survive. Psychologically there is ample reason why a person would want to feel himself distancing from his injured body. By becoming emotionally detached from the body that is wounded, observing the body from above, one becomes more equipped to handle the situation without panic. It affords him the ability to call forth new potentially life-saving energy from within.

As a matter of fact, any memory of our selves is simply a recalling of what has occurred to us as seen from a kind of removed 'bird's eye' view. A part of our consciousness is always somewhere in the background bearing witness to any event that we are experiencing. We remember ourselves doing something but it is as if we are a separate entity, a third person, watching ourselves while doing that act.

Wishful thinking is another counter-argument against the authenticity of the near-death experience. The hypothesis is that seeing one's body from a detached location is simply a fantasy of sorts. A deaf, blind or handicapped person, whether actually or imaginably, may visualize himself inhabiting a flawless body. The same is true with those who were in an accident and severed a limb. Having been knocked unconscious they may observe their physically ravaged bodies lying on the ground and simultaneously wish into existence an ethereal-like replica of themselves, which is perfect and whole.

Autoscopic vision, a self-seeing hallucination, is another issue that needs to be discussed. An autoscopic hallucination is where people see a reflected image of themselves as an external entity. It may occur when a person suffers from a brain tumor, stroke, migraine headache or epilepsy. Or when a reflection of the self is seen elsewhere, which is a psychological disorder referred to as derealization. This phenomenon has been recorded throughout the ages. Some years back, Aristotle spoke of a fellow Athenian who would walk the streets of Athens and see himself in the crowd.

Yet, autoscopic hallucination and body-vision in the near-death experience are quite different. There is a clear distinction between the two. In an autoscopic vision the person sees the body alive and vibrant, even perhaps talking back to him. In the near death experience, however, one sees the body as a lifeless unresponsive carcass. What's more, in an autoscopic hallucination the awareness occurs from within, observing the self from one's own eyes, as it were, perceiving a projected image of oneself. Conversely, in the near-death experience the center of awareness appears to be 'outside' the body. One sees the body lying there as if from another location unrelated to the body.

Stage Five — Six — Seven:

Tunnel vision is one of the most well-known phenomena associated with the near-death experience. Precisely because of its popularity there are numerous theories and counter theories regarding its validity and authenticity.

Eye deterioration, which occurs during the shutting down of the brain, is one hypothesis that is quite commonly cited. There are also scientists who speculate that tunnel vision originates from a dim 'birth memory,' when the person passed through the birth canal.

The next progressive phase in the near-death encounter, the sixth stage, is that of seeing 'light entities,' often perceived of as family, angels or even G-d. To continue the metaphor of birth, as cited above in the example of 'tunnel vision,' this stage of 'seeing the light' would be parallel to the next stage of birth, i.e., following the journey through the birth canal. After the infant passes through a dark birth canal there is an abundance of light, like a light at the end of a tunnel, so to speak. Essentially, according to this hypothesis, the light entities are nothing more than birth memories of the sunlight or of the light of a fluorescent bulb at the time of being born.

Today most researchers dismiss this theory, and for various reasons. First of all, we now know that the eyesight of a newly born child is too underdeveloped, if there is even any eyesight at all, to visually register its experience in the birth canal. Besides, infants are usually born with their heads pressed down on the canal and their eyes are tightly closed. Rarely is a child born looking forward with eyes wide open.

What is more, according to this hypothesis, those who were born via caesarian would not experience this vision during a near-death encounter, as they would not have had this primal tunnel and light experience. But this does not seem to be the case when compared to the experiences of people who have had near-death experiences. In addition, birth can hardly be considered a peaceful experience. Being pulled or pushed into a cold unfamiliar world from the warm security of the womb does not register as a pleasant experience, and yet the near-death experience is most often utterly peaceful and pleasant.

Others speculate that the sensation of passing through a dark tunnel can be explained by cerebral anoxia or oxygen deprivation. Additionally, some researchers conjecture that a mixture of neural activation and inhibition produces labyrinthine patterns in the cortex of the brain that, due to what is called 'retinocortical transformation,' materializes as tunnel-like images in the visual field. The trouble with the cerebral anoxia theory is that there are many people who have experienced tunnel vision in a near-death encounter and yet they have not suffered from any oxygen loss.

Oxygen deprivation is also used to explain the resurfacing of old memories. The problem is that oxygen deprivation is known to cause dizziness, fuzzy thinking and vagueness, but nothing like the rematerializing memories of the near-death experience.

Various chemical conditions are also employed to explain the encountering of loved ones during a near-death experience. When the brain becomes overloaded and is in disarray it will release old memories or project inter-

nally sourced dreams. Meeting loved ones occurs when the brain repro-
duces the memory of the loved one. While perceiving the Creator, angels,
old mentors or religious figures is the mind clinging to its most secure and
fantastic dreams and images in a time of devastating crisis.

Intellectually this theory of clinging to positive memories may resonate,
but empirically it is quite refutable. Some noted researchers have testified
that from all the children who have reported experiencing a near–death
experience, not one of them saw their mother or father during their experience, unless that parent was no longer alive. This apparently shows that
the idea of hanging on to our fondest memories in order to help alleviate
a life threatening situation cannot be the source of the memory. More
shocking is the fact that some people see relatives that they did not even
know and could not have known existed — like a brother or sister, uncle or
aunt who were born and died long before them, and were never spoken of.

Stage Eight:

Following these ethereal light 'entities' — whether they are previously deceased relatives bathed in light, angelic figures or for that matter, Hashem— there is, as we have established, a kind of life-review.

There are a number of logical methods available to explain this most fantastic of phenomena. The neuro-physiological explanation is as follows:
Through the gradual depletion of oxygen, which occurs near death, minor
seizures of the temporal lobes may occur and, as a result, old memories
may rematerialize. In fact, probing the temporal cortex and stimulating it
with a mild electric shock brings to consciousness previously lost or hidden memories.

When, in the 1950's, a Canadian surgeon passed a mild electric current through electrodes connected to certain regions of the visual cortex, patients began to remember events and occurrences of the past in detail and as if they were reliving those events with all their sights, sounds and smells. Once the current was shut off the induced memory was instantaneously lost. Yet, every time that region was once again stimulated the entire memory came back and, interestingly, it did not continue from where it left off previously, but started all over again. It was as if there was a place in the brain that records incidences as they occur. This was referred to as the "experiential response," a full reenactment of a previously lived experience.

As sensible a theory as it may seem, there are some loose ends that do not add up. There are researchers who contend that the images that are conjured up through seizures are generally not known to be arranged in a chronological order, they do not appear in the mind as in the order of life. While on the other hand, for those who experienced these images during a near-death encounter the order of the events was in fact chronological.

Beyond the physiological there are also psychological reasons that are offered to explain this phenomenon. One theory is that in order to help the conscious mind escape the horrible reality of death, the mind automatically reverts to and revisits old childhood memories. Again, the issue that this explanation does not make clear is why the mind would produce images in the same order as they occurred. If it is a way to deal with the pain, why would being two years old resurface before one recalls being three years old? The preference should be the pleasantness of the memory, not its chronological sequence.

Stage Nine – Ten:

Throughout the near-death experience there seems to be an absence of time or space, one appears to be operating in a dimensionless reality.

This concept of spacelessness and timelessness can also be somewhat explained scientifically, without resorting to the paranormal. The premise is that once certain regions of the brain begin to deteriorate and cease to function properly the perceptions of time and space become less pronounced.

There are studies that demonstrate quantifiable phenomena that explain why people who enter deep meditative states or prayer or even deep thinking, experience a sense of spacelessness or oceanic boundlessness. This sense can be summed up, as the great physicist Albert Einstein once said, as the feeling that "the universe is a single significant whole," or, as the quantum physicist Edwin Schrödinger wrote: "you and all other conscious beings as such are all in all."

By mapping the brain before and during meditation with a computer scan to portray the brain's activity in red and yellow colors, research has found that there occurred a striking color change in a certain part of the brain during peak moments of meditation and relaxed focus.

On the left side of the cerebrum, right behind the crown of the skull, there is a region in the brain that is called the posterior superior parietal lobe. When a person is in a regular mood of consciousness this part of the brain shows up on the computer as flaming red. However, during peak moments of meditation this area becomes a deep azure, which shows that there is a substantial decline in that region's activity. This is the part of the brain that helps us orient ourselves in time and space and gives the body its sense of physical limits. It is precisely this parietal lobe that helps us locate ourselves in space, assisting us so we do not walk into walls. When there is a substantial decrease in this region's activity, and there is no longer a vital sensory stimulus to clearly define the borders between us and the world around us, the brain perceives and concludes that the self is endless and is truly interwoven with everyone and everything.

In all honesty, with all the attractiveness of this theory, the issue remains unresolved and it is still open for further exploration. The question that can never be truly answered is this: Is this experiential phenomenon of dimensionless being a physical manifestation of a spiritual occurrence, or is this merely a physical phenomenon, which is interpreted as a spiritual event? In other words, is the physical experience in the brain the cause of the experience or the effect? Is it simply an external symptom of a spiritual phenomenon, or is the external sensation the source and generator of the experience itself?

The truth is that we can draw a parallel between this and any experience we have. Let us take for example the experience of looking at a physical object. If we recognize and map the brain to see how it works in a particular manner when observing an outside object, this would not deny the fact that there is an external object that is being observed. All we have done is shown what happens to the brain when it is observing. The same can be said with these mystical types of near-death experiences. It can be argued that all science is telling us is what happens to the brain when it is going through a mystical experience, not that the brain activity is the actual cause of the experience.

Issues such as these, open-ended and unresolved as they are, must be left for each individual person to decide on their own. To some extent, a person's interpretation will be based largely on his own predispositions and personal inclinations. It is a subjective matter and not so much an objective one, though we may believe otherwise. Therefore it is an issue that can never be fully resolved with a consensus amongst all people and must be decided by each person individually.

Overall it is difficult to completely dismiss the near-death experience as illusory and a mere figment of the dying person's overactive imagination. There seems to be a profound difference between schizophrenics and other related psychoses and the near-death experience. The former is generally negative, with a propensity to bring the person down or for them to feel unrealistically high about themselves, while the latter is positive and often empowering. Illusionary perception causes one to think either extremely negatively about himself or quixotically positive, such as thinking that he is a famous Emperor, King or Tzadik, with the end result being despair and depression; while the near-death experience appears to have the converse affect. It tends to inspire and make the person a healthier functioning human being — kinder, nicer and ever more loving.

In addition, and in absolute contrast to the psychotic experience, people who undergo the near-death experience have quite a good handle on life, and are in no way out of touch with reality. To the contrary, they observe and report details that were otherwise overlooked. These people, unlike those who suffer from distorted perception, seem to operate in a heightened sense of awareness with quite a keen sense of focused perception.

On a more scientific note it is also problematic to attribute the near-death experience to mere hallucination. Essentially, in order to hallucinate there needs to be some level of brain activity, and yet some people have experienced near-death encounters while their brainwaves appeared to be flat. Within the reported cases of near-death experiences there have been some people who went through the experience while being connected to an electroencephalograph, and all throughout there were no signs of any brain activity.

The World as our Mirror:

Having explored the particulars of the experience from a scientific perspective, its arguments and counter-arguments, there is still one more principle issue that needs to be broached and clarified. Upon closer examination it becomes fairly obvious that there is a major inconsistency regarding the details of the near-death experience. Although as a whole the experiences recorded throughout history are similar, the details of the experience are greatly dissimilar. In fact the entire experience appears to be culturally conditioned. What is encountered varies from one place and time to the next depending on the geography, history, and Weltanschauung of the people of which the person was a part.

From the little that is known of the past it seems that people who reported experiencing what we today call a near-death experience, experienced it quite differently than today. Years back people spoke of first undergoing a series of trials, judgments and tests before they were allowed to enter heaven. They also often spoke of passing a gate or bridge with a beastly powerful animal protecting the entrance.

A hell of fire and brimstone is another phenomenon that seems to have been quite a popular trope years-back. The ancient Egyptians spoke of Anubis, a dog-headed deity who escorts the soul throughout the journey of the afterlife, and other cultures as well spoke of barking dogs who did not allow the soul to enter into the realm of the afterlife. Many ancient people spoke of the soul crossing a river with a boat or of going over a bridge. Also the vivid image of a 'tunnel' per se is not found at all in ancient recordings, although the general idea of transition is present, but it was expressed in different forms and images. Keep in mind that the idea of passing through a dark tunnel was common in medieval times, whereas today, less than ten percent of people interviewed say they encounter a tunnel. All in all, many of the concepts spoken of today are not found in the literature of times gone by, and many of the adventures found in the writings of yesteryear are not found today.

Even today what is experienced varies from one people/culture to the next. People from different parts of the world encounter diverse experiences. Most of the research has been done in the West where people tend to think along similar lines. The little research that comes out of the East is unsurprisingly different. In the East people report that they are first escorted by a spirit messenger, and later on in the process they speak of encountering a 'man with a book.' Once it is discovered that a mistake has been made and the person's time to pass on has not yet arrived, the person is escorted back down to earth by a messenger or departed relative. The idea of viewing the body from another location and seeing the body from 'above' is very rare; also the panoramic life review is completely unknown in the east.

Within each culture itself the experience varies from one person to the next. No two people describe the same experience as the other. The inconsistency and apparent discrepancy has been a major challenge to verifying the authenticity of the near-death experience. In defense of the legitimacy of the experience it is important to keep in mind that not every near-death experience is in fact genuine, and it may indeed be an imaginary fantasy. But more importantly, people see in their dreams what they are accustomed to seeing during their waking hours, and the near-death dreamlike vision is no exception.

Take, for example, the idea of going through a dark tunnel. Scores of medieval artists depicted the journey of the afterlife in terms of going through a dark tunnel. Among the more famous is the sixteenth-century painting by the Flemish artist, Hieronymus Bosch, entitled "The Ascent into the Empyrean." As a result of this reoccurring cultural image and archetype, either subconsciously or by osmosis, near-death visions were almost always accompanied by such tunnel visions. When the above image no longer captivated audiences, tunnel visions subsided and other metaphorical images arose. Essentially, images and metaphors are a reflection of their times, although what they represent is a truth beyond it.

What is more, even authentically revelatory experiences are funneled through the consciousness of the human being. Perception, no matter whose, as long as there is some measure of 'ego' and 'self' involved, is always bound to the physical senses and connected to some material structure. Every experience, even a genuine one, is anchored in one's personal understanding and conditioned according to each person's power of discernment and personal proclivities. For this reason, even amongst the master prophets, no two experiences are alike, and they all speak of sensing alternative spiritual realities. Yeshayahu/Isaiah saw one thing while Yechezkel/Ezekiel saw another. Both are true and valid expressions of the Divine, and yet each prophet could only observe the experience according to his own level of consciousness and consistent with their own set and setting — i.e., their prior mindset and culture/environmental conditioning (Chagigah, 13b). Incidentally, after the experience itself, what they attempt to describe in 'conventional' transmittable language, replete with relevant and relatable imagery, is pale in comparison to the actual experience that took place on another dimension of reality.

Fundamentally, the way people observe life is to a large degree dependent on their biography, education and environment. Certainly the various descriptions and imagery of 'otherworldly' realities are founded on the ways such a person navigates through this time-space realm of existence. The 'light' that awaits a person shines through the vessels of the various images one holds dear. The expressions of the experience are channeled through the cultural structure of the experiencer.

The world is full of mirrors. We see in others, images of who we are. The world is our mirror (*Keser Shem Tov*, Hosofos,152. *Meor Einayim*, Chukas). This is true not only of other people, but even with the Divine. Hashem appears and is understood by each person differently. "Hashem is man's shadow," Dovid HaMelech says (*Tehilim* 121:5). As such a shadow, each individual person experiences the Divine according to the proportions of his or her own internal paradigm (*Kedushas Levi*, Parshas Nosa. *Nefesh HaChayim* 1:7). Inconsistency of near-death imagery only reinforces the beautiful truth that each soul is truly different and unique; each person is operating with a distinct mind and individuated power of imagination. Each individual finite soul represents another facet of the Infinite Oneness.

Ultimately, all opinions agree that at the time of death many people undergo a promising and pleasant experience, one that is true, at the very least, to the experiencer. These experiences are often reported to enhance and change lives for the better, and indeed in our context, this is what really matters.

CHAPTER 6
Soul Leaving Body

The Soul Entering and Leaving in Stages

The soul reaches and penetrates all levels of existence. There are elements of the soul that remain above the body's standard mode of operation, while there are soul sparks that are intimately integrated within the body.

Souls are multi-dimensional and multi-faceted. There are both transpersonal and individualized sparks, there are purely transcendent dimensions of soul as well as embodied aspects that animate and give life to the body. As mentioned — Na'ra'n (the Nefesh, Ruach and Neshamah) constitutes normative consciousness. There are also deeper, higher and more expansive states of soul that envelop and encircle the human being. There is the

Makif Ha'karov/Immediate Surrounding, and there is the Makif Ha'ra-chok/Distant Surrounding.

As intelligence and human development evolves over the course of life, the soul as well enters and impacts one's being in progressive stages. The initial connection is at conception, but ultimately the soul only becomes more assimilated at maturity - twelve or thirteen for girls or boys respectively - and then again later on at twenty and only fully at forty. The process reverses itself in death, meaning that the soul also leaves the body in phases.

There is a severance from the body of the most apparent manifestations of soul at the moment of death, and yet still, while the body lies lifeless, the soul does not instantaneously disintegrate or completely disappear — it still exists and is in some way still present. The more conscious aspects of the soul retreat from the body at the moment of death and yet traces of soul-energy remain attached to the body for a longer period of time.

There is a gradual procedure of how the soul enters and exits the body. The process of the soul leaving the body begins prior to the actual clinical death. Even before the essential separation and severance that occurs between life and death (i.e., the moment that divides physical life from the next world), there are soul properties that will have already begun to detach from the body.

The Tzeil / The Aura

Every human being possesses a Tzeil, which can be translated as an 'aura,' a shadow of sorts, the ethereal body; and that Tzeil is what departs in advance of the actual moment of death (*Zohar* 1, p. 217b, 220a. Bamidbar 14:9, Ramban and Rabbeinu Bachya, ad loc. *Safer Chassidim* 547. *Sefer Ha'emunos* 6:4). The Tzeil ascends and unifies with the Tzeil of the Ohr Ein Sof/Infinite Light thirty days before death. From this teaching we can discern that death does not occur suddenly and there are no accidents. No matter the circumstance of a person's death—whether it was a natural death, or one caused by an accident or illness—thirty days prior to their death, parts of their soul have already begun to slowly ascend.

There is a spiritual phenomenon that is referred to as Hargashos Ha'avir, literally translated as, 'sensing the atmosphere' (R. Shem Tov Ibn Gaon, *Keser Shem Tov*, Ki Tetze. *Recanti*, Ki Tetze. Rebbe Yoseph Shlomo Delmedigo, *Metzareph LeChachmah*, p. 15b). Highly sensitive and refined individuals can discern this Tzeil, this 'aura' or surrounding light, that envelopes a person, and through it they can peer, as if through a prism, into another person's psyche.

One of the primary spiritual teachers of the thirteenth century was Rebbe Yitzchak Sagi Nahor — Rebbe Isaac the Blind. The Hebrew words Sagi Nahor literally mean 'excess light' or 'excess vision.' This phrase was employed as a euphemism referring to people who were visually impaired. But in the case of Rebbe Yitzchak, this was meant quite literally. For although he was physically blind, on a spiritual level, his vision was quite clear and penetrating. In fact he was known to be able to both observe other people's thoughts, as well as to 'sense the air' around them, meaning that he could perceive and then impart a person's soul-type or soul-root. He also had the ability, through sensing whether the aura is with the body or not, to discern whether death was looming and imminent.

Sensing one's own Tzeil as it is departing is also a real possibility. There are many people who seem to sense their immediate physical demise, whether by the things they do or the thoughts they express. In such instances, and for such people, there appears to be a deep precognition that their death is immanent (*Medrash Rabbah*, Bamidbar, 19:17). This phenomenon could be a result of the person being super spiritually sensitive, possessing an acute awareness that their Tzeil has parted thirty days prior (*Ohr Hachayim*, Bereishis, 47:29). It is also possible for a person that has a highly evolved consciousness to be aware when another person's Tzeil has already left them (Chasam Sofer, *Torahs Moshe*, Vezos Haberachah).

The Tzeil is said to appear as a person's literal shadow, so one can detect its disappearance by observing its absence in the moonlight. Yet, generally speaking, we should not pay attention to such matters (Ramah, *Orach Chayim* 664:1), as most people simply do not know how to really look for such a phenomenon.

According to the Zohar a person's Tzeil will ascend from his body on the night of Hoshanah Rabbah - the seventh day in the holiday of Sukkos, and the twenty-sixth day from the beginning of creation - if they are destined to pass from this world within a year (*Zohar* 1, p. 220a. *Zohar* 2, p. 142b. *Ramban*, Bamidbar 14:9. *Tziyoni*, Shelach). Later on, after the holiday, the Tzeil returns to the body and stays with the person until thirty days before they are actually going to pass on. And, as mentioned, on the thirtieth day before their death it ascends for good.

Once the so-called aura/shadow leaves the body it is only a matter of time before the more manifest aspects of soul begin to depart. But, as always, through the power of Teshuvah/Reintegration and Self-Reconstruction everything can be readjusted and all decrees can be overturned. Even though there are meta-physical principles within the world of the spirit, and, as with the physical dimension, once something is set into motion the law of inertia takes hold, even still, through Teshuvah we have the ability to halt the quasi-mechanical causality of the spiritual world and suspend the apparent immutability of determinism. Simply put, through Teshuvah we have the power to reverse that which has been commenced and the Tzeil can thereby return to the body.

Nehurah / Pillar of Fire

Death occurs when there is a physical meltdown of the body and the Na'ra'n (Nefesh, Ruach and Neshamah) levels of soul dissipate. Discussing the soul's exit from the body, the tenth century sage Rebbe Saddiah Gaon explains that we are not able to visually observe the soul ascending from the body because of the soul's air-like transparency, similar to the heavenly spheres above (*Emunos VeDeyos* 6:7). Although, interestingly enough, according to Rebbe Saddiah the soul is actually a kind of 'physical substance,' albeit an undetectable one (although see, Alter Rebbe, *Likutei Torah*, Berachah, 98a). Furthermore, the mystics explain the soul as a kind of substance that is itself insubstantial. To capture this paradoxical idea they often use the poetic image of the soul being a spark of the Infinite Light. Although, there have been reports throughout the generations of someone actually seeing something that appears as a pillar of fire rising from the body at the moment of death. The Talmudic term for this light is Nehurah (*Kesuvos*, 17a). Clearly, this sighting is not optical in nature, but rather it is observed with the third eye, as it were. In other words, it is detected by a higher sense.

In the sixteenth century, following the expulsion of practicing Jews from Spain in the year 1492, the holy city of Safed, under the rule of the Ottoman Empire, found itself to be an oasis of spirituality, a hub for mystics, poets, philosophers and codifiers of Jewish law. One of the great luminaries of that period was the Ramak, Rebbe Moshe Corodovero. In the year 1570 as the Ramak was about to pass on to the next world he informed his close disciples that the person who will notice a pillar of fire at his funeral should become their next mentor. During the funeral precision a bystander by the name of Rebbe Yitzchak Luria, later to become known as the Arizal, noticed the column of light and accordingly directed them to the place where the Ramak was to be buried. Soon thereafter, when his vision became known, the students of the Ramak accepted him as their new teacher and master.

Sightings such as these have been reported throughout the ages and across numerous cultures. Countless witnesses attest to seeing luminous rays of light surrounding bodies after their death. In fact there are scientists who suggest that 'the light from the body' is a physical phenomenon and not necessarily a spiritual one and is therefore observable with the naked, though trained, eye.

In 1908 a French physician distributed pictures he snapped of an apparent haze rising from a lifeless corpse. While it piqued great interest neither he nor anybody else were ever able to retake new photographs of such a phenomenon. Soon thereafter these pictures were dismissed, either because they were a result of a mechanical error or the camera merely picked up a shadow of something. Others speculated a more scientific interpretation. There are various gases of decay; for example, phosphorescent hydrogen, which can be luminescent especially during the warmer parts of the year. Perhaps the image of the photo was of this luminescent gas. Yet, from traditional Kabbalistic sources it seems that the Nehurah is a 'spiritual' phenomenon, and not a physical fire that can be captured in a photo.

The First Three, Seven and Thirty Days After Death

At the moment of death the Nefesh, Ruach and Neshamah rise upwards whereas the body continues to linger on. It is only much later that the physical properties of the body rearrange themselves and merge with the elements of the earth. The dimensions of soul that depart at death are the 'animating' aspects of the soul, what remains are the 'sustaining' aspects. Nefesh is subdivided into Nefesh Ha'mechaya/the vitalizing energy and

Nefesh Ha'mekayem/the sustaining energy (Rebbe Rayatz *Safer Hamaamorim* 5694, p. 29). The former leaves the body at death, the latter remains temporarily still vested within the body.

Earlier the idea of a cord was employed as a metaphor for the soul. In its highest reaches the soul is part of the All, it is one with the Ein Sof and extends 'downward' to animate and sustain corporeal existence. Once the cord is severed and the energy flow is cut off, so to speak, the higher dimensions of the soul ascend upwards and the power of the sustaining soul slowly diminishes. Nefesh Ha'mekayem can only relay energy 'below' to the body as much as it is fed from a higher source. Nefesh is a transmitter of energy not an originator. In time, the energy diffuses and becomes dimmer and the body, as a result, slowly begins to disintegrate and fall apart. A helpful example of this would be to pull the plug of a lamp out of its socket. For the first few moments the light still shines, then slowly it dims, and finally fades.

Having been housed in a body for an extended duration of time the soul grows comfortable in such a situation, therefore when it needs to leave (i.e., during the process and moment of death), a longing to remain in close proximity to its former home ensues. For the first three days after the severance of body and soul the soul/consciousness lingers on next to or right around the body. Despondently, the soul hovers above its body hoping to return. When, after three days, the soul notices the disfiguring face and how the body is beginning to decompose, the soul starts to rise from the presence of the body (*Yerushalmi Moed Katan*, 3:5. *Medrash Rabbah Bereishis*, 100:7). Mirroring the soul's own grievances, Halacha/Jewish law imbues the first three days of mourning with particular significance; this period has its own set of laws and distinct customs (*Moed Katan*, 27b). These are known as the "three days of weeping." These first three days constitute the initial period of mourning and they serve as a double consolation; comforting the soul that has left this world and, at the same time, consoling the bereaved that were left behind.

Slowly weaning itself from its dependency on the body the soul begins to move about more freely, although, the 'movement' is somewhat restricted and primarily revolves around familiar locations. For the first seven days after death the soul wanders about to and fro, roaming back and forth from the house it lived in to the grave, and from the grave to the house (*Zohar* 1, p. 218b–219a. *Likutei Torah*, Vayechi). Reflecting this process is the dedicated time frame of seven days of Shiva, a time to offer comfort, consolation and healing both for the disembodied soul and for the grief-stricken mourners. This consolation is given through the various practices of Shiva, the mourning rites and rituals following death.

While the general understanding of Shiva is that it is a time in which to comfort the living, it is in fact even more that that. During the Shiva period, the soul may be feeling deep regret and lack of fulfillment which causes it to cling to its earthly form, unwilling to let go. When the mourners, and those who come to comfort them, speak of the departed's accomplishments and good deeds they are feeding these words to the soul itself, allowing the deceased to accept that his or her earthly task was completed. And as such, the soul feels free to rise.

Sheloshim, which is the longer period of thirty days following death, is the next timetable of mourning. Once again, it has its own set of laws and particular customs. Gradually becoming more acclimated to spiritual reality, the soul starts to loosen its ties with the trivialities of physicality. Yet, for the first thirty days the soul is still found roaming around the more earthly realms of existence, only ascending slowly and progressively (*Zohar* 2, p. 199b).

The final stage of mourning is at the conclusion of the first year. During the duration of the first year the soul ascends and descends, rises and returns. (There is a tradition from Rashi that in the first year following the passing, the soul will frequent its former place of prayer, such as its shul.) Once the year is completed, the body by now has generally dissipated and the soul rises much more easily. After the year the soul feels free to soar upward without being pulled down; the soul ascends without the nagging need to descend (*Shabbos*, 152b). As the body decays, rearranging itself into new forms and elements, the soul too goes through its own transformation and reassuming of its original form as it rises higher and deeper (*Tz'la'ch*, and *Ben Yehoyada*, Berachos, 18b).

Following the Year

Still, even following the cycle of the first year, the soul retains a degree of awareness and is very much connected with the people it loved and cared for. Whereas the soul increasingly releases its bond with the insubstantial qualities of this universe, such as the car it drove or the job it had, and it no longer misses 'things,' the soul never loses its connection with its loved ones.

The sages explain that this kind of awareness of the happenings in the physical realm is retained through the Nefesh that remains with body (*Zohar* 1, p. 81a). As we previously explained, a small part of the soul does in fact stay connected with the grave via the Luz bone. It is then through this Luz bone that souls in the higher realms of existence are able to observe and be aware of what is occurring in the lower realms.

Generally speaking, after a person passes on and sheds their physical form the soul continues to be quite conscious of the people and the universe it has left behind. But, as time goes on — following the cycles of three days, seven days, thirty days, a year, and then still further — slowly the soul ceases to 'hang around' this dimension. In time, as the people the soul knew and loved also begin to pass from this world and the world continues to change, as it always does, the departed soul becomes less and less focused on or concerned with this world. Once souls are reunited with their loved ones above, even the positive qualities of this universe capture less of their attention. As consciousness progressively abandons the mode of grasping experiences characteristic of this world and is fully adjusted within a non-dimensional reality, it begins to lose interest in the physical.

Interestingly enough, although it is not the prevailing opinion, there are traditional sources that suggest that a Yartzeit/memorial for a person's passing (observed through the saying of Kaddish, studying Torah or lighting candles) does not need to be observed by the living relatives after a period of fifty years. The explanation is that by this point the soul has attained a secure place, as it were, and does not need any more assistance from related souls below. Ultimately, everyone agrees that after exceptionally long periods of time it is not required for one to observe the Yartziet of his or her great-great grandmother, for example. The argument in this case is only about how long after a family member's passing must a Yartziet continue to be observed.

In due time souls that were once embodied become entirely accustomed to the purely spiritual levels of existence. Although they will never relinquish their 'individuality,' they will become disinterested with a world and with a people that are unknown to them. Even so, they will forever have the potential to once again reconnect to this world via their Nefesh – the tiny measure of soul that continues to reside at the place of their burial. For this reason, people continue to pray at the gravesite of relatives, certainly if the deceased was a Tzadik, many years after their passing.

CHAPTER 7
Reincarnation

The concept of reincarnation seems to conflict with some of the basic tenets of Torah, such as the concepts of heaven and hell, eventual resurrection and general accountability for one's own actions. Assuming reincarnation suggests that the '*same*' soul journeys from one body into the next, reincarnation and personal immortality seem to contradict one another. How does reincarnation correlate with the notion of a personal, individual afterlife journey?

The question, "Where is the soul once it leaves the body?" — is a question that has been asked of and by Rebbes, philosophers and mystics for hundreds of years. Is the soul on a higher realm of existence somewhere 'up' there or does the soul reincarnate, re-embody and come to inhabit another human being down here? (*Teshuvas HaRashba*, Teshuvah 418. *Minchas Kenaos. Nishmas Chayim*, 4:15).

To reconcile this apparent contradiction we need to delve more deeply into the issue. The best place to begin would be with the first human beings, the first possessors of a human soul — Adam and Chava/Eve.

The Root Soul

Adam, the way he is described at the genesis of his creation, was both male and female. Physically or metaphysically speaking the prototypical human being, Adam, was neither all male nor all female, he/she was both (*Bereishis*, 1:27. *Eiruvin*, 18a). Adam was therefore a synthesis of both the male and female genders, similar, but not completely the same as a hermaphrodite or androgene.

Today, these two aspects of the male/female dynamic are present in the protoplasm of all human cells, those of men and those of women. Considering that Adam was the first human being, the father/mother of the whole human species, all humans can trace their DNA to this one ancestor; he/she is the genetic embodiment of all further articulated gene sequences within the human line. Practically speaking, all people are understood by the Torah to be genetically related and descended from a single ancestral being much like modern biologists surmise — all forms of life ultimately descend, through the process of evolution and various mutations, from a single form of life.

A general Torah principle is that physicality is merely a reflection of spiritual conditioning. As Adam is viewed as the material parent of humanity, he/she is also the spiritual primogenitor. Adam's soul is the collective and universal soul from which all human souls emanate (*Sha'ar HaGilgulim*, Hakdamah 12. *Ramak Shiur Komah*, Chap 2. See also *Medrash Rabbah*, Shemos, 40:3. *Tanchumah*, Ki Tissa, 12. *Tanya*, Igeres HaKodesh, 7). Adam's soul is therefore the source-soul from which all individualized souls are derivatives. Adam was a cosmic figure of sorts, containing elements of all the souls of every person who would eventually be born.

All souls are contained within the primordial soul of Adam, hence, once the eating from the Tree of the Knowledge of Duality occurred, followed by the ejection from Eden, the sparks within the collective soul of Adam were scattered throughout all worlds and all people. Ever since then the purpose of reincarnation is to restore the integral wholeness of the Root soul, thus creating a Tikkun / fixing / attunement of the mystical and primordial image of Adam/Humanity.

Putting the Puzzle back Together

Adam, before eating from the Tree of dualistic Knowledge, was at-one and unified, existing within the shade of the Tree of Life, basking within the glow of the Light of the Creator. Once Adam ate the fruit and identified with the reality of duality, separation occurred.

Let us delve a little deeper.

Before eating from and identifying with the "Tree of Knowledge of Good and Evil," which represents the world of opposites, the "body" and soul of Adam was one unified existence. There was no internal dichotomy and no separation between his body and soul. Adam existed in the garden of the "Tree of Life," defined as the reality of wholeness and Unity.

Even within the physical reality itself there was no separation, there was no separation between his body and the world outside of him. The body of Adam "stretched from one end of the earth to the other" (*Sanhedrin*, 38b). It was one, unified and "everywhere."

Being unified with the Tree of Life, the reality of Unity, Adam's body was a unified entity wherein even his fingers were not separated, but rather connected by skin, creating a mittened hand, as it were (*Sader HaDoros* 1, *Eleph* 2; 56-58). The skin of Adam was transparent, similar to the fingernails we have today (*Yalkut Shimoni* 15; 27. Alshich, *Torahs Moshe*, Bereishis). The primordial "Body of Adam" had a shining, transparent skin (*Targum Yonasan. Pirkei Rebbe Eliezer*). Adam's body was even more brilliant than the light of the sun (*Medrash* Vayikra, 20:2. *Tekunei Zohar*, Hakdamah. Note: *Baba Basra*, 58a).

The eating of the Tree of Knowledge in Eden caused a shrinking, a breaking apart of the one great body/soul into myriads of shards and sparks of light. The once unified body of Adam became pixelated into multiple pieces. Each shard became another specific and finite soul/spark. These Sha'ards/sparks are diminished from their original state for two reasons: 1) they are no longer a singular unified reality, and therefore as a result, 2) their individuals lights are not as potent as they were when they were part of the whole.

As a particular finite expression of soul/spark from the primordial body/ soul of Adam becomes embodied in a physical form, the task then becomes to fully actualize this distinct soul potential. One by one, through subsequent reincarnations and lives lived, all sparks become brilliant and bound together again. When a person lives his or her life and completely expresses their soul/spark, their particular shard of soul is Zahir/illuminated. After this soul completes its journey through physical life, the now illuminated soul/spark returns to the great Body/Soul of Adam.

After the eating and internalizing of duality, the Body/Soul of Adam fell apart; it became pixelated into many individual pieces, like a broken puzzle. Our job is to recreate the great Body of Adam, to put back the pieces of the puzzle so that it can brilliantly shine again.

Over time, each soul that has completed its task returns and thus recreates the one great and unified Body/Soul of Adam. Like pieces of the puzzle, each distinct soul expression is another part of the whole, and when all pieces of the puzzle are 'returned' and fit perfectly back into the primordial body of Adam we will enter, once again, into a unified reality sustained by the Tree of Life.

So far we have been describing and discussing the collective aspect of the Tree of Life, although every individual who lives his/her deepest truth also connects with the Tree of Life on a personal level.

The body is the physical imprint of the soul (*Choker U'Mekubal*, 1). Body and soul mirror and reflect each other. The literal structure of Adam's body was analogous to the spiritual form of his soul. As the body can be divided into various compartments, the same is true on some meta-physical level in regards to the soul. There are souls that are rooted in the head of Adam and there are souls that stem from the hands of Adam, there are souls from the heart and souls from the feet. Accordingly, 'head souls' are inclined toward intellectual pursuits and 'hand souls' show signs of physical dexterity, 'heart souls' brim with emotions and 'feet souls' are action or movement oriented. All in all, there is a particular soul-root within Adam for every individual distinct consciousness.

Family Souls

Herein is where the idea of group or family souls comes into play (*Safer HaGilgulim*, 12. *Shiur Komah, Shit Alfei Shnin* 3, *Shallah, Kedushas HaGuf V'Damim. Tiferes Yonashan*, Vayigash). A group soul would be those individual souls that all share the same root within the primordial all-encompassing Body/Soul of Adam. As a physical representation of this truth they will gravitate towards each other in this temporal realm, either as a family, group, network, or more macrocosmically, as a nation. Physical nearness, whether via blood, friendship or even geographic location is indicative of spiritual connection. Souls that share a common root on a spiritual plane will transmigrate together on a physical level as well. These souls are bound together physically and spiritually by a common purpose, as they originated from the same archetype-aspect within the primordial Body/Soul of Adam.

An interesting detail regarding the immediate family dynamic is that although the nucleus of a family is constructed of souls who originate from the same broad area in the all-inclusive body/soul of Adam, still, not all members will share the exact same soul-root. At times a friend may share a closer soul-root than that of a relative. Diversity and individual expression within the context of the family unit is a result of the divergent sources and soul-roots of some of the members of the family.

Most members of a family will spring from the same area or same root of Adam's soul/body, but some souls will travel from other parts within the great body/soul of Adam and come to join a particular family unit for a specific incarnation and purpose (*Sha'ar HaGilgulim*, 10. *Ohr Hachayim*, Ki Sisa 32:27). For this reason we find that within every family assemblage, although collectively they may share general common interests, some family members may go in different, and occasionally even opposite, directions. Most of the family will gravitate towards one profession or live in one climate or environment, while there is always the one or two members of the family who seem to be singing their own tune and doing their own thing. For example, the whole family may be doctors or lawyers, while one child is a musician or painter.

A healthy unit is where each member of the family lives in accordance with their own particular soul inscription and where each member of the group is influenced and spiritually nourished by the individuality of the next, collectively creating a veritable rainbow of personalities and pursuits.

Parenthetically, many erroneously believe that if a child is born and named after a loved one the child will then automatically possess the same soul energy as the one who departed. True, we have many ancient teachings attesting to the ways in which our names affect our behavior (*Yumah*, 83b, *Berachos*, 7b. *Tanchumah, Ha'azinu. Zohar* 1, p. 58b). A certain number of these teaching also suggest that when parents name their children they do so with Divine inspiration and intuition so that the name will be suitable to the characteristics of the child's soul (*Sha'ar HaGilgulim*, 23; *Emek HaMelech, Sha'ar* 1:4. *Chesed LeAvraham*, 5:6. *Agrah DeKalah*, p. 107). Additionally, still other teachings indicate that when a child is named after a righteous person who has lived, that righteous soul who resides in the world of pure spirit is aroused and an affinity of souls is then forged between these two that can have positive results (*Noam Elimelech*, Bamidbar). Still, all this does not guarantee that a child who is named after someone else will inevitably have a spark of that soul. Though that can certainly occur, it is not the rule. Names are influential, but not necessarily definitive.

People who are Similar

Whereas family members may not all share the exact same soul root, there are others outside the family, community or even nation who do share the same spiritual DNA. Even outside the family there are souls who share roots within the great body/soul of Adam, and when these two meet up they will unavoidably and almost reflexively experience attraction and serious magnetism for each other; although it is not always necessarily a positively charged attraction (*Sha'ar HaGilgulim*, 20).

When two similar souls encounter each other for the very first time there will often be a kind of aversion of or even dislike for one another. Being of the same ilk their internal chemistry is too much alike; it is like taking two objects with the same exact magnetic energy field and trying to fuse them together. These two souls may feel challenged by each other, if not consciously, then on a deeper level. A 'spiritual' type of jealousy may arise, pinning one soul against the next, struggling to see who can acquire more energy from their source.

If, however, these two individuals attain a more evolved measure of spiritual maturity and they are highly developed individuals who experience Ruach Ha'kodesh/Divine intuition, then instead of an abhorrence and dislike a beautiful love can be nurtured and flourish between them (Ibid. *Pri Eitz Chayim*, Sha'ar Hanhagos HaLimud. *Kehilas Yaakov*, Machlokas). Supposing these two powerful energy sources do in fact coalesce and manage to resonate with each other the vibrations that are created would be eminently more powerful. Much like light that is generated via friction and discord can be fiercer than light that is produced in harmony and uniformity. (See also, *Noam Elimelech*, Vayechi)

Actualizing Our - Soul - Potential

In relation to the concept of the body/soul of the cosmic Adam and the notion of a soul root that we have been discussing, our sages intuit that the human form is subdivided into six hundred and thirteen parts; two hundred forty-eight main organs and three hundred sixty-five principal veins and arteries. Which of the body parts or veins/sinews are included in this count and which are left out was never fully disclosed. Perhaps this meta-biological construct of the Rebbes is related to the Neijing's description of the 365 acupuncture points on the body. Either way, whether understood physically or metaphysically, this is the way the sages deciphered the human form. As soul animates body and spirit enlivens matter, the soul too, like the body, is comprised of six hundred and thirteen energies and attributes. And it is specifically through spiritually oriented activities that utilize the body that the soul is able to achieve its full crystallization, self-articulation and actualization. Although we must also keep in mind that as the soul is a spark of the Infinite, its essential core is neither reducible nor dividable.

Correlated to the six hundred and thirteen body parts and soul energies are the six hundred and thirteen Mitzvos of the Torah, which are comprised of the two hundred forty-eight body parts and the three hundred sixty-five days of the solar year (*Bechoros* 45a. *Makos* 23b. *Zohar* 1, p. 170b). Aligning oneself with the Mitzvos, which serve as the inner purpose and directives of creation, whether by actively participating in particular actions or refraining from others, allows the soul to soar to the most exalted and elated heights possible.

The full array of Mitzvos grants one the opportunity to fully bring to fruition all of the various aspects of soul as they are expressed through the body. Each distinct Mitzvah taps into another reservoir of spiritual-energy and sets the soul free, allowing for the soul to express itself in the most expansive way. By physically performing a particular Mitzvah the corresponding attribute within the soul is activated and as a result the soul as a whole attains an even greater and more comprehensive state of completion and articulation than when it existed as pure spirit prior to descending into human form.

Generally speaking, the Nefesh, Ruach and Neshamah unfold and become consciously felt in a progressive fashion. First a person develops on a level of Nefesh and then works his way up to Ruach, and then eventually graduates into the level of Neshamah. Only once the entire structure of Nefesh has evolved and been entirely articulated through the correlating Mitzvos, will the Nefesh level be transcended and included with that of Ruach. And then the same process repeats itself moving from Ruach to Neshamah. Reincarnation occurs when sparks of soul that were not fully articulated in one lifetime resurface in another human form to be worked on and fully expressed.

Mitzvos are the tools through which soul attains excellence in this world. Theoretically, our aspirations should be to achieve excellence in all aspects of life, yet practically we achieve perfection – or as close to it as we can get - in only certain areas of our life. Every individual person has at least one Mitzvah that he or she is "Zahir Tfei/ultimately careful in performing" (*Shabbos*, 118b). Zahir can also be translated as illuminating or shining. This concept can then be understood as implying that there is at least one Mitzvah that every person is connected with; one positive area that he excels in. That one Mitzvah becomes the source of his or her personal radiance.

Overall every person displays some degree of uniqueness and specialty, even if it is only in one area in life. There are some people, for example, who are remarkably compassionate and wonderful humanitarians, and yet they have a challenging time relating to their own family; while there are others who are fantastic in interfamilial relationships—i.e., they are good parents/children, brothers or sisters—but they experience difficulties when it comes to parting with their hard-earned money.

Whatever the Mitzvah is, it is that correlating energy within the soul that one becomes intimately connected with and joined to. In fact we find that the one, two or three areas that one excels in are the primary focus of that person's spiritual development and all other goals, aspirations and achievements flow from that particular domain. All of one's life, including their own interpretations of experiences and expressions, is founded on their own uniqueness and individuality.

Notice that whenever you are asked to capture or encapsulate in one or two words another person you will always discover something unique to say about them. For instance, employing some basic generic terms, one person you would say is gracious, another thoughtful, one is serious and responsible, another light hearted and cheerful, one is a good parent, and another is a good friend — each person expresses their own uniqueness. There are always traces of positivity within people and often this positive aspect of character is so powerful that it appears that everything else in that person's life is an extension and derivative of that particular trait.

Individual Personality

Individualized sparks of soul that a person connects with in this life become their 'own' soul — in this life and the next. As in life, when others think of this individual they think of him or her in a certain way; the same is true in death, the individuality within will continue to exist and extend eternally in the afterlife.

Individual/personal immortality is experienced when the soul of a person, the unique spark of a person's soul that they expressed in life, lives on for eternity in higher/deeper realms of existence. Having traveled through life the individualized spark of soul has now become ever more colorful, accumulating all of life's experiences and knowledge. In the afterlife that integral entity will journey onwards to ever increasing measures of awareness. What reincarnates into other human beings are the sub-conscious or 'beyond conscious' aspects that exist within the soul, the elements within the soul that were not activated or articulated.

Nothing is reoccurring. There is no repetition within creation and each person is born with the potential for a radical new expression.

The innate individuality, the spark of soul that fashioned the person's uniqueness does not generally reincarnate. The principium individuas of a person, what makes people unique and guides them to their special destiny, will not re-embody. What reincarnates are the aspects of soul that one had little experience with, the elements of the multifaceted soul-energy that one had little association with. Clearly one's soul contained all the possible energies and the entire soul resided somewhere within the person, nevertheless, on a day-to-day level of awareness the person was only consciously affiliated with the uniqueness of his own soul, and nothing else. As such, it is this uniqueness of soul, coupled with a life full of memories that were imprinted on the soul that journeys on in the afterlife.

The soul 'divides' itself in the afterlife much as it did during life. Just as in this realm of existence there were sparks of soul that one connected with and there were others that remained dormant, in the afterlife this very same phenomenon continues. The sparks that were consciously activated in one's soul in this life remain with one's soul in the afterlife, while the other sparks reincarnate and gradually become individualized souls for other people. The unifying factor between all these incarnations is that they all collectively constitute 'one soul,' meaning that there is one overarching thematic interest, goal, drive and propensity that can be found in all manifestations of that 'one' soul.

Picture a tree with multiple branches. One tree with one root, yet with branches extending in all directions. Each of these individualized soul's share the same root and are in essence part of one continuous unfolding field of consciousness; one soul, which unravels and becomes apparent throughout the course of many lives as individual spiritual energies are activated by different individual people.

The Spark that contains the Whole

Though the soul keeps on dividing and subdividing itself, still, in each incarnation it retains integral wholeness and a sense of completion. Not only is the soul complete and all-comprehensive with all six hundred and thirteen energy forces as it had in the first incarnation, but subsequently in each incarnation the soul remains 'perfect' as it was in its previous embodiment. Even after the first possessor of soul passes away and the elements of soul that became exclusively his remain his, only the remainder of the soul reincarnates, and this 'remainder' is also complete. Think of the soul in terms of a hologram, where the part is like the whole and the whole is present within each part, every pixel mirroring the total picture.

As the collective spirit of Adam contains six hundred and thirteen soul energies, so too, all individual consciousness that stem from Adam's soul contains six hundred and thirteen aspects (*Sha'arei Kedushah*, 1; 1). The micro or the part, is like the macro — the whole.

Additionally, each specific soul energy can be further divided into six hundred and thirteen aspects, and they in turn into another six hundred and thirteen. This is a dynamic referred to as interinclusion, wherein each part of a larger structure actually contains the whole structure in miniature within itself. The core of soul is one with the Infinite and no matter how often infinity is divided it always remains infinite. Every 'slice' of infinity is infinite. Infinity cannot be divided (*Kuzari*, Maamor 5:18. *Chovos Halevavos*, Sha'ar HaYichud, 5), and thus when you grasp a 'small parcel' of infinity you grasp the totality (*Keser Shem Tov*, 111. *Toldos Yaakov Yoseph*, Yisro. Yavatz, *Avos*, 4:2). Regardless of how often the soul is divided or subdivided it will always retain its signature shape and form as the general root soul, it will forever encompass all six hundred and thirteen branches of the single tree.

Practically, the fact that an individual's personality and primary soul- connection is the attribute of kindness does not necessarily mean that such a person is lacking in all other areas of life. It merely means that for him kindness is the center of his being, the foundation and root cause from which everything else in his life flows. The multiple multi-dimensional aspects of his soul are channeled and funneled through his individuality and uniqueness, his soul-connection of kindness.

Most, if not all people go through life and succeed in tapping into at least one aspect of soul. It seems that there is always one Mitzvah that is essential and vital to each person (Rebbe Rayatz, *Safer Maamorim*, Tof Shin Ches, p. 240). There is always some positive life affirming force, a raison d'être that compels the human being to carry on and move forward through life. The individualized spark of soul that a person activates in this life through their one unique Mitzvah is what gains him/her their place in Gan Eden (Rambam *Pirush HaMishnays*, Sanhedrin, 10. *Avudrham, Hilchos Shabbos*. Alshich *Toras Moshe*, Shemini, 9; 5–6. *Mei Hashiloach* 1, p. 177), and is thus the part of their soul that remains his or hers throughout their afterlife. It is the uniqueness of self that will journey onwards for eternity.

Once the soul in its entirety, its divisions and subdivisions, has been elevated, activated and articulated the soul will then cease to return into this earthly terrestrial realm of existence. The soul will stop reincarnating. How long this process of elevation takes, whether it is in one lifetime or hundreds of lifetimes, essentially depends upon the individuals who possess that soul and what they do with it.

There is no limit or set amount of times the soul may descend, so long as even the slightest measure of development is being achieved during each subsequent incarnation (*Sha'ar HaGilgulim*, 4. *Mishnas Chassidim*, Seder Nashim, Meseches Gilgul 2:3). When no perfection and elevation whatsoever has occurred in a lifetime, the soul will only descend another two times; it has three tries. If no perfection and elevation were reached in the subsequent two lifetimes the distinct soul will never reincarnate into another human being again (*Zohar* 3, p. 72b. *Tikkunei Zohar* 32. *Ramban*, Bereishis, 4:1. *Shivilei Emunah*, Nosiv 3. Chayit *Ma'areches Elokus*, 10. *Magid MeSha'arim*, Iyov. *Alshich* Devarim, 7:9–10. *MaHarsha*, Shabbos, 152b). But even if a slight elevation is achieved in every subsequent incarnation, the soul will incarnate indefinitely. As long as there is work to do and work is being done, there are lives to lead.

The passage in the daily morning prayers, "The soul that You have given me is pure" (*Berachos*, 60b), is intended to be taken quite literally. Each soul that comes down to this world is pure, immaculate and unsoiled from any previous deeds of past incarnations. For the most part each person begins life with a clean slate. People are born innocent, neither good nor bad, holy nor evil, but simply innocent with the innate ability to choose their path. With regards to the spark of soul that belongs exclusively to each individual, this incarnation is considered the very first one; for it is the first time that these particular spiritual energies are combined in this proportion, making up this unique soul and articulating themselves in this novel manner.

Mending Past Lives

In the world of souls, much like any other reality, there are rules and there are exceptions to these rules. The rule is that souls do not reincarnate to rectify previous misdeeds or to complete someone else's story, but rather to reach their own actualization and individuation and write their own story; articulating another element of the one soul in each evolving incarnation.

Reincarnation from one human being to the next is for the purpose of self-elevation and not so much to correct errors from past lives. Errors are amended for and fixed in the afterlife not here on earth. If a soul does reincarnate in this world to rectify past wrongs it will be in other life forms, not within a human body. The exception is that occasionally souls will reincarnate in human form specifically to make amends for that which was done in a previous life. But this is the exception to the rule.

The postmortem purification mechanism, i.e., Gehenom/Hell, has no dominance over the Tzadik (*Chagigah*, 27a). For this reason a Tzadik who has erred and passed away and now needs to unburden himself of negativity must do so by reincarnating once again into a human body and correcting that which was wronged rather than being purified in the temporary fires of Gehenom as most people would.

Tellingly, there are countless stories of bereaved parents who have lost young children and have gone in search of consolation from the great Rebbes, such as the Baal Shem Tov. These Rebbes often revealed to them that their child possessed the soul of a previous Tzadik; informing them that their son/daughter was the soul of a noble righteous person who needed to descend to this world for only a short period of time to rectify something done in their own previous lives.

When an actualized soul does reincarnate into another human being it is usually the soul of a wholly integrated Tzadik who has only slightly erred and needs to achieve a minimum of soul fixing. For everyone else there is the afterlife.

Reincarnation & Monetary Issues

Just as the Tzadik is the exception to the rule and may require reincarnation to achieve Tikkun, the converse is also true. At times a person may have done something so spiritually damaging that the only way for him to enter a state of Gan Eden is by returning to the so called 'scene of the crime,' descending once again into this world and repairing that which was marred (*Sha'ar HaGilgulim*, 8 *Reshis Chachmah*, Sha'ar HaYirah, 13. *Medrash Talpiyos*, Gehenim. *Be'er Mayim Chayim*, Chaya Sarah). This is particularly the case with regard to issues between man and man, in contrast to issues between man and his Creator - i.e., spiritual/ritual issues that can be worked out on a spiritual plane in the afterlife journey.

Interpersonal matters, especially monetary issues, cannot be 'fixed' in a world of souls. If money was stolen, for example, during the course of one's life and the thief passes on without ever returning the money, he will need to return again to this world and return the money to the person from whom the money was stolen (*Gra*, Mishlei, 14:25. *Even Shelomo*, 3:8). When one steals from another, the deed is not forgiven until one actually returns what was stolen (Rabbeinu Yonah, *Sha'arei Teshuvah*, Chap 1). For this reason, they will both reincarnate and they will meet up and the money will be returned to the rightful owner, whether this will be done consciously through one's free choice or by 'accident.'

Not only theft, but even owing money to another person can be a reason for needing to reincarnate. We need to be careful and scrupulous about money matters.

It must be mentioned at this point that if you were on the receiving end of such a transaction, i.e., money was stolen from you or owed to you, and if you feel like the other person is incapable of repaying the debt, whether they literally do not have the funds or because they are crippled by their own narrative, you may want to forgive the debt and forfeit the money. This is purely an act of piety and compassion, not demanded by Torah law, but ultimately beneficial both in this life as well as the next. If someone still owes you money after both of your journeys in this life they will need to repay you in another incarnation and you too will need to reincarnate in order to receive those funds.

There is a spiritual principle that states: "[The Creator] causes auspicious events to occur on dates that have a history of auspicious events and inauspicious events to occur on dates that have a history of inauspicious events" (*Taanis*, 29a). Positivity attracts more positivity and negativity attracts more negativity. "Curse cleaves to the cursed and blessings cannot attach themselves to curse" (*Rashi* Bereishis 24:39). Blessings follow the blessed and curses follow the cursed, and ultimately these categories are both self-defined and self-fulfilling. We must therefore be extremely cautious in how we craft our narratives and identities. Negativity attracts people, ideas and events of that kind. This is not to blame the victim, but rather to acknowledge that there is a greater and higher force in the universe and nothing happens by mere accident. We cannot always control what happens to us, but we do have the power and even responsibility, for our own sake as well as others, to control our responses. This in turn will effect what may happen next.

It is necessary to point out that if something negative happens to you, you do have the choice of whether to release it or not. Although it is also important to keep in mind that at times it is beneficial to forgive, and in other circumstances when the issue is larger than you, you are actually not allowed to forgive.

Reincarnation of a complete soul identity — meaning not just the returning of the unarticulated aspects of one's soul, but indeed the whole soul — is warranted when the soul being re-embodied was deceitful to another human being and caused the other person physical or mental harm. The path along which the perpetuator of pain attains Tikkun is traveled by coming back to this sphere of reality, reenacting the scene and then undoing that which was done or not done. Only by reliving the events and altering their outcome can optimum Tikkun be achieved.

Rebbe DovBer, the Maggid of Mezritch, once requested his teacher, the holy Baal Shem Tov, to reveal him the secret of reincarnation (*Devarim Areivim*, Mishpatim, 18. *Degel Machanah Ephrayim*, Mishpatim). The main passage in the Zohar that elaborates the mystery of reincarnation is in the portion of Mishpatim, which speaks of monetary laws. The Zohar begins: "'These are the laws;' this also refers to the mystery of reincarnation." The Maggid wondered: "What is the connection between monetary issues and the reincarnation of souls?"

The Baal Shem Tov encouraged him to travel to a certain location and that when he reaches a tree with a stream nearby he should rest there until the evening, observe what transpires and then return. He was clearly instructed not to interfere or participate, but rather to simply observe; and that is exactly what he did. He traveled to that particular location and sat down. Sitting there he noticed a traveler passing by. The traveler put down his bags, rested for a bit and ate something before continuing on his way. When he left, the Maggid realized that the man's wallet was accidentally left behind. But the Maggid also remembered that he had been instructed to observe and not to participate. Along came another traveler who rested in the very same place. While lying there the second traveler noticed the unmarked wallet. He picked it up, put it into his own pocket, and left. A few moments later a third person came along. He had just sat down to rest his tired body when along came the first person that had lost his wallet earlier. Assuming this man had found and pocketed his wallet, he asked him for it back. When the man rightfully denied any wrong doing, the first person lost his temper and beat him.

Puzzled, the Maggid returned to the Baal Shem Tov and asked for an explanation. The Baal Shem Tov explained: In a previous life the first person owed the second one the amount of money that was found in the wallet but refused to pay him. When they went to their Rebbe, the third person in this event, the Rebbe callously and carelessly ruled incorrectly and did not demand the first person to pay up. Each one was now repaid appropriately.

It should be pointed out that even in a predicament such as the one mentioned above, the individual with the reincarnated soul is not enslaved to nor held hostage by the past. The past is not an inevitable indicator of how life will develop and flow in the present. Past-life experiences may impress upon or shape the direction of one's life, but they do not completely define one's destiny. We have the power to radically transform ourselves in the moment and the effects of such a transformation may ripple out into the future and echo back into the past. The soul may indeed need to work out some past issues, but by doing so the soul liberates itself and profoundly alters its trajectory in all directions of time, effectively impregnating the future as well as reinventing the past in light of the renewed present.

Knowing Our Purpose

A person who possesses a soul that has embodied in order to purge itself of past-life negativity will be able to discern which areas in life require readjustment by noticing the natural patterns of his behavior and discovering where his instincts lead him. The negative behaviors or tendencies he is inclined toward should be his barometer. Precisely the self-destructive behavior he has most trouble distancing himself from and the areas he struggles with most are the territories that most need to be worked on (*Shiur Komah*, p. 166. *Kol Eliyahu Yonah*, 4:3. *Sheivet Ha'Musar*, 1:23. *Tzidkas HaTzadik*, 49). The exact area one finds most challenging may very well be the purpose for his soul's descent, returning precisely to refine that area or that aspect of character.

Every soul has its unique purpose and mission, whether it is a soul that has reincarnated to mend previous behavior or simply an ordinary case of reincarnation wherein 'new' sparks of the soul embody in order to be articulated. Often we find that parallel to the importance and magnitude of one's goal is the inner struggle confronted in the quest to achieve those accomplishments. According to many Mekubalim we choose the ambiance for the life we are going to lead (however the definition of we is understood), we choose whether we are going to be rich or poor, strong or weak, beautiful or the opposite (*Chesed LeAvraham*, 4:11. *Midbar Kadmos*, Yud). And the reason we chose the circumstances we have was to help us reach our own soul–actualization and attain our own perfect and personalized Tikkun. Wealthier people are working on the attribute of kindness, openness and giving while the less fortunate wrestle with learning to become more content and not to covet (*Derech Hashem* 2, 3:1). Perhaps, some measure of reassurance and comfort can be gained by realizing that it is we who elected this lot. Each person, each soul is aspiring to achieve their own Tikkun through their own area of struggle, whether it is being fabulously wealthy or devastatingly destitute, and everything in between.

Whenever we encounter difficulties and challenges along our path of life we ought to keep in mind that everything has a purpose and there is a reason 'why' we were born, including to whom we were born and at which time and place we were born. Even our physical/mental genetic makeups work in conjunction with our psychic/inner dynamics of soul. Our physical prowess mirrors our spiritual potential. Intrinsically, although we may not notice it at first, our nature and nurture are all working with us toward the articulation of our distinct soul-type.

To attain our maximum development it is pivotal that the soul is placed in an environment that is conducive for such actualization, and so it is. Everything within us is conspiring, so to speak, and assisting us in our Tikkun.

There is a basic spiritual principle that states: "The master of the universe does not approach man in trickery"(*Avodah Zarah*, 3a), and therefore "demands only as much as man is capable" (*Medrash Rabbah*, Shemos, 34:1). Essentially, everything in life is working to help us, at least as far as the tools are concerned. Environment/culture/genetics are all ingredients that support and assist us to bring forth our individual soul-type in the best possible way.

As mentioned above, although it does appear that the importance and magnitude of our goals runs parallel to the inner struggles we encounter in our quest to reach them; this is only true with regard to our shallower modes of perception. To a large extent the only power that works against us is our own surface 'self,' the outer shell self which has been traditionally referred to as the Yetzer Ha'ra – the ego, or selfish inclination. The obstacles that may exist are not from the external world around us, rather they emerge from our internal world, emanating from an ego space within, which gives rise to all inner doubts, uncertainty and skepticism.

The Yetzer Ha'ra is nothing but an impostor whose secret desire is for the transcendent elements of the self to prevail and render it transparent.

Obstacles are only there to challenge and provoke a marshaling of all of one's inner strengths and resources to persevere. Looking at life from this vantage point we begin to realize that our entire scope of reality is working toward helping us attain Tikkun. When a person has, on whatever level, overcome this inner strife he will come to the astonishing epiphany that all of life was forging towards perfection all along; even his setbacks were for the sake of progress and refinement. And when he finally acts upon this realization he will find his true sense of self–worth and inner contentment. Simply put, he will discover and rediscover his soul.

Beyond the collective responsibility of repairing this broken universe by perfecting the imperfect vessels so that they too can absorb the Ohr Ein Sof /Infinite Light via our good deeds and Mitzvos, there is a distinct and separate mission and purpose for each specific person related to the Mitzvos that speak to that individual in particular. Every person intuitively knows what his higher purpose in life is. Occasionally he may acknowledge it and at times he may choose to ignore it, but deep down the awareness is always there.

Overall, all the tools that are needed to achieve our maximum spiritual potential are apportioned. Both nature and nurture work in sync with our soul–type. Every person has areas in life for which they have a natural gift, things they love doing, even if or despite them being challenging. Having a gift does not mean that it comes easy. It takes inspiration and a lot of perspiration to achieve one's full soul potential. Still, in the greater scheme of things it is these challenging areas that we are soulfully connected with and through them we are able to attain our perfection.

All of the above is nested within the domain of the positive, indicating that these territories are part of our overarching Tikkun. But by the same token there are also negatively charged attractions and they too are soul indicators. Just as when we sense a powerful surge toward positively inclined actions we should pursue them, the converse is true with regard to negatively inclined actions or desires, our work is to refrain from them. The area in a person's life wherein lies their greatest fault or deficiency is that very place wherein resides the potential for the greatest merit just waiting to be actualized through appropriate action and expression (*Tzidkas HaTzadik*, Os 70). Whenever we feel a peculiar pull towards certain negative behavior and conduct — be it lust, greed or anger — we ought to realize that these are precisely the areas that we must pull ourselves away from in order to achieve our Tikkun.

In time, we will come to the amazing realization that these certain attractions emanate from a surface level of self, while from a deeper space within they reveal themselves as merely trials to test our resolve, meant to call-forth greater reservoirs of energy and striving.

The areas we are drawn to and feel a strong connection with, whether positive or negative, indicate to us that this is where our soul's mission is located. When the attraction is positive we should follow it with all our heart, pursue it and then pursue it more. When the attractions are negative we ought to distance ourselves and run from them and do so with all the strength of our being.

Knowing When to Pursue & When to Refrain from Attractions

Most often there are clear markers that separate a positive from a negative inclination and attraction. A positive action is a Mitzvah or more broadly speaking an attraction that when followed brings about a greater sense of connection and unity with one's deeper self, with others, with creation and with the Creator. A negative inclination and attraction is an Aveira or more broadly speaking an attraction that when followed brings about more friction with and separation from one's deeper self, with others, with creation and with the Creator. Occasionally it is not so clear-cut whether a particular action is positive or negative in its ultimate impact.

Sometimes it is unclear whether one should pursue an inclination or stay away from and overcome the temptation. The subject matter is not necessarily a Mitzvah or an Aveira and, for that matter, it is not clear if the action will bring about greater or lesser unity and connection.

Beyond the obvious, there are other indicators that can help us know if something is a desire worth pursuing or one that is better left alone. In addition to learning to become aware of the subtle sensations of feeling either contracted and constricted or conversely, expansive and alive, there is also—in a time of deicison making—the possibility of taking notice of whether the world around you is supporting or contesting your decision (*Mei Hashiloach*, Parshas Balak).

Practically this means as follows: Sometimes we make a decision — for example, whether to buy a particular home or enter into a relationship with another person — and then once that decision is reached or maybe even prior, everything goes smoothly. There are very little bumps in the road and the whole world, as it were, seems to conspire to allow you to purchase the home or go deeper with the relationship. And sometimes the exact opposite is true. You make a decision to do or buy something or be with someone, for example, and right away obstacles and hardships set in. It becomes a labor filled experience.

Overall, there are logical and spiritual "certainties" and logical and spiritual "uncertainties." In simple terms a "certainty" means you know that this is the will of the Creator; it is a Mitzvah for example, or related to a Mitzvah, a good deed. An "uncertainty" is when it is not to your estimation either a Mitzvah or the opposite.

Let us take the example of wanting to purchase a home. If logically, emotionally, mentally and spiritually it makes "sense" that you should buy a home (i.e., you have the funds put aside, it is a buyer's-market, you need to live near that home either because of schools, education, family, or community), than ignore the hardships. No matter what pursues or ensues in the wake of your attempt to buy the home. Even if it comes with great difficulty and challenge do not say, "Well if it was meant to be it would be much easier." With regard to "certainties," do not allow "uncertainties" to guide you.

But then there are times — again using the example of buying a home or entering into a relationship — where, in truth, you are "uncertain." There is no overwhelming logical, emotional or even spiritual argument to pursue the home or the relationship, and yet it seems so natural and easy. If everything around you seems to conspire and help you move along with the purchase or the relationship, then pursue it. This is a sign, as it were, to follow course. (Note, Rashi, *Chulin*, 95b, regarding Rav).

When it is "certain," do not let the "uncertainties" of the world distract and dampen your enthusiasm. And when there is "uncertainty," use the "certainty" of the world around you to show you the way of what is right for you and what is not, what you should or should not do.

If you are uncertain and it is easy or it comes with ease, move forward and pursue it; if there are setbacks and hardships, walk away.

Inheriting Qualities from Past Lives

Aside from the unique inclinations and intentions that we each feel a strong connection/attraction to, there are other aspects of life wherein impartiality is put to the test. Certain people seem to be instinctively "better" than others. For example, some people appear to be biologically conditioned to be more charitable or innately less prone to anger than others. This by no means suggests that one person is more spiritually enlightened or evolved than the next. What comes to a person naturally is not to be confused with the spirituality that comes through hard work and toil. Good and 'natural' easy behavior is perhaps nothing more than a remnant of a past incarnation.

A soul that has achieved actualization in the area of charity in a past life will find giving charity in the next life unchallenging, they will contribute almost with a sense of indifference, so long as they have the means to share and are not financially deprived. True, unarticulated sparks of soul that return to this world recreate themselves and become complete in their six-hundred and thirteen dimensions, still some measure of residue of past lives are left. The actions or non-actions that come about with ease, without strong feelings for or against them, are manifestations of the effects of one's past lives.

Combination of Souls

In today's world most souls are not one or even two-dimensional. In general, people are very influenced by the world at large; they are multi-dimensional and trans-geographical. This is truer today, in contrast to say a hundred years ago.

As the world becomes a smaller and smaller place, more and more people are interlinked. This inter-inclusiveness and linking of people across the globe is a physical manifestation of the soul reality. On a soulular level, souls today are composites of various souls of the past. Because of the multi-dimensionality that exists currently on a soul level — expanding from times past and even into the future, across cultures and geographies — people today are more multi-dimensional.

Generally speaking, in this generation we are completing the repair of the great soul of Adam. Whereas people in times past were working to manifest and actualize the "head" or "arm" souls within the great cosmic body of Adam, today we are working out the last details within the great soul of Adam. This time in history is specifically known as the time in which we are manifesting and repairing the "heels" of Adam. The cosmic body is almost complete.

Souls today are more composite, as they are made up of various souls from within the great soul of Adam. For example: Let us say a soul from the "head" of Adam has in their past life reached a ninety percent Tikkun, elevation, articulation and actualization and another soul from the "heart" of Adam has also attained a ninety percent Tikkun in a past life; additionally, another eight souls from the "hands," "arms," "liver" and so forth have also reached a ninety percent Tikkun. Ten percent taken from each of these ten souls comprises one soul, and that is the shape of most souls today. This is also another definition of "heel" souls, the final aspects within the great soul of Adam that need elevation.

Combinations of small amounts of soul energy from various souls are what characterize the spiritual makeup of souls today. Even though, as mentioned many times, each aspect of the whole is itself whole. So every percent of soul is total soul and has the entire structure of the soul with all six hundred and thirteen dimensions.

A Generation of Heel Souls, Desiring to be Tickled

This generation is referred to as the "heel of Moshiach," because we are on the cusp of the Great Tikkun for the entire world - the last generation before the great Redemption. The final letter of the name Adam is Mem, which is the first letter of the word Moshiach. We are at the end of one cosmic phase and approaching the dawning of the next stage of humanity's spiritual evolution.

Psychologically, there is something about this generation that is deeply connected with the "heel."

The heel, because it carries the weight of the entire body feels a lot of pressure. And to relieve this pressure, whether real or assumed, the heel likes to be massaged and tickled.

We too are a people, a society that likes to be massaged. We want things to be smooth and easy, to feel good. At the first sign that something is challenging we tend to shy away.

We also love to be tickled. Our collective sense of enjoyment is shallow and superficial like tickling.

We want things to be easy and we like to be tickled, amused, entertained. Our spirituality is thus generally very shallow. We want to be spiritually moved a little bit, but then we want to move on with our life. This is the main Kelipa/concealment and challenge of this generation: to learn to overcome this shallowness and superficiality. But there is also a positive aspect to the "ticklish nature" of this generation. For just as the experience of being tickled represents a cheap and easy way to be stimulated, we too are easily moved. We can be whipped into a frenzy of fear or faith without much prodding. True, this can have negative consequences as well, but it could also be a good start to stimulating and inspiring positive growth.

Perfected Souls Incarnating into "Imperfect" Bodies:

There is another unique case of reincarnation that warrants mention and that is the re-embodiment of a completely elevated soul. Normally a soul will return to attain a deeper and more expansive level of articulation. In each subsequent incarnation another aspect of soul energy will become the one most apparent. Yet, from time to time souls settle into this realm of existence, not for themselves per se, but rather to help those around them to attain their own Tikkun and reach their soul's destiny.

There are clusters of souls that gravitate toward each other physically as they are spiritually linked, Sha'aring the same soul-roots. Occasionally, a 'perfected' soul will descend to assist those souls that it is connected with to reach their maximum spiritual potential.

This idea relieves a somewhat perplexing and disturbing phenomenon. Sadly, we find too many beautiful children that are born mentally or even physically handicapped, incapable of performing any of the normal day-to-day life chores. The question immediately becomes: What purpose do they fulfill in the scheme of personal Tikkun. How does a mentally impeded or a physically impaired person actualize their soul potential? As Mitzvos are the means for soul actualization and articulation, what happens when the body is crippled and does not allow the possibility of doing Mitzvos?

One of the ways to make sense of this issue is by realizing that occasionally a perfected Tzadik's soul will re-embody, not for its own sake of Tikkun, but rather to teach, inspire and help those around them attain their soul's mission (*Sha'ar HaGilgulim*, 8. *Magid MeSha'arim*, Miketz. *Tiferes Shelomo*, Rosh Hashanah, 40. *Mishnah Berurah*, 23:5). These souls have unique relations of affinity and are able to help the others in their 'family,' as they are all sourced in the same root within primordial Adam. Clearly, their selflessness is abiding as their sole intent of descending to this often harsh reality is not for their own personal purpose, but rather to assist the people they love and are spiritually bound to.

Living selflessly and completely for another can also be a gradual state that a person matures into. At times, a person who has completed his soul task while in the midst of his life journey, or even at a very young age, will continue to live on solely for the purpose of helping others attain their Tikkun (*Yismach Yisrael*, (Alexander) Hagadah, p. 45). Those who are born healthy and later on in life become utterly paralyzed or entirely incompetent, continue to live on so that their care-takers and those in their sphere of influence can attain proper soul articulation and spiritual development.

Transmigration: Reincarnation into Other Forms of Life:

Death is never absolute, rather it is merely a recycling of energy. At the time of bodily death the spirit does not perish but rather enters into new channels of life. For most souls this translates as entering higher/deeper realms of existence without ever returning to this world, and what reincarnates are the elements of soul that were unarticulated. Yet, for other souls, in order to re-attain their perfected state and enter Gan Eden they need to come back into another form of life, whether animal, vegetative or inanimate existence, and through these forms of life, attain their Tikkun.

Transmigration is quite different from the normal course of reincarnation. Unlike the usual scenarios where only sparks of soul reincarnate as the individualized elements of soul journey onwards into higher/deeper realms, here the actual individual conscious level of soul descends and inhabits a variant shell of existence. In this situation, the soul experiences vivid memories of its previous life while embodied within human form (*Safer Cheraidim*, 33. *Sheivet HaMusar* 14).

As the human soul is enclothed within another form of life it does not become the soul energy of that creature or object, it simply resides and settles therein. In addition to the animal/vegetative/or sustaining soul that exists there is now a human soul trapped within. A 'human' configured energy confined within an unfitting vehicle that is non-conducive for its full self-expression.

The manner in which deeply ingrained negativity can be erased is through the process of transmigration. Purity of soul is a natural gift and our birthright. The question is only how we choose to interact with and express our soul. Whereas the higher reaches of soul remain completely unscathed by our destructive behaviors, the more intimate aspects of the soul can in fact be somewhat tarnished or dimmed of their brilliance. So while the light of one's soul can never be done away with, a temporary eclipsing is possible. Negativity coats and paints a mask over one's soul, so that its natural light does not shine forth.

Just as we have the ability to activate our innermost resources of soul and through those powers elevate all that we come in contact with, the converse is also a possibility. Much like the rest of the zoological kingdom who act, or better yet react, instinctively by reflexively seeking their own survival and aggrandizement, man has the ability to shut out his deeper soul and operate from his base instincts, thereby joining the animal kingdom. Man has the choice to surrender to the ego and give in to the automaticity and habitual patterns of life. In essence, natural instincts are amoral, neither good nor bad, yet when a person weakly yields to his reactive nature the laws of inertia dictate that unchecked selfishness will lead to innocuous vice and perhaps to vile and aggressive actions. It is a slippery slope from ego-based actions to evil based actions.

In accordance with the way the soul lived life here on earth the soul will journey onwards through the afterlife. Souls enter levels of existence parallel to their progression and spiritual development or lack thereof during life. Operating on a zoological plane of existence — ego ridden, reactive and reflexive — the soul will eventually transmigrate into an animal. Acting as an animal the person will eventually become an animal. Whereas being stoically indifferent and completely lifeless in regard to matters of the spirit will cause the soul to enter such inanimate objects of existence. Being stone-like in life, the soul will ultimately end up in the form of a stone. A person becomes in the afterlife what he is in this life.

The late eighteenth century teacher Chassidic Rebbe, Reb Pinchas of Koritz, once explained, perhaps in jest, why self-centered egotistical people reincarnate into buzzing bees (*Medrash Pinchas* p. 81). "I Am this"... and "I Am that"... is the phrase an arrogant person has most on his lips. If he were to be speaking in Yiddish, as most Eastern European Jews would have been in the late eighteenth century, he would be saying, "Ich Bin Das.../I am this..." or "Ich Bin Yence...I am that..." In Yiddish the word Bin means am, but can also refer to a bee. As such, the arrogant person who goes about saying, "Ich Bin" is also saying, "I am a bee," and so, after years of saying he is a bee he will finally become one.

Our Next Life or Body as a Continuation of this Life

Another way of perceiving this dynamic is to look at the transmigration phenomenon in terms of self-development and spiritual evolution. We are all born with an inanimate soul, a vegetative soul, an animal soul and a human soul. These four souls or aspects of soul correspond to the four forms of life — the inanimate, vegetative, animal and human. The inanimate is a reality completely enclosed within itself. It appears as Domem/Silent, with no apparent movement or vitality. The vegetative kingdom is more (apparently) alive, vibrating and moving. Plants grow and expand. The animal kingdom is even more alive and teeming with movement. Not only do animals grow in their bodies, like vegetation, but they also move about freely, they are not "planted" in one place. The human being, the Medaber/ Speaking Creature is the highest, most complex and revealed level of life, movement and growth. The human exists like stones, grows like vegetation, roams freely like animals, and communicates in symbolic language like only humans can.

The inanimate soul, as it were, is our basic core reality, representing the minimum spiritual energy required to exist. There is no movement, no growth, just the will to exist. Experientially it is totally selfish and ego-based. The more advanced level of soul is our vegetative soul, represented by the spiritual energy that propels our physical expansion, like vegetation. Experientially, the vegetative soul is our survival instincts, much like the instincts of a tree to bend towards sunlight. Even higher is the animal soul, reflected in the spiritual energy that allows us to physically move about the world freely. Experientially, the animal soul is reactive and impulsive.

Our soul reincarnates into the next life according to the level it has reached in our current life. If someone has only lived on the level of vegetation, meaning that they expanded and grew physically, but were guided purely by their selfish instincts, much like a 'selfish' tree (although this is not as a moral judgment of trees, as everything, besides the human being, is always perfect, existing exactly as the Creator intended it to be), after this person passes on they will move into a period of vegetation. The same will be true of a person who was merely reactive during their life, like an animal; after they pass on they will reincarnate into the body of an animal.

Either way, the reason why a soul may descend into the various forms of existence is for the lessons the soul can acquire. Once the lessons have been learned the soul re-attains its purity and is able to enter Gan Eden. Take, for example, the arrogant and contemptuous individual. One of the ways this self-centered person can reach his Tikkun, purging himself of the appended negativity, is by entering into the body of a bee. By its very nature bees live less for themselves as individuals and more for the entire hive. Simply through residing in the body of a bee the soul acquires this most important lesson; it learns selflessness and becomes accustomed to Sha'aring.

Essentially this kind of soul reincarnation is a kind of cleansing and re-finement process. There is a sort of anguish the soul experiences existing within another form. Beyond the psychological embarrassment that some sources speak of, there is also a genuine discomfort and disturbance the soul undergoes due to its inability to express itself fully or even partially.

Body and soul are designed to fit each other. The human body is a visible projection and physical representation of the spiritual structure of soul. The body is a mirror reflected image of the soul. Existing in any other form of existence will undoubtedly cause great upheaval and agitation for the human configured soul (Alter Rebbe *Siddur Im Dach*, p. 48). The amount of distress depends on the quality and quantity of expression the soul will be allowed to show in its new life. Residing within an animal where it has limited room for expression, as animals possess some form of intelligence and emotion, is not as tormenting as occupying inanimate entities where there is no outlet for human-like self-expression.

Refinement through Transmigration

Transmigration is for the purpose of refinement. It is an act of Chesed/ Divine kindness intended to ease the soul's torment and help it regain its original brilliance. The numeric value of the Hebrew word for reincarnation, Gilgul, is seventy-two (Gimel/3, Lamed/30, Gimel/3, Vav/6, Lamed/30 = 72). This is the same numeric value as the Hebrew word for kindness, Chesed (Ches/8, Samach/60, Dalet/4 = 72). Gilgul is in fact a Chesed (Chayit *Ma'areches Elokus*, 10. *Likutei Torah L'Arizal*, Yisro. *Megalah Amukhos*, 11. *Emek Hamelech*, Hakdamah 2:3). Through the experience of being embodied within another form of existence and not being able to fully or even partially express itself, the soul is able to re-attain its harmoniously integrated state and can enter and reenter Gan Eden, 'paradise.'

Silencing and muting its own self-expression is one of the ways a soul that exuded negativity can heal and restore itself. A person who has lived a completely immoral and ungodly life, radiating negativity and vileness, is able to cleanse himself by being put in a condition that does not allow for self-expression, thereby entering a form that is totally and radically inconsistent with his soul's makeup. The silencing is itself the Tikkun.

Sometimes after existing within a rock, for example, a person is given the full chance to reincarnate within a human form in order to undo and elevate the past life. When a person uses the power of being human (i.e., speech) for negativity he descends to the level of the inanimate and will reincarnate into the form of a silent stone (*Sha'ar Hagilgulim*, 22). This is what is taught regarding Naval who spoke disparagingly against King Dovid (*Shmuel* 1, 25:10). It says about Naval that, "His heart died within him and he was a rock" (*Shmuel* 1, 25:37). He became a "rock." The mystics teach that Naval was a reincarnation of Bilam/Balaam, the infamous magician who wished to use his speech to curse the people of Israel in the desert, but instead he blessed them. He then reincarnated into the world of the inanimate, as a stone. Later he was given another chance and reincarnated into Naval. When Naval repeated the same mistake, i.e., when he used his mouth for negative speech, and his wife reminded him about this, the verse says, "His heart died within him and he was a rock." His heart died when he remembered that he was once a rock - i.e., within a rock. For this reason the verse does not say, "He became a rock," but rather, "His heart died…he was a rock." His heart died when he remembered that he was a rock and was given another chance to live within a human being to fully undo his past actions, but his messed up. He did not achieve his Tikkun.

Think of the above in terms of a teacher attempting to initiate a student into a newly discovered scientific theory. Provided the student has a basic understanding of science the teacher may formulate his teachings based on his previous knowledge. However, if all the student possesses is an askew understanding of science the teacher may ask the student to 'forget' everything he had ever learnt about science and start anew. In this way, the teacher would attempt to have the student deconstruct the old paradigm in order to reconstruct a new understanding. Sometimes the only way to build or rebuild anew is by first demolishing the old, knocking down the previous faulty structure to construct a new one.

This healing process is comprised of two aspects. The first is the washing away of the appended spiritual toxicities. This is achieved through the soul being silenced, as explained. And second, by simply existing in another form of reality other than man, the soul re-attains and reveals its true transcendent nature. All of creation, outside the human, is completely in sync with its spiritual life energy.

Within nature, unlike within humanity, there are no conflicting desires between body and soul. Take an animal for example. Animals, to the best of our knowledge, are integrated creatures. Their actions and being are one and the same. They do what they are. They act instinctively and reflexively, without meditated choice, and that is because the Creator has already chosen for them. A human soul, by simply residing within an integrated animal (or any other non-human element within creation for that matter) achieves its Tikkun by submissively manifesting the will of the Creator and getting in touch with its own true nature.

The length of time that a soul needs to spend within another form of existence depends on the degree of negativity that needs to be eradicated and erased. If a soul needs to reside for a year within an animal, for example, and that particular animal dies, the humanoid soul will then be transferred into the body of another animal. And when its fated time is completed it will automatically return to its Source. Such is the process without human intervention. However, with human interference the entire procedure can be accelerated. A human being that consumes a product that contains a human soul has the power to set that soul free even prior to its original prescribed time.

A human being has the potential to alleviate and liberate trapped souls provided that there is a soul-to-soul connection, such as a shared soul-root, between the eater and the eaten. The person consuming the food must share a spiritual kinship with the soul he is literally internalizing. To a certain degree this is much like a catch 22. For the most part, the very reason one is attracted to those particular tastes, as opposed to others, is because the soul yearns to reach out, connect with and elevate those specific sparks that it are contained within those foods.

More than animating and giving life to the body, the soul informs and guides the body/mind to pursue that which it is inherently connected with. Physical likes and dislikes — whether people, foods, objects or subjects of interest — are all tangible manifestations of the soul's desire to connect. The alleged natural inclinations toward certain areas in life are a result of the soul's desire to join with the spiritual energies that exist in those areas and elevate them. This attraction, resonance and consonance extends into all aspects of life, ranging from the friends one chooses to the job one has, to the place one lives — all of life is included within this parameter. Everything that a person has or is inclined to have contains sparks that are connected to the root of his soul.

Throughout life we find that there are some people that we are instantly attracted to while others immediately rub us the wrong way. Sometimes we meet someone for the very first time and we are mysteriously and inexplicably attracted to that person. Instantaneously we feel safe in their presence and we sense that there is no reason to continue wearing the usual masks we throw on and project to others. We feel as if we have always known such a person, and on some level we have. In the world of souls there is a deep soul-to-soul connection. It is not that we share the exact same soul root as that would potentially cause friction as previously mentioned, but there is some kind of deep soulular connection, some undeniable magnetism. In this way, both souls need each other to reach their own spiritual development.

Eating becomes a sacred activity as we become aware of how we can assist trapped souls in their elevation through this very act. One's natural attraction towards certain foods is one soul (the eater) being drawn to the other soul within the food (the eaten). Yet, it is clear that simply devouring food will not engender any positive reorientation of the confined soul. In fact, it may even cause harm to the eater (*Shiur Komah*, Shit Alfei, 4. *Sha'ar Hamitzvos*,

Ekev, 43. *Safer Hagilgulim*, Sader Gilgulim, 4. *Yaros D'vash*, Derush 1). To truly inspire an elevation and have a positive effect on the soul trapped within, and not the converse, one needs the proper Kavanah/intention. A requisite for elevation is a measure of intentionality before, during, and after eating. The recitation of a blessing and the acknowledgment that through eating one will have the strength to serve both Creator and creation with more vitality and vigor is the bear minimum that is required to stimulate a release of soul energy within any given food.

Intentionality during consumption is only a necessary ingredient with regard to human beings. Animals, however, can inspire the elevation of souls contained within grass, hay or any one of their foods, by simply eating. Since animals have no independent free will, everything they do is in accordance with the will of their Creator. As such, their pasturing is a divine and holy activity by its very nature, thus stimulating the required elevation through mere grazing.

In summary: there are two fundamental types of reincarnations, and they should not be confused. One is the usual course of reincarnation (from one human being into another), and the other course of reincarnation is from a human being into another form of existence. In the latter, the individualized aspects of soul reincarnate in order to be refined and cleansed. This kind of reincarnation is somewhat uncommon. In the former, which is more common and universal, new elements of soul continue to reincarnate, not for punishment's sake, but rather to articulate and actualize original, unexplored and untapped resources of soul.

CHAPTER 8
Individual Memory, Collective Memory

The Self at Birth

The best way to understand who we are in the present, in our entirety, is to say that we are in our memories. All of our experiences and knowledge, the way we think, feel and interact is all stored in our memory. Not only are our thoughts and the way we think contained within our memory, so are our external realities. Even the presence of something outside our bodies is only a reality to us because it exists in our minds.

Though memory is accumulated through the senses, we are more than what our senses tell us we are. Not everything can be accounted for by sensation alone. Hobbes' assertion that, "Nihil est in intellectu quod non fuerit in sensu – there is no conception in a man's mind which has not at first been begotten upon the organs of sense," is not quite accurate. It is more akin to what Leibniz added in response, "Nisi intellectus ipse – except understanding itself." There is knowledge that we are born with and there is knowledge that we collect through the perceptions of our senses which we further develop through continued reflection and analysis.

Mind is not undistinguished at birth. There is a you/soul before birth and even conception. The very reason we are inclined toward certain thoughts and experiences and not others, or that we intuitively interpret events in a particular fashion and not another, is because we possess individualized soul–types. Although our memories are founded on the various experiences of life, they are also very much colored and funneled through the prism of our soul's particularity, which we have from birth.

The Medieval Latin term Tabula Rasa, which literally means 'scraped tablet,' or as it is known colloquially, 'blank slate,' is an inaccurate definition of the mind at birth. The mind/psyche/soul is not, as the Empiricists such as Locke would want us to believe, a "white paper, void of all characters, without any ideas." Nor does "existence precede essence," as Sartre would like us to think. Rather there is an essence to who we are. And to rephrase the quote, "essence precedes existence."

There is an essence or a soul reality with specific defined properties, even prior to our existence within the body (*Rabbeinu Bachya* Vayikra, 18:29. *Sefer Ha'emunos*, 6:1. *Magen Avos*, 3:4).

Today we understand that even genetically our minds are 'hardwired' at birth. As the genetic pattern is a reflection of the spiritual construct, spiritually speaking, each of us is born with a distinctive and unmatched soul-type. The soul is more like a colored sheet of paper with a distinct essence upon which life's experiences are written. The writings, our experiences, are imposed upon our essence. During the course of life we are in our memories; we are that which is stored and indelibly impressed upon our soul's fabric.

There is what can be called the "autobiographical self," the self that is comprised of combinations of our memories and past experiences. This self can only exist once life begins to unfold. And then there is the "essential self," the self that is already somewhat preconditioned or hardwired at birth, which, as explained earlier, is consistent with our soul make-up and divine purpose.

Brain Memory vs. Soul Memory

At our inception we possess an infinite soul sans finite physical experiences. As we go through life we slowly become the sum total of our 'soul plus life experiences.' This totality of who we are in the present is stored in our memory-bank. The brain contains all our memories. Whether memory is localized in the brain and dependent on two small pieces on either side of the brain called the hippocampus, or, as science understands today, it is distributed throughout the entire brain which is more like a hologram, is of no importance. Either way, the brain is the physical organ that retains our memory.

There are two types of memory recollection, with a marked distinction between the two. One can be called 'brain memory' and the other 'soul memory.' 'Brain memory' is generally inaccurate, partially or fully fragmented, and distorted. 'Soul memory' is always accurate, complete, and precise. The former is the memory we most often experience during embodied life while the latter is reserved primarily for bodiless existence.

Brain memory does not retain memory faithfully. Modern research has shown that by and large people do not recall the past with accuracy. Memories of the past, even if it is just a few days or even minutes ago, are colored by the present condition of the brain. Memory is more an interpretation of an event than an actual recall. Memory is a creative act in the present looking back into the past. Indeed the present is always different from the moment that just passed, and to remember a past experience while standing in the present is to see it through the bias of one's present conditioning. A modern, brilliant, but rather deranged philosopher once put it this way: "Pride and memory had an argument. Memory said: 'It was this way.' Pride said: 'It couldn't be.' And pride won." Pride and ego always win.

Soul memory, by contrast, is not defined or limited to physical properties and is therefore accurate and precise at all times. This subliminal soul memory receives and faithfully records all our world experiences, it picks up everything that the mind did not register or even notice. When the physical brain dies what remains is the 'soul memory,' containing not only the total package of the present person (including how he exists at the moment of death), but the total recall of the person's whole life from the day of their birth.

Every life experience imprints itself upon the soul, some permanently, others temporarily. The soul is similar to raw material. Some experiences scrape the surface, while others chisel themselves into its very fabric. Some things in life have become so ingrained into one's consciousness that they become indistinguishable from the person himself, while some merely remain on the exterior.

Ultimately, that which is indelibly imprinted upon the soul is only the positive and virtuous acts one does during this life, and they too become eternal and everlasting. Not only do positive deeds and attitudes stay with the person in this life, but they also journey onwards and upwards into the afterlife. Antithetically, negativity never truly becomes part of the person's constitution and psyche. Any negativity that a person may have exhibited or experienced throughout their life is not indicative of their personality, it is always viewed as an artificial appendage that can and will be removed, either in this life through one's own free choice, or in the afterlife.

Negativity is not Nitzchi/Everlasting (*Tanya*, Chap. 25). Lodged in a finite universe of time and space it will and eventually must perish or dissolve; the question is only how and when. A person who passes away with negatively charged memories — that is, with negative and destructive thoughts, feelings or behaviors that now exist as memory — will need to go through a process of ridding himself of that memory. That process itself will be explored later on, and is referred to as Gehenom.

It is important to keep in mind that through the power of Teshuvah/Reintegration and self-reconstruction we have the ability to liberate ourselves from the negative choke hold of our past and erase that past from our 'soul memory.' One who embarks on the path of Teshuvah is considered a new person, with a new sense of identity (*Sifri*, Vaeschanan, 30. Rambam *Hilchos Teshuvah*, 2:4. *Semag*, Mitzvah 16). What's more, not only do we have the capacity to undo or eradicate the past, we have the power to transform past malice into merit and liabilities into assets (*Yumah*, 86b).

Individualized Teshuvah for particular deeds or misdeeds exonerates those specific deeds performed either by commission or omission. Yet, Teshuvah of a higher order is to experience a total radical transformation, wherein one shifts their very beingness, and through that change all negative experiences are transformed, or 'recycled,' so to speak, into something positive and useful.

Accurate memory is a G-d-like quality. Such memory can only exist in an Infinite space unfettered by the lapses of time and distances of space. When a person transforms themselves through Teshuvah these un-godly memories, these regretful and negative experiences, are totally obliterated as there is no "memory" of them any longer (*Tzidkas HaTzadik*, 99). On an even deeper level, they too are now integrated and included within a more positive frame of reference.

Genuine choice, such as true movement and radical transformation, is only present within this operating sphere of existence. Once a soul enters higher/deeper states of being these options are no longer available; one no longer has the power to transform (*Zohar* 3, p. 178a. *Shabbos*, 30a). This world is created and founded on Divine Chesed/kindness and Divine compassion. In this world of Chesed, a world of forgiveness and compassion, Teshuvah is a real possibility and actions do not have inevitable reactions. In the world of "truth," the afterlife reality known as the world of Gevurah/severity and judgment, there is no room for change, for undoing what was put into motion (*Derech Mitzvosecho*, Viddui Teshuvah, 4. Tefilah, 45). A soul that enters such a world with negative baggage needs to unload its burden before it can fully integrate with its Source. Ridding itself of these negative experiences that have become part of one's memory and presence may be part of such a soul's exhausting, albeit liberating, journey toward Gan Eden, Paradise and eternal bliss.

Individual Memory, Collective Memory

Memory, the totality of who we are, lives on following the death of the physical brain within the all-encompassing 'memory' of the Omnipresence. This 'memory' space can be viewed as a type of matrix of the totality of all memory and information within the universe and beyond.

Personality exists as a distinctive constellation of memory within the vast and limitless expanse of the Creator's 'memory.' Individual sense of self, characterized by the distinct memory, does not lose itself or become completely consumed within the vastness of the Whole, but rather continues to exist in its distinction, as a sliver of particularity within the Whole.

The individual memory, the fullness of the person, flourishes and functions as a paradox and contradiction, as it were. On the one hand the memory exists as a distinct individual with a unique set of experiences; on the other hand, that very distinct memory is now part of the wider web of life, the Whole System. The person, in the form of the memory (present in the Guf Dak and within his soul), continues to exist as a distinct and finite self and yet it is subsumed as part of the greater infinite memory. The finite, distinguished self becomes eternal and its eternity is experienced within the infinite and the indistinguishable.

Imagine a drop of water flowing back into the ocean, and yet retaining its existence as a drop. The ocean can be viewed as a seamless flow of water, an infinite expansiveness, which is the way we normally see it; or it can be viewed as billions or even trillions of individual drops of water. The aspect of eternity that the soul experiences is of the deepest levels, as it becomes one with the ultimate unity, the inclusive transcendence. Here the oneness, the infinity, is so beyond distinctions that it penetrates even finitude and does not view finitude as a contradiction of infinitude. As an expression of this deepest truth the soul does not surrender individuality, but rather retains its sense of selfhood, experiencing finite memory within the womb of the Infinite.

In simple words: We continue to exist as we know ourselves to be now, for all eternity.

Gan Eden-Active Intelligence:
The Revealed Space of Wisdom and Purpose

Several Medieval sages speak of paradise as existing in a state of Seichel Ha'poel/Active intellect or Seichel Ha'kelali/Universal intellect, a type of reservoir of intellectual consciousness, an expression of the Divine flow of wisdom (*Akeidas Yitzchak*, Sha'ar 7. *Magen Avos*, 3:4. *Machir Yayin*, p. 16). The logical conclusion of this perspective would be to argue that only philosophers, pursuers and lovers of knowledge and those who acquired intellect during their journey through life, could and will experience Paradise. Yet the Torah ensures that Gan Eden is not reserved exclusively for intellectuals. Gan Eden will and can be experienced by all good and decent people, each person according to his own level of appreciation (*Sanhedrin*, 10:1. *Kesef Mishnah*, Hilchos Teshuvah, 3:5. *Ohr Hashem*, 3. *Moreh Nevuchim*, 2:27. *Safer Haikkarim*, 4:31). Cognitive ability and intellectual genius is not the only yardstick with which to measure a person's goodness or spiritual achievement. Every person has his or her own particular way of actualizing their soul potential and through that articulated aspect they achieve eternity. This can be through Iyyun/delving deeply into the mysteries of creation and the Torah, or Mitzvos/good and noble actions, or both — Intellect and Action. (Ralbag, *Melchemes Hashem* 1:2. *Akeidas Yitzchak*, Sha'ar 6).

This "active intelligence" could and should be seen as the Divine limitless flow of wisdom. Creation occurs through an active Divine life force, a Shefa Eloki/Divine flow that continuously flows from the Infinite One into creation. This wisdom is the revealed purpose of why there is a creation in the first place. Everything in the world contains Divine wisdom, innate intelligence, and a guiding principle to fulfill its purpose. Whether a person is an intellectual or not, whether they work with their brain or with their hands, is not the sole measurement of a person's connection to the Divine Shefa or the Divine purpose and wisdom of his/her creation, as Divine wisdom is present in all levels of reality including even the physical. This is why admission to Gan Eden - although it is a place of revealed understanding, purpose and wisdom where life finally makes "sense" - is primarily dependent upon one's good deeds and Mitzvos performed in this world, as well as on the Torah that they learned.

Gan Eden:
A Reality of Becoming

The level and quality of our experience of the afterlife in Gan Eden will be commensurate with the level and quality of our actions here in this world.

From a deeper perspective, not only is the 'there' a place/state one enters as a result of the work and action done 'here,' but Gan Eden/World to Come is a reality that is created by our actions done in this world. There is no objective independent reality called Gan Eden, as it were. Rather Gan Eden/World to Come is the objective correlative reality corresponding to our actions done in this world.

Our sages say, "All of Israel has a portion L'Olam Ha'Ba/in the World to Come" (*Sanhedrin*, 10:1). Grammatically, the words "L'Olam Ha'ba" do not translate as "IN the World to Come," but rather, "TO the World to Come." A person may state, "I own property IN New York," but it would make no sense to say, "I own property TO New York." Yet, this is exactly how the sages phrased it, that all of Israel has a portion To the World to Come. That is because the World to Come is in a state of becoming, it is in a constant state of being created. Unlike a piece of land that one can purchase, settle and enter, Gan Eden is continuously evolving according to the actions of each individual person who is creating it (*Ruach Chayim*, Avos, Mishnah Kaal Yisrael. *Nefesh Hachayim*, 1:12).

Gan Eden exists within the divine "attribute" and sphere of Binah, the quality of intelligence and understanding (*Sha'arei Orah*, Sha'ar 8). After a person's body passes on his memory will continue to function within the realm of Binah, within the mind of the Creator, so to speak. As the aspect of Binah is in a constant state of movement, flux and fluidity, the soul/consciousness, which is housed in Binah will also continuously advance, expand and progress. The soul, the defined sense of self, will survive in an active mode of being. In the world of the spirit there is constant movement. There is no room for complacency or dormancy. In the words of our sages, "the righteous experience no rest; not in this world nor in the next" (End of *Berachos*. *Tanya*, Igeres Hakodesh, 17).

All ascents in the after-life are determined by the degree of spiritual development and merits accrued here on earth. Parallel to one's spiritual and moral achievements is the level of one's celestial abode. So, whereas the soul is stationary in that it is defined by its identity and can only progress in accordance to the life it led below; still, based on the experiences of this life the soul will ceaselessly continue to move and expand eternally (*Zohar* 1, p. 185a. *Shulchan Aruch Harav*, Talmud Torah, 2:13. *Safer Hamaamorim* Nun Dalet, p. 232). The ladder that leads to the Infinite is itself infinite. The soul in its fixed state of being will constantly be in a state of becoming, becoming ever more connected and committed to its supernal Source.

Transparent Memory & the Selectivity of the Brain

Recently a theory has been put forward that speculates that the mind is more selective than indiscriminate. The mind perhaps sees everything but absorbs only what it needs for survival. One of the proofs of this is offered from art appreciation. It does not take an artist to value art. Most people, when they see a beautifully depicted landscape are awestruck — the question is why. The painting could be a depiction of our very own neighborhood, and yet, although in our own day-to-day experience we may not find our neighborhood very charming, in the artist's rendition we do, why?

According to the theorists who explain the workings of the mind, this phenomenon, as mentioned above, is proof that even though we see our neighborhood every day we really do not see it at all; certain details are never fully registered or noticed. The artist acts as a 'revealing agent' who points out some of the details that we may have otherwise never observed, and that is why we are impressed and appreciate the art. We can see everything but only a little is filtered through the screening mechanism of our brain. A motion picture camera can serve as a good analogy. When it records it picks up everything the lens is aimed at. Later on, when the tape is played and viewed, not everything that had been captured is detected by the average viewer.

This selection process that the brain exercises is a paradoxically creative, or at least curatorial act, although on some level it is automatic and unconscious. Its creativity lies in the process of weeding out a specific something from the everything of experience; and yet it is automatic in that the selection is based on the viewer's predisposition based on past experiences, their mood in the moment, and essentially what their notion of survival consists of.

Selectivity of the mind of course extends beyond the visual. In the domain of ideas the same selective process is extant; the mind chooses what it considers important or not. The brain in a way shields the person from every little bit of information that it finds unimportant. So beyond helping the person acquire the necessary information, it blocks out all stimulus that it deems unnecessary. The brain thus serves as an editor. Just like the lungs do not produce air, and the stomach does not produce food, similarly, the brain does not source thoughts; rather it absorbs and edits what it deems vital. Much like the rest of the body the brain is not the originator. The brain is thus not the creator of consciousness, but rather functions more like a filter or screen through which creation passes into consciousness and the back out again.

Most contemporary brain researchers agree that the human brain receives far more information than what is actually registered. It is estimated that the unconscious mind processes something like ten billion bits of information per second, whereas the conscious mind process something like ten to thirty bits a second. Whether or not this theory holds up, the relevant point here is that in the afterlife the mind/soul is free and non-constricted by any jamming devices. There is no ego and no sensory functions and the mind, which has now joined up with the 'mind of the Creator,' is completely open and transparent. The reduction valve or filter has been totally removed and the whole of reality becomes available.

Once the filter and limiter is gone there can be a total recall of memory and unified level of consciousness. All of life becomes crystal-clear and the person is able to view and recall all of life, the good as well as the opposite.

Beyond the selectiveness of the mind it is the five senses that are by and large the windows to our reality. True, there is knowledge that is not 'at first begotten upon the organs of sense,' but most of our day-to-day perception and definition of what is is founded upon our senses, i.e., the empirical way we see, hear, taste, smell and feel.

It has been alleged that terminally ill people whose sensory powers have drastically declined are able to peer into the future due to the strengthening of their imagination (*Magen Avos*, 3:4. Rebbe Menachem *Recanti*, Vayera). They are no longer distracted by the interference of their sensory abilities. Genuine clear-minded and lucid perception is available when the body altogether ceases to function and there is no interference of the sensory powers whatsoever. In such a state, the soul-mind experiences the most transparent perception possible, becoming exponentially more aware of itself and of total reality.

To a certain degree through meditation a meditator can switch off the body's sensory interferences, effectively blocking them out from their mind and experiencing objective reality in its truest form. Yet it is only once the soul and body part ways that the soul can observe reality with such ultimate clarity and maximum precision. Without the selectiveness of the ego or the obstruction of the various senses, the mind is entirely open and the whole of life becomes transparent and most apparent; everything that has ever occurred, even if only slightly registered on the radar of consciousness, becomes manifest.

Souls interacting with the Living

Growth and perpetual movement are constant dynamics of the soul. Once the soul leaves the body it forever expands and attains deeper and more profound levels of D'veikus/Attachment with its Source; the journey, mirroring the destination, is infinite and endless. Yet, even though the soul continues to progress and advance 'upwards' it still knows and even feels the pain of the reality from which it graduated, the physical world (*Zohar 2*, p. 16b. *Maharam Shik*, Orach Chayim, 293).

Souls retain earthly awareness in various ways. The dead are aware of the living (*Berachos*, 18b. *Shabbos*, 152b). On the most elementary level when the soul is nested within the Omnipresent 'memory of the Creator' it has the ability to unambiguously observe and perceive all of reality, both 'above' and 'below.'

More specifically, an unembodied soul is able to connect with this physical realm of existence via the Nefesh, the element of soul that is eternally bound to physicality. The Nefesh is the most reified and dense level of soul. It is the spirit that is permanently tied up with the location of the body's burial (*Zohar* 1, p. 81a). While the soul continues to rise and ascend it can observe and interact with this plane of existence by way of the Nefesh.

In some cases the soul may even assume a physical presence and make itself 'observable' by other living beings (*Safer Chassidim*, 1129. *Ma'avar Yavak*, 3:25. *Avodas Hakodesh*, 2:26). On occasion, for the purpose of transmitting a message, a soul may vest itself within the distilled form of the Guf Dak/Refined Body and the living may then sense their presence. Those observing the Guf Dak may even experience a sort of unclear or obscured vision in the form of an apparition or silhouette of the soul's previous physical figure. A soul will do this to effect some type of physical change in this world. For otherwise, being as they are totally without a body they cannot influence the physical world (*Sheivet HaMusar*, 35. Ma'hara M'Fano *Maamor HaNefesh*, 2:12).

A dream is another mode of spiritual communication and can serve as a conduit through which the world of souls interacts with the world of bodies (*Reshis Chachmah*, Sha'ar HaYirah, 12. *Migdal Oz*, Chibut Hakever, 5. *Tur (Perisha)* Choshen Mishpat, 255). Talmudic sources mention various sages who were visited by their colleagues in dreams to transmit messages or teachings from beyond the grave (*Moed Katan*, 28b. *Baba Metziah*, 85b). Though certain types of post-mortem communication are a possibility, "permission is not granted for souls to convey the heaven's decrees to their loved ones" (*Safer Chassidim*, 1133). Certain eternal truths are intended to remain mysterious and hidden from the perception of mortal man.

During the course of a dream the brain-wave activity is quite different from the brainwave activity of a waking state. Delta—which occurs during sleep—is the slowest of the brain wave frequencies, whereas Beta is the fastest. As the Beta state slows down, the normal 'rushing around' modality of daily life becomes less prominent. Additionally, one's three-dimensional fixation becomes less pronounced as one enters a more ethereal and relaxed mode of awareness. From this more fluid state of consciousness souls of one's teachers or loved ones may henceforth communicate. While dreams are constantly and unconsciously generated, what is required on the part of the living dreamer is to become more receptive and fine-tuned to this mental frequency or brain state. Literally, one must be open and sensitive to such an experience.

Ibbur:
Becoming Impregnated with a Perfected Soul

Beyond dream communication, bodiless souls may re-embody in order to assist embodied souls. In fact, the world receives continuous sustenance through the intercession of the pure souls above (*Zohar* 2, p. 16b). A person's life in this world may be impacted by the work of his ancestors in other dimensions of reality, whether physical or spiritual.

At times, perfected souls on high will intercede on behalf of souls they are related to. Not only are souls aware of what is occurring on this plane of existence, they may even come to help, support or give guidance to souls who are struggling in their earthly journey. One of the ways this phenomenon transpires is through Ibbur/Impregnation. Ibbur is a guest soul that descends to assist, or at times to be assisted by, the soul it inhabits to reach their proper elevation and articulation.

Fantastical shifts of mood or temperament can occasionally be attributed to Ibbur. If a person has been feeling consistently depressed, confused or uncertain and then wakes up one day and feels inexplicably empowered, focused and secure; or if one day he struggles immensely to simply go about his chores and the next day, after a night sleep, he feels on the top of the world beyond psychological reasoning — the spiritual explanation and root cause for this empowerment is Ibbur.

As 'perfected' souls sense their related souls struggling to achieve their potential they may re-descend and infuse the person with an extra dosage of spiritual stamina. At times one may even experience an Ibbur from one's very own soul, that is, from the elements of one's total soul–type that have been previously elevated. At these heightened moments where a person feels overwhelmingly empowered he may be experiencing an infusion of his own higher self. In such a case the sparks of his soul that have been perfected in previous lives have returned to assist the other sparks to express themselves fully and articulate their essence.

Whereas the normal course of Ibbur originates from an 'arousal from above' (i.e., it is bestowed upon one in a way that is beyond his or her control), working to draw forth an Ibbur in a manner of 'an arousal from below' is also a possibility. We can actively call forth other souls to impregnate us (*Yaros D'vash*, 16. *Tanya* 14). Souls that resonate with each other to the extent of forging a steadfast unity between them may impregnate one another. Simply by doing a certain positive deed that a particular person excelled at could influence the soul of that person to come and impregnate the living earthly doer of the deed.

The telling thing about these peak Ibbur experiences is that they come instantaneously and go away just as quickly. They are transient, ephemeral and rarely permanent. Enduring experiences are the ones that come from within, achieved through effort and generated from elements of self that are part of our normative consciousness and not from experiences that arise due to 'awakenings from beyond.' Stimulating and exciting as they may appear, the real and lasting valuable highs are the ones that come through hard work and exerted toil.

CHAPTER 9
Afterlife Journey

The process of the individual and distinct memory existing within the Mind of the Omnipresence, gradually drawing ever closer to its Source, is Gan Eden. To enter Gan Eden is to exist consciously as your unique-self/soul-identity/composite-memory while at the same time being at home within the trans-personal Infinite memory of the Creator. While for some souls the transition from an ego-based reality to unifying with the Infinite Transcendent One is swift and seamless, like moving from room into another, there are others who need to go through an elaborate afterlife progression to arrive at Gan Eden.

Gehenom /Hell

Gehenom, which has been loosely translated as hell, is the all-inclusive description for the various spiritual processes a soul may undergo in its afterlife journey. Although, keep in mind that Gehenom, and for that matter, Gan Eden or Heaven are states of reality and not literal locations. They are, more accurately, metaphysical landscapes or spiritual topologies unrelated in any way to any of the properties of a four–dimensional universe.

The Hebrew term Gehenom stems from the words Gai Henom/the valley of Henom. Henom was a gorge just outside of Yerushalayim, which in Tanach times was the known site of many human sacrifices offered by various groups of pagan Canaanites. Later on, during King Dovid's rule, the pagan altars were destroyed and it soon became a dumping ground where the city's waste was burned. In time, the term Gehenom was introduced as a metaphor for a fiery 'place' were a soul disinfects and cleanses itself of any accumulated 'dirt' or schumtz so that it can once again return to and reintegrate with its Source in Gan Eden.

Understandably, Gehenom is not a place somewhere up there in the galaxies or down below in the middle of the earth. There is no underworld or subterranean universe where doomed souls wander about aimlessly. The notion of an underworld amounts to nothing more than pagan mythology. And yet, the way people give language to and describe these events are very much physically referential — as in souls descend into hell or ascend up to heaven. Take the colloquial phrase: After people pass on they go to another world. The word after implies time; go indicates a space; and another means an other in contrast to this world, as if there is a parity.

Spoken language is comprised of symbolic sonic gestures that are intended to convey information that is spatial and time-bound. Being that the verbal idiom is the most comprehensive mode of communication at our human disposal, difficulties emerge when we attempt to express, through conventional language, that which is beyond linear logic. So while the terminology, imagery and descriptions of the afterlife seem to be expressing a material reality, they are in fact mere metaphors attempting to depict a spiritual process that has no physical equivalency.

Existence in the afterlife is an organic continuation of this life, minus physical form. The individuality of the person, defined and contained as a memory unit, lives on. The entire personality of the person — which is comprised of their pure and primordial soul-type plus all the unique experiences of life that have been imprinted on that soul — survives.

The measure of reintegration within Gan Eden experienced by the individual 'soul memory' after death is commensurate to the level of soul actualization manifested during life. If one has lived in complete harmony with his soul the transition is immediate, while those who have lived a more out of balance and misaligned existence may need to travel along a longer route in order to reach that 'place,' although, eventually, all souls 'get there.' All souls come full circle and return to their origin.

Individual immortality is by no means a contradiction with the previously explained idea of reincarnation. What, in effect, incarnates into newly conceived embryos are spiritual sparks or sub-conscious elements of soul that were not fully articulated during the course of one's life. The aspect of soul that was individuated, and was his personal soul, retains its individuality in this life and in the next.

Between Gehenom & Gan Eden:
Heaven & Hell

Before the afterlife journey is further explored let us begin with a folk tale. A story that is certainly true on some level, if not literally, than at least for the message it imparts.

Years ago, in a small and rather poor village in Poland there lived a wealthy and pious man by the name of Yankel. One day, Yankel invited all the leaders of the community to an evening banquet, promising them a feast worthy of Gan Eden/Paradise. Upon their arrival each of the guests was escorted to the table, which was set magnificently with a place setting for each person. As soon as Yankel entered the room he sat down and summoned the butler. Carrying a bowl of hot soup he walked over to the master of the house and placed it in front of him. Oddly enough, soup was not offered to any of the other guests. Sipping his soup Yankel exclaims, "Oh, what a delicious soup! I am sure my friends that you have never tasted such a tasty soup." After the soup the next course was brought in, and once again the guests weren't served. Again Yankel exclaimed how delicious the food was. Losing patience, one of the guests blurted out: "Reb Yankel, have you invited us to make a mockery out of us. You promised a feast worthy of Paradise, and here, not only did we not get to eat but we have to suffer watching you eat." Gently, Reb Yankel smiled. "Indeed, this meal is worthy of Paradise. Paradise," he said, "is a place/state where people love each other enough that they can take pleasure in another person's happiness. There is no envy or jealously in Paradise, only love and understanding. Now that you have understood the paradisal part of the feast, dinner can now be served."

The blissful feeling of heaven or the agonizing dread of hell is based on the choices we make. Throughout life we can either pick heaven or choose hell.

Heaven is inclusive, hell is exclusive.

In a heaven paradigm it is me and you, in hell it is me or you.

To exist in heaven is to live in the open embrace of transcendence. A living hell is when every person we meet is suspected of being an enemy, and every experience we have is potentially threatening.

Hell is to live in a state of total conflict — with oneself, with others, with the Creator and with all of nature. Heaven, on the other hand, is to exist harmoniously with others, with oneself, with all of creation and with the Creator.

Interpersonally, heaven is where one is mature enough to realize that another person's enjoyment does not come at the expense of his own misery.

Here is another poetic image that attempts to describe the essence of the afterlife journey: Imagine a group of people sitting around a lavish table loaded with delicacies and the finest foods. Everyone is smiling and beaming, just so happy to be present at such a feast. The time for eating, indulging and enjoyment has arrived. Each person looks down only to find an unusually long eating utensil by their plate. In fact, the utensil is so long and unwieldy that no one is able to get food into their mouth. This is hell — the experience of having everything you have ever wanted laid out in front of you and being unable to access or enjoy it. Heaven is the exact same set-up, except that instead of desperately and unsuccessfully trying to contort themselves in order to find a way to shovel their food into their own mouths, each person has realized that the oddly shaped eating utensil is just long enough to reach across the table and feed someone else. This is truly Paradise.

Beyond offering a glimpse into a future existence, this metaphor is intended to enlighten us in regard to the present moment. It teaches us how to live now, in a heavenly way in the present.

To live heavenly is to experience self devoid of ego, aggression or resentment; the converse is hell. In hell, according to the above metaphor, one is completely wrapped up within himself, imagining the self as an autonomous and separate I, with everyone and everything else as a foreign invasive other.

With regard to the afterlife journey keep in mind that "between Gan Eden and Gehenom there is but a hairbreadth" (*Yalkut Shimoni*, Koheles 976). Put more dramatically — one soul's heaven is another soul's hell (*Kesones Posim*, p. 6d. *Toldas Yaakov Yoseph*, Bo. *Tzafnas Paneach*, Beshalach).

To some degree, all souls return to the same 'place.' For some souls merging with the light is transcendently ecstatic; whereas for others souls, those accustomed to being ego-oriented and self-centered, the very same experience is encountered as a kind of hell.

As individual soul memory moves on within the collective memory, the distinct unit will increasingly experience a movement 'upwards,' expanding and coming continually closer to its source. The soul reengaging with its deepest self participates in that which is most divine, the continuity and fluidity of life and awareness. Soul memory lives on as it enters Gan Eden in the sphere of Binah, a perennial condition of growth, understanding and evolution.

Afterlife movement and direction is determined by the soul's success in this life. The process is similar to how things work in a quasi-causal manner in this life. For instance, it is often the case that how a person acts or thinks in their elder years is generally (though not necessarily) a reflection of who they were when they were younger. Similarly, in the afterlife, what is experienced 'there' is a reflection of what was accomplished 'here.' The soul advances from one level of awareness to a higher/deeper one in accordance to the life it led. Although, it is important to mention that souls can be assisted in their afterlife journey by actions performed in their memory by the living, such as saying Kaddish or giving Tzedakah in their name or memory.

Life, both in this world and in the next, is a journey towards the Infinite One, and thus it is a journey that is itself infinite.

The Light of the Shechinah: Warming vs. Burning

To loosely paraphrase the Zohar (*Zohar* 3, p. 53): When a soul is about to leave the body the Shechinah appears in a brilliant radiance, and the soul goes out in great joy and open love to greet her. If, during the soul's sojourn here on earth it has become entrenched and immersed in materialism to the extent that it derived its identity from the externals, the Shechinah drifts away and the soul is left mourning.

Regarding the near-death experience one of the more popular tropes is that of encountering a comforting and embracing 'light.' Most near-death reports are strictly positive, yet there are isolated cases where people interviewed speak of hellish experiences. This phenomenon is referred to as an inverted NDE. In the inverted experience everything is reversed — fear sets in instead of love and dread overwhelms one in place of peacefulness.

Fear is a by-product of the ego and its dire need for attachment. Observing the light from an ego prism is fearful, as one desperately clings to their center of self and wishes not to surrender. A tension arises with the realization of the transient nature of the ego and that it no longer serves a purpose on the threshold of the next world. The need to give it up provokes anguish, fear and uncertainty.

To experience consciousness devoid of ego and unrelated to the senses can be wonderful for some and misery for others. One recognizes the light and approaches it with love, the other shies away in dread. A person who has lived a transcendent, godly and noble life immediately senses the beauty of their experiences and expires. Others who have not lived this way retract, recoil and turn aside. In the inverted process the presence of the Shechinah remains apart and one senses a devastating absence and emptiness. Altogether, for such a person, the experience is quite frightening and nightmarish.

For a soul that has lived a disharmonious existence the light of the Shechinah may be similar to sunlight being absorbed without the proper equipment or screen; it is exquisite and picturesque, but it is a light that is nonetheless blinding. Light that is too intense blinds the observer and by doing so becomes the source of darkness and confusion.

Gehenom is the absence of light, also known as darkness (*Tanchumah*, Noach, 1), not because the Creator's light is not present, but rather because the light is too powerful to be appreciated by any misaligned or spiritually estranged inhabitants. "There is no Gehenom in the time of Redemption, rather the Creator will take the sun out of its (protective) shield, the righteous will rejoice and the unrighteous will be blinded" (*Nedarim*, 8a). The same light that can be warm, embracing and illuminating for one, can burn, overwhelm and blind another.

Hell is a transitory condition where a soul is not yet equipped to absorb the bright lights of Heaven. Gehenom is where a soul is operating in a dis-united and disingenuous manner. The soul is unable to merge with and is blinded by the infinite light. The image that best represents this hellish experience is that of the Shechinah turning aside, as the soul is not yet able to become unified with the light. Part of the anguish is knowing the truth, but being unable to live it. In due time Heaven becomes available to all.

Upon one's passing and one's shedding of physical form, consciousness assumes a non-corporeal essence comprised of our emotions, thoughts and intentions. This unified ethereal-like form or astral body is compatible with the level of integration one achieves during their life. A disconnected and fragmented person's astral body will also be 'handicapped,' so to speak, and shaped in a disfigured manner. An imperfect ethereal-body, such as this one, will be an unsuitable vessel to fully soak up the wholesomeness and perfection of the infinite light.

Gehenom is nothing else but darkness, an absence of all light. It is an incomplete and unfinished entity, a creation that is intrinsically lacking wholeness (Maharal *Tifferes Yisrael*, 18). For a spiritually immature person or a soul that has, through their travels and travails in life, allowed the pure brilliance of their soul to be eclipsed, the experience of feeling the Divine's presence can be more humiliating and disturbing than uplifting and delightful.

Ultimately the eternal bliss of Gan Eden is beyond our conventional intellectual grasp. In fact, one of the reasons offered for why the Torah does not unambiguously address the afterlife is because issues such as these are beyond normative human comprehension (*Rabbeinu Bachya*, Vayikra, 26:9). In the words of master prophet Yeshayahu/Isaiah who, speaking of a World to Come, said: "No eye has seen and no ear has heard, O G-d, besides You"

(64:3. *Berachos*, 34b). Similarly, when Moshe was asked what could be expected in the future he humbly replied: "I do not know, but what I can tell you is that you are fortunate for what is awaiting you" (*Sifri*, Devarim, 356).

A blind person attempting to fathom colors or a deaf person trying to appreciate music is one of the many metaphors employed to describe the lack of any accurate description or comprehension of the world to come (*Pirush Ha'Mishnoyos*, Sanhedrin, 10:1). Being human and lodged in a four–dimensional universe we can never fully grasp a reality that is dimensionless and infinite.

Gehenom: A Process to get into Gan Eden

Whereas Gan Eden is the destination, albeit one that goes perpetually deeper and higher (like a moving target), Gehenom is essentially the process of getting there. The former is an end unto itself, the latter is merely a means to get to the former. A process, by definition, suggests something that has a time limit or trajectory; the question is only 'how long?' Gehenom is not forever.

There is no 'eternal damnation.' Souls are not condemned perpetually to a world of darkness.

Certainly, Gehenom has nothing to do with torture or perpetual infliction of pain or distress. And no, an adulterous is not permanently trapped in the moment of passion, and one who has committed suicide is not forever marooned in the situation that led up to their death. There is no eternal condemnation, as all souls will, eventually, return to their Source Above.

Heaven is the state we are born from and to which we will all ultimately return.

Some of us retain this primordial purity throughout our life and immediately following death return to our Source, while others may require a more elongated process or winding path in order to return. For some souls the process of re-learning and re-membering is quick, for others it may extend a bit longer. Generally the time limit is twelve months and in some extreme cases perhaps longer, but sooner or later all souls regain their original brilliance.

Since the essential quality of a soul is immaculate, beyond being sullied or circumscribed by any events or actions, there is thus no place for eternal punishment or condemnation. Gehenom is equated to a sponge. It absorbs all negativity that may have attached itself during the soul's journey on earth, allowing the soul to regain its 'original condition.' Gehenom is a learning station, a didactic undertaking and an experience the soul eventually graduates from and advances out of.

Incidentally, what allows consciousness to continue to exist even after the body/brain has ceased to function are the sparks of goodness that have been articulated and crystallized through one's life and actions. Every human being has at least some measure of goodness that affords him a degree of immortality. A large variety of Mitzvos (613) are made available so that each person can discover at least one positive good attribute or action to latch on to and excel in - although we should of course aspire to do them all - and through that particular Mitzvah they may reveal and connect with Eternity.

At this point some of the actual processes will be explored and we will see how these procedures in a nether world can assist the soul to rid itself of unwanted and debilitating negativity. Some souls, though only a rare few, experience all of the below, while others go through one or more of them. All of the processes listed below are only necessary so the soul can regain its original condition and pass into a world bathed in purity and transcendence, a reality where the soul reintegrates with its Source and becomes at one with its truest nature. This is the realm of Gan Eden

Olam Ha'dimyon-World of Imagination

A smooth transition for the soul would be to exit the material form and instantaneously find itself within the memory of the Creator as an individuated entity with its own distinct character and memory. There are, however, souls that leave their bodies, yet remain confused as to their present state. The term used for this condition of chaos is Olam Ha'tohu/World of confusion, otherwise referred to as Olam Ha'dimyon/World of imagination.

A soul that is operating within a world of imagination and confusion thinks it ought to continue doing the things it has being doing throughout their life on earth (*Keser Shem Tov*, 26. *Likutei Torah*, Pinchas. *Chayei Maharan*, 2, 9a. *Peulas Hatzadik*, 680). The soul is in a bewildered state of disorientation with a distorted perception of the reality of their new situation. Thinking that it is still alive in a body, it may desire to take out the garbage, fix the car, go to work and perform all the other trivialities of their life. If, during their life the person had a job on Wall Street their soul will continue to go there. These souls will go about doing their ordinary business. All the while, living in an imaginary self-perpetuating state and for the most part not being recognized nor acknowledged by the living.

Once, a sorrowful looking fellow came to visit his teacher, the Chassidic Rebbe Rebbe Yissachar of Volbroz, to tell him that his wife had recently passed away and he needed some money to remarry. Puzzled, the Rebbe looked at him and

said: "How sad that you do not realize that you are no longer alive!" When the man refused to believe him, the Rebbe demonstrated to him that he was no longer amongst the living. Later on, the son of the Rebbe asked his father, "And how do I know that I am not in the world of confusion? Perhaps I too exist in the world of imagination?" "No," his father responded. "You know you are not, because you are asking. The simple awareness of the very possibility of being in this confused reality is the greatest proof that you are not there."

Olam Ha'dimyon is typically the first reality one experiences once one is no longer alive in the body. It is where disembodied souls imagine themselves to be still existing enclothed within a body. After many years of the soul inhabiting a body, it begins thinking that the body is an integral part of its continued existence, and even after it departs from the body the soul continues thinking that it is with body.

Being that it is difficult for a person to visualize himself without the features of his body, his soul creates a phantom image of the body as a kind of post-mortem coping mechanism. It is in a state of utter confusion and existential limbo. Oddly, the soul continues to interpret and dissect reality as if through the prism of the five senses, acting and reacting as if still within the body.

In the Talmud there is mention made of bodiless souls being fully absorbed and interested in the trivialities of life (*Berachos*, 18b. *Avos De'rebbe Nasan* 3). Incongruously, such a soul exists in a world of souls, a world that is dimensionless and endless, and yet is preoccupied with and anchored in a reality that is physical and dimensional. Because of this paradoxical reality that includes both infinity and physicality, everything that exists in this imaginary world exists in an infinite way. If cars were what one focused on in this realm of reality, he will continue to enjoy cars in the first stages of his afterlife and will have an infinite amount of powerful cars.

Most times, souls graduate from the world of Dimyon/imagination and journey upward/inward to a higher/deeper state and in a subsequent order. Perception becomes clearer and less obscured as the soul moves forward and deeper into the world of souls. Yet, occasionally, though not the norm, the soul may not want or is not yet able to truly appreciate and feel comfortable in the higher levels of Gan Eden and so it 'descends' for a period of time into the realm of Dimyon until it desires to advance.

On one of the Baal Shem Tov's storied journeys, the roads were treacherous, and the distance to cover was great. It was Friday morning and there was still a great distance to travel to get to his destination before sunset. The horses, pushed as they were to the brink of their strength, began to weaken, and one of the horses passed out. But still the driver continued on with his second horse and somehow managed to arrive at the destination before Shabbos. After Shabbos the Baal Shem was notified that the second horse died as well from exhaustion and that the wagon driver, realizing his dire situation, was grief stricken and fell seriously ill. Upon the Baal Shem Tov's request the best doctors in town were summoned, all to no avail. Sadly, the driver passed on. When his soul ascended on high it was immediately admitted into Gan Eden, but the soul did not find any pleasure whatsoever from the deepest of spiritual delights that were present. And so he was sent into the imaginary world where he was offered four handsome horses with a beautiful carriage and was placed on a straight level road with no obstacles. This made him very happy. All that the wagon driver was able to enjoy, at least initially, in the first stages of his afterlife journey were things of his own world such as wagons, horses and paved roads.

Dybbuk-Attachment

Once the soul realizes that it is no longer joined with the body, the soul may want to attach itself to a variant physical form and that is where the idea of Dybbuk comes in. Dybbuk is a relatively modern Hebrew term for a diabolical possession (*Sefer Habris*, 1:17:15). This is otherwise known as a Ruach Rah/bad spirit (*Rashi Eiruvin*, 41b), or metempsychosis. This too is a form of reincarnation (*Mishnas Chassidim*, Seder Nashim, Gilgul, 6:4), but it is a primarily negative version of Ibbur/soul impregnation.

The word Dybbuk, literally translated, means becoming attached. Out of desperation a wandering and bewildered soul may seek another living body as refuge. 'Naked souls,' those who roam about, neither entering permanent residence within Gan Eden nor temporary residence within Gehenom, search to find other locations within which to relocate and self-express.

A soul would be considered 'naked' due to its lack of good deeds or comportment. Good deeds that are perpetuated in this world weave spiritual garments enabling disembodied spirits that have passed on and left their bodies to receive and absorb the Infinite light. At some point, a naked and homeless soul may re-attach itself to a body on earth. Not knowing where to 'go' and what to 'do' such a lost soul might latch on to a body that resembles their own conditioning. These souls look for bodies that are metaphorically soulless with regard to the aspects they wish to express. Being a bodiless spirit desiring expression through physical form, it inhabits a body in which it can articulate itself.

People who suffer from a Dybbuk perceive the force as an externally invading entity that is malevolent, hostile and disturbing. Often, those claiming to be 'possessed' are not being overwhelmed by exterior forces, but rather are suffering from internal mental breakdown. In such a case it is merely a psychological disorder that needs to be dealt with through medication not meditation; i.e., it requires a physical treatment not a spiritual exorcism. Although, there is also the opinion of the Rebbe of Lesk, the son in law of the Sar Shalom who holds that every mental illness is in fact a form of Dybbuk.

In today's age it is very uncommon for there to be a real Dybbuk. Rebbe Chayim of Volozhin once quipped that there will come a time of such deep spiritual exile and alienation that even Dybbuks will cease to occur.

Assuming it is a real Dybbuk, the actual details of exorcism are beyond the scope of this discussion, yet there is a way that it can be done and in the scheme of things it is a relatively straightforward technique. Souls who wander about homeless do so because they are unable to unshackle themselves from a tremendous gravitational pull earthward, which is a result of their own negative baggage. The way we can help these souls begin their journey is by finding merit for such a soul, and as a result allow them the opportunity to shake themselves free and start their movement heavenwards. Additionally, this entails that one takes notice of the negativities spewing from the possessed and respond by doing the precise opposite on their behalf.

A possessed individual was once brought in front of Rebbe Schneur Zalman of Liadi, the celebrated eighteenth century Chassidic Rebbe. Examining the situation the Rebbe began to speak favorably regarding the murderers of the prophet Zecharya. Zecharya was the prophet who was murdered during the period near the end of the first Beis Hamikdash. The murderers' motives, the Rebbe explained, were somewhat justifiable, as they wanted to prevent the prophet from pronouncing his vision of the destruction of the Temple due to the transgressions of the people. They believed that once the prophecy was verbally articulated it had a much greater chance of actually occurring. Having concluded his discourse it became apparent to all those around that the Dybbuk had left the body.

The concept of Dybbuk/attachment should not be confused with the more positive soul visitation of Ibbur/impregnation. Whereas Dybbuks are possessions of souls that have not yet found their lasting peace, Ibburs are souls from Gan Eden that 'descend' to inhabit bodies in order to help them.

An Ibbur occurs when a soul — either one from above that shares a common root with the soul below or in some cases, other manifestations of one's soul that were articulated in previous lives — 'comes down' as a guest to assist or at times to be assisted by the body it occupies. Dybbuk, on the other hand, is felt as an invasion, a negative infringement of an un-elevated consciousness causing confusion and chaos. During an Ibbur the person remains in full control of his faculties, and what he experiences is a sense of clarity and spiritual uplifting. As an Ibbur comes to help, occasionally the host may not even be aware that there is another soul within them.

Kedushah/holiness empowers; Kelipa/negativity overwhelms. Dybbuks, which are bodiless, homeless and un-elevated souls, seek to occupy and overtake a body. Ibburs, on the other hand, are elevated souls desiring to offer and contribute, providing an extra measure of support to the person they inhabit so they can attain their maximum soul potential. While being possessed one loses or struggles for self-control; while being impregnated one remains in full control. Being possessed is wrenching, mentally exhausting and debilitating; impregnations are overwhelmingly positive and non-invasive, leaving the individual feeling more empowered, competent and able.

Chibut Ha'kever- Pounding the Grave

The next evolving stage in the process for those who have gone through the first two stages - existing in the world of imagination and inhabiting other human forms - is Chibut Ha'kever/the pounding of the grave. The pounding of the grave means that the soul recognizes that it is its own body lying there in the grave that is now decomposing. Most souls come to this realization immediately following death, others come to this realization in due time.

"Worms are as painful to the dead as needles are in the flesh of the living" (*Berachos* 18b. *Shabbos* 152b). This is another way of describing Chibut Ha'kever (*Emunos VeDeyos*, 6:7). Some commentators speak of Chibut Ha'kever in physical terms. At death, while the normative levels of soul depart the body, the levels of soul more closely connected to the physical - the levels of Nefesh - continue to linger on with the body. As the body begins to putrefy, the Nefesh, the bioenergetic aspect of soul, experiences a cleansing pain which purifies the soul of all bodily based negativity (*Zohar* 2, p. 141b–142a). All of the coarse, unrefined 'grime' that has become attached to one's soul is disposed of via Chibut Ha'kever.

Most opinions however view Chibut Ha'kever in psychological/mental terms unrelated to the physical (*Maharatz Chayos,* Shabbos, 13b. *Teshuvas Ha-Rashba*, Teshuvah 369). It is a mental anguish similar to knowing that one's childhood home has been destroyed (*Emunos VeDeyos*, 6:7), or, like watching a loved one being harmed (*Nishmas Chayim*, 2:24). Either way, Chibut Ha'kever is psychosomatic and spiritual, not literal or physical.

The intensity and anguish of the Chibut Ha'Kever experience is in direct correlation to the measure of one's association, or better yet fascination and indulgence with their body and its aggrandizement during their lifetime. For a soul who acquired its sense of selfhood and identity primarily from the body it resided in, the grief will be greater than for a soul who viewed the body as a mere tool and vehicle for soulful expression. This can be explained using the nature of people's relationship to material belongings.

People who are more attached to their possessions will become more aggravated when they lose them or they become damaged, whereas others who are less attached to their material belongings will become less agitated in such an event. The pain is a healing pain of a soul that has become immersed in sensual identification and pleasure as it is being ripped away from the body so that it can experience an infinitely higher, deeper and vaster satisfaction of reuniting with its Source.

The transition from being embodied to a bodiless existence can either be smooth or fraught with difficulty, depending on the soul's level of attachment to the body. The measure of trauma or lack thereof in the initial phases of the afterlife journey is in direct proportion to the soul's perception of present reality. Death for the wholly righteous is painless. In the words of the sages, "it is similar to having a hair removed from a glass of milk" (*Berachos*, 8a. *Moed Katan*, 28a). For the fully integrated human being, the Tzadik, there is no Din Chibut Ha'kever/judgment of the grave (*Sha'ar HaGilgulim*, 23). One state of existence leads smoothly to the next, one door is thrown open as the other door closes just as easily.

In the world of psychology there is a phenomenon that is referred to as phantom sensation. A phantom sensation would be to lose a limb and continue to think that it exists. As a result one would then experience pain from that very location. A more common illustration of phantom pain occurs when one visits a dentist. Dentists numb the gums before any serious work is done on the teeth and yet oddly the moment the drill touches the gums most people squirm from pain. There are no feelings in the gums, as they are absolutely frozen, still, one reacts as if they were really 'feeling' the pain. In such a case, the 'pain' one is reacting to is purely psychological.

The older we become, and the more memory that is stored associating drilling with pain, the Sha'arper we will experience phantom pain at the dentist. Chibut Ha'kever works much the same way, the soul/consciousness may experience phantom-like pain when it observes its body's disintegration. Commensurate to the level of the soul's association with the body is the intensity of Chibut Ha'kever. For some people death means the cessation of the entirety of how they knew themselves throughout life. For others, coupled with the awareness that their real self continues to exist, there is still a terror and dread in realizing that everything involving their body will no longer be. The Tzadik experiences no pain whatsoever, as a Tzadik's estimation of self is not materially oriented. For a Tzadik the transition of death is like walking from one room to another.

Kaf Hakela

Following one's physical demise and the eventual awareness of death is a process called Kaf Hakela, which literally means the cup of a slingshot (*Shmuel* 1, 25:29. MaHarsha, *Shabbos*, 152b. *Avos De'rebbe Nasan*, 12). Kaf Hakela represents being thrown to and fro, ricocheting from one state of existence into another, and then back again.

After leaving the body a clearer picture of truth emerges. For some souls the truth is what they have lived by their entire lives; for others the new found epiphany throws them out of sync with who they were throughout their life. For those people who have lived in complete harmony with their deeper selves there is no Kaf Hakela. However, for those who were out of touch with their deepest self, awakening into a higher awareness may give rise to a tremendous sense of inner strife, turmoil and discord. On the one hand they now desire to live with this deeper truth and they long to move upwards; on the other hand, they still wish to cling to their distorted vision of reality, as it is the reality they are most accustomed to and they are therefore mightily weighed downwards. A sense of deep dichotomy and internal schism arises and one feels as if they are being pulled in polar opposite directions.

The painfulness of the experience lies in the soul untangling itself from materiality, thus allowing consciousness to find a 'new life.' In the metaphor of the slingshot the soul is being thrown around — from the material to the spiritual to the material again, back and forth relentlessly and with no rest.

As with all other aspects of the afterlife journey Kaf Hakela has psychological ramifications and is a state in which a person can operate during this lifetime as well. To be spiritually attuned to life is to live life harmoniously, without dichotomy or internal friction. A purpose of the Torah is to codify this integrated life style, allowing for an alignment of the human with the being, making complementary what would appear as conflicting energies. When this does not occur Kaf Hakela is the end result. The experience of Kaf Hakela is defined by the experience of feeling scattered and splintered, with one's energies, ambitions, talents and capabilities being pointed in numerous and even divergent directions. When a person is in a Kaf Hakela condition he exists without a sense of wholeness or unified oneness.

Memory & Forgetfulness

Oddly, one of the greatest gifts humans possess is the propensity to forget (*Chovos Halevavos*, Sha'ar Habechinah, 5). Without memory loss no sorrows would be healed and no tragedy would be put to rest.

In a universe of total recall, life as we know it would be unbearable and intolerable. If every past negative experience would be lucid in memory how would any sense of happiness ever occur? Conversely, if peak moments of joy are perceived in the memory as present how would one be able to go on living his day–to–day life, which is by definition, not a 'peak' experience, but more like a valley. Without memory lapses we would be hard-pressed to honestly experience love or joy, or even to truly mourn or feel sad when appropriate, as we would be too caught up in the past to authentically engage with what was currently happening.

In a linear progressive universe as time moves forward, experiences of the past become memories of the past and thus become less and less vivid. Memory loss is a derivative of linear time. In a universe of souls, where there is no elapsing of time, there is no forgetfulness. Souls remember everything as if it is occurring in the present. In the spiritual world all time is simultaneous. At the moment of death the brain, which was the storage house of memory, ceases to function, while 'soul memory' continues to live on. On this soulular level, memory and consciousness are not just epiphenomena of the brain extinguishing at death, but are everlasting. The 'soul memory' after life contains more than the totality of the person the way he existed at the time of his death. It is an 'open memory' operating without the filter of the brain and thus able to experience a total recall of the person's life from the day he was born until the day he died.

In the life of the average man some experiences are positive and virtuous whereas some are negative and destructive. Positive thoughts, words or actions attach themselves permanently and become one with the fabric of the soul for all eternity, while negative attachments must be dusted off. Negativity does not and cannot endure. To move 'upward' the soul must unburden itself of all negativity through a total erasure of the effects of all destructive behavior. Assuming five percent of a person's life was defined by negativity, this five percent of conscious memory needs to be uprooted and cleansed from memory. That is precisely what is accomplished via Kaf Hakela.

Experiencing a complete recollection of life with all its accumulated experiences may cause great discomfort for the soul as it realizes that certain images were better forgotten. The process of awareness is not intended to torment or afflict, but rather to heal and cure. The best way to describe this would be to envision this procedure as therapy. The soul recalls all the foolishness of life so that it can re-attain its perfect brilliance. There are schools of therapy that proclaim that the way to rid oneself of past negative experiences is to bring them back to memory and then flush them out of the system. Similarly, this is what transpires in the afterlife journey. To help the soul rid itself of unwanted baggage the soul recalls all its past experiences and through the resulting anguish and embarrassment erases them. Reviewing one's life helps flush out any worthless information, thereby purging oneself of all the accumulated 'dirt,' and ultimately revealing one's truest essence.

A grand editing of the book of life is experienced in the hereafter — this is Kaf Hakela. A soul at birth is similar to a sheet of paper, clean and ready to be written upon by the author of life which is you. There are many images of life. Some speculate that the world is a harsh battlefield and man is its ultimate warrior, others suggest that the world is but a stage and man its primary actor, or that the world is nothing but a circus and man its designated clown. Yet the Kabbalistic image is that the cosmic and microcosmic world is a Sefer/book and every human being its Sofer/scribe and author. We write our story and the story is life itself.

Every experience, along with all our knowledge and wisdom is imprinted on the soul's fabric. As the body fails and the soul untangles itself from the material reality an editing is performed. Whether there is a light or strong editing, or no editing at all, depends on the story that was written during one's life. For some people their book is complete and perfectly authored, others may need a little more fixing up before they are ready for a final and eternal 'publication.'

Gehenom Shel Aish, Gehenom Shel Sheleg: Hell of Fire, Hell of Ice

Classic sources refer to a Gehenom of Aish, a cleansing through fire, and a Gehenom of Sheleg, a refinement via snow and ice (*Tanchumah*, Re'eh, 13. *Yerushalmi Sanhedrin*, 10:3. *Yalkut Shimoni* Tehilim, 40:37. *Rabbeinu Bachya* Bamidbar, 16:33). There are numerous degrees in each of these unfolding processes. In Kabbalistic texts the number of gates or portals within Gehenom itself range from seven to thirteen to eight hundred and fifty (*Zohar Chadash*, p. 33. *Ginas Egoz* 2, p. 244. *Reshis Chachmah*, Sha'ar HaYirah, 13. *Megalah Amukhos*, Emor. *Safer Haplia*, *Bnei Yissochar*, Shabbos, 8:17). Being that no two stories are the same, each soul, if need be, must be adjusted and reoriented according to their own condition of misalignment.

No two lives are identical within this realm of existence or within the next. Each soul is repaired and re-attains its original brilliance differently. Eventually all souls return and become re-unified within their Source.

As physicality is a reflected mirror image of meta-physicality and meta-physicality is projected within physicality, parallels can be drawn between the two. Regarding the laws of kashering un-kosher utensils the Torah says, "Everything that comes into the fire, such as cooking utensils, you shall pass through the fire and it will be purified…and everything that did not come in to contact with fire, such as drinking cups, you shall pass through the water by immersion within a Mikvah/purifying ritual bath" (Bamidbar, 31:23. *Rashi*). That which was used in fire ought to be cleansed with fire and water is sufficient to wash away that which was used with water.

Spiritually speaking, souls may need to undergo the process of cleansing or kashering in accordance to how deeply negativity has become attached and ingrained into one's consciousness. In this sense too, fire removes fire and ice counters ice (Alter Rebbe, *Maamorei Admur Hazoken*, Inyonim, p. 212).

Fire represents fervor or passion, while ice bespeaks of coldness or indifference. The choice of whether one comes to life with passion for the spiritual or the material, a measure of indifference regarding the material or coldness to matters of the spirit is entirely the prerogative of the chooser. In this life there is absolute radical freedom.

One's choices determine how a person lives and responds to life. And these very choices affect the person in this life as well as in the next. Positive choices are internal and eternal, negative choices are external and ephemeral. The positive indelibly imprints the soul's constitution with the seal of the eternal, whereas the negative is temporal-bound and thus needs to be disposed of so that the soul can journey smoothly as it 'flies' onwards and upwards.

While most commentaries view the fire and ice of the afterlife as metaphoric images, strictly describing a spiritual/mental process in an unphysical reality (Maharal *Be'er Hagolah*, 5. *Tifferes Yisrael*, 8), there are some authorities that take these imageries quite literally. Some opinions speak of a 'distilled' version of fire that has the potential to affect a spiritual substance, such as a soul (*Ramban* Bereishis, 3:22. *Toras Ha'adam*, Sha'ar Hagmul. *Ginas Egoz* 2, p. 197).

To better comprehend this position it would do well if one were to recall an earlier discussion regarding the body. While the body that is most apparent is the Guf Gas/coarse materialistic form, there is also a Guf Dak, an ethereal-like luminous form. After the soul leaves the body the Guf Gas withers away and the soul-consciousness assumes its identity within the Guf Dak. It is the Guf Dak that serves as a medium through which a physical substance can impinge upon a soul. The so called 'fires' of Gehenom, though certainly not comprised of the basic four elements that constitute a physical object, do have a bearing on the afterlife of the soul via the Guf Dak (*Avodas Hakodesh*, 2:33). Remember the Guf Dak, the astral light ethereal body, contains all of our impressions, all our thoughts, words and actions, essentially our entire selves.

Notwithstanding, most authorities maintain that the cleansing process of the hereafter is purely on the realm of the spiritual and there is, therefore, neither fire nor ice in a universe unrelated to the material. Still, the imagery employed is physically bound so that the issues can be more easily grasped and understood.

Shame is one of the various experiences a soul may encounter in the afterlife (*Kiddushin*, 81a). Fire represents shame and embarrassment, as when one is shamed he becomes crimson and flush. Once the soul leaves the body and there is no longer the protecting veil of the ego/brain it gains a new and unguarded perception as such a complete clarity and openness is made manifest. This newly discovered transparent clarity allows the soul to accurately view and review all of life including everything that has ever occurred. If during life there had been an inconsistency between what a person truly is and how he behaved, a sense of self-embarrassment and shame will arise. If the authentic inner self was not expressed in one's exterior outer conduct, the soul, in its clear state, unbridled by the senses, will experience fire, which results from a sense of being consumed and enveloped in an overwhelming condition of embarrassment.

As a consequence the 'fires' of Gehenom are not externally generated, objective fires, but rather these are fires that rise up from within (*Zohar* 2, p. 150b). It is man who inflames the fires of Gehenom (*Yalkut Shimoni*. Yeshayahu

247, 437:30. *Lev David* 10). A human being that has lived disharmoniously and has become misaligned, such as one who has perpetuated negative thoughts, speech and actions will ultimately be aflame with his own passions and negative desires and thereby experience embarrassment upon becoming aware of his own indiscretions. The soul will function within a condition of fiery Gehenom until it is cleansed of all its dirt and reoriented within the Light of the Creator.

Within shame itself there are two expressions, one more emotional and the other more intellectual. As mentioned, fire represents fervor and passion, ice coldness or indifference. The metaphor of a fiery Gehenom is employed to describe the process of eradicating negatively charged passion and its offspring of negative behaviors. The Gehenom of snow is meant to remove negativity founded on coldness and indifference. The former is emotionally based, the latter more intellectual.

Intellectual, as opposed to emotional, embarrassment is a 'cold' form of embarrassment. If a person were to be caught passionately involved in an unbecoming act then that person would become red in the face. If, however, a person stands idly while another person is harmed and he had the ability to help, later on when he recalls, or is forced to recall, such an incident he may become ashamed of himself, but he won't turn red. This type of embarrassment is a shame for not getting involved, while emotional fiery embarrassment is for being too involved. One form of Gehenom purifies from physical and emotional based negativity, and the other purifies from mental and intellectual wrongdoings.

Essentially, the anguish of the experience comes about through the soul recalling the acts it has perpetuated from a more expansive perspective and experiencing shame because of them. Once the soul experiences this kind of embarrassment as a result of viewing its actions from the perspective of its higher self, it cleanses itself, either intellectually or emotionally, and can therefore move on and into Gan Eden.

By and large the abovementioned procedures work for most souls, yet, there are isolated cases where souls have accumulated such heaps of negative baggage that the only way they can attain Gan Eden is to first enter other, nonhuman forms of life. A soul that has been quite expressive negatively in this realm of existence may need to transmigrate and enter another form of life that has less, if any, potential for expression. And through that very inability to express itself, it can thereby re-attain its brilliance. In this type of reincarnation the entire so-called 'personality' of the soul descends and embodies a new lifeform. In addition to the animal, for example, possessing her own soul there is also a human soul, with all its memory trapped within it and working on its own Tikkun.

In the same way that the journey has many levels there are also infinite levels within the destination. Just as Gehenom has various degrees, Gan Eden does as well. Broadly speaking, the higher/deeper Gan Eden is dedicated to the expansive pleasures of Divine contemplation. The less intense aspect of Gan Eden is more of an emotional form of delight. The level the soul attains immediately following death depends on the measure of spiritual attainment it has reached here on earth.

A soul that finds itself too confused or bewildered to enter the higher/deeper dimensions within Gan Eden may first experience lower grades until it becomes fully acclimated (Seforno, *Kavanas HaTorah*. Ramchal, *Maamor Ha'ikkarim*, Gan Eden V'Gehenom). The lower Gan Eden serves as an orientation, allowing the soul to become accustomed to its new bodiless existence until it becomes able to reintegrate with the infinite light of the Infinite One.

CHAPTER 10

Eternity &
Corporeal Existence

Death is present in all of nature. Nothing avoids death. It is a universal concept.

Birth, maturity and death are natural courses of life. No aspect of creation escapes unscathed from its grip. Nobody leaves this realm of existence alive. No–body lives forever. No one goes through life without relinquishing their physical form at some point.

There are recorded instances in the Torah and in later sources where human beings were reported to have ascended to Heaven, as it were, without experiencing any form of corporeal death, most notably the prophet Eliyahu (*Melachim* 2, 2:11. *Yalkut Shimoni*, Yechezkel, 247:367. *Baba Basra*, 121b). But as a whole, at the end of life the body melts down and slowly disintegrates into its constituent elements. In fact, the Torah statement, "earth you are and to earth you shall return" (*Bereishis*, 3:19), is not only a prediction or an inevitable conclusion to life, but is very much a part of life itself.

The cycle of life is birth, the emergence of one life, death, the returning to the elements and then rebirth and resurrection. The Baal Shem Tov once declared that he had the spiritual power to enter paradise with his body and soul in unison, however, he did not do so for he desired to go through the natural process of 'earth returning to earth' (Rebbe Rashab, *Toras Sholom*, p. 46).

Just as death is part of the life cycle, so is the idea of physical and even bodily eternity. In the most elementary manner, corporeal immortality can be interpreted as the body living on as part of the whole. Earth rejoins earth and the individual elements of the body rearrange themselves to become part of the entire ecosystem. Yet, there is also the idea of bodily resurrection, implying an eventual revival of the body and a perpetuation of that same body in its distinct shape and form. There will come a time when there will be a recreation, an ingathering of the elements or a reconstruction of the DNA, if you will, and bodies of old will once again resurface to roam the earth and live again.

The Resurrection & Manifestation of all "Past" in the Present

Time — which is comprised of a past, present and future — is another by-product of the Tree of Knowledge and Duality. In the Tree of Life, representing the reality of unity, all of 'time' occurs simultaneously. When the world eventually attains a full Tikkun, when each individual soul is perfected and becomes whole again, as well as when all individual souls return to their root in the one body of Primordial Adam, time will be one and unified as well. At this point there will be the great Resurrection of the dead. The resurrection is not simply that our souls will return into our physical forms once again. But on a deeper level, since it will be a perfected unification of time, all of the 'past' will become present in the moment.

Assuming you are a forty-year-old person, where is the "you" when you were thirty nine? Or, for that matter, the "you" of a moment ago? And where is the world of a hundred years ago?

Because we live in a three-dimensional universe, with the fourth dimension of time existing in the paradigm of separation, the 'past' only exists in and as memory. But in a unified reality the fourth dimension of time will be manifested entirely within the three dimensions of space. There is thus a total conservation of energy, but moreover, everything of the 'past' will be manifest in the present, and thus, of course, there will be a resurrection of bodies of the past. There will no longer be any past, for everything will exist within the eternal, unified moment. All of our selves, and all of what has passed will be present.

Reviving the Cold Intellect

On another level, resurrection can be understood as a metaphor of reviving the spirit. Just as a lifeless body is frigid and cold, similarly is the human intellect. Intellect can be cold, detached and apathetic. When a person, however, meditates and enlivens his intellect, imbuing it with holy passion and Divine rapture, this is a form of resurrection (*Hayom Yom*, 11th of Sivan). Likewise, if through deviation and transgression one detaches the self from the Source of Life and becomes spiritually insensitive and lifeless, then when that person re-engages, reintegrates and re-embarks on the path of Teshuvah he is in a sense experiencing an internal resurrection (*Derech Chayim*, p. 95).

While these life lessons are certainly appreciated, clearly the notion of Techiyas Ha'Meisim/the resurrection of the dead is intended to be taken quite literally. By recognizing the intrinsic value of the human body, and for that matter all physicality, and viewing the body as a potential instrument and vehicle for soul expression it becomes axiomatic that the body is not something to be disregarded or overlooked. Undoubtedly, the body too has a place in a world of ultimate goodness and spirituality. Bodily resurrection is so much a part of Torah that according to many opinions the resurrection of the dead is one of the basic fundamental principles of the Torah.

Resurrection & Olam Habah / The World to Come

The Ramban, a thirteenth century legalist and mystic otherwise known as Nachmanides, equates the period of resurrection with the ultimate state of Olam Habah/the World to Come (*Toras HaAdam*, Sha'ar Hagmul. *Targum Yonoson*, Yeshayahu 58:11). The peak of goodness and spiritual delight will be experienced in a time when body and soul are re-joined as one, in total harmony and unison.

Realities mirror each other. The universal law of cause and effect is a truth in the world of spirit as well as space. Mankind labors intensely and is challenged to transform physicality to spirituality by taking tangible objects and hallowing them. The results of such actions are a complete material transformation. The ultimate transformation of 'things' will become apparent in the state of Olam Habah, when the body will also participate in the greatest/deepest of spiritual revelations and become an equal partner in receiving, absorbing and then projecting the Light of the Infinite.

To phrase it differently: If individual immortality is the goal, than the soul experiencing eternity alone in Gan Eden, without the body, is not satisfactory. A human being is a total package comprised of soul/mind and body, any exclusion of any one of these dimensions renders the immortality incomplete. Soul immortality is not individual immortality since elements of the individual, such as the body, are still absent from the equation.

In addition, rewards — which are the consequence of actions — should be given to those who deserve them, which in this case is the soul and the body both. Being that it was the conglomeration of the body and soul that worked on engendering physical transformation, in all fairness, the result of such labor should be enjoyed by the body as well as the soul. If the body is left out of the picture the reward is incomplete and inadequate.

In stark contrast to Gan Eden where souls exist in bodiless states, resurrection, which is a reward and the end result of one's physical actions and spiritual state of material transformation will be experienced when the soul and body are re-joined as one. The way to stimulate physical transformation is through the Mitzvos (*Torah Ohr*, Yisro). Mitzvos are the spiritual tools that were gifted to help humanity tap into the vast energies of soul-consciousness in order to engage that awesome power of spirit and inspire a total reorientation of physicality. The latent powers of the soul are made apparent by the Mitzvos. Once these forces are unleashed one has the amazing godlike ability to create and recreate, to take something physical and transform it into something spiritual.

Though some people perform more Mitzvos than others, still, as our sages testify, "All people of the nation of Israel are filled with Mitzvos as a pomegranate is filled with seeds" (*Chagigah*, 27a). Which, even if not quantitatively true, is at least true qualitatively. In other words, most people have a least one area in life that they excel in. Most people have at the very minimum one Mitzvah that is their specialty, and it is through that particular glimmer of soul that they achieve their physical transformation and thus through that they will eventually feel the inevitable ramifications of their actions in resurrection.

Olam Habah is not reserved for the elite, but rather all moral, good and decent human beings will experience Olam Habah (*Medrash Rabbah*, Bere-ishis, 13:6. *Yefa Toar.* Tosefta, *Sanhedrin*, 13). It is through the spark of goodness that becomes one individualized self that each person will be ultimately resurrected. From within the entire spectrum of the soul, only one or two aspects become manifest as a person's particular identity, and it is through those individuated sparks that a person lives and expresses themselves. The same is true for the afterlife and in the time of resurrection. Each body will be re-birthed with the sparks of soul that had become theirs and theirs alone.

In this way, reincarnation does not preclude resurrection and these two are not mutually exclusive. Every time a soul incarnates, a new and unexplored dimension of the cosmic soul becomes apparent. Each person manifests a new aspect of soul and it is with this individualized spark of soul that each body will experience revivification and resurrection.

In truth, even those souls that may have departed from this world with-out articulating or actualizing the individualized aspect of their soul can attain their Tikkun through the assistance of those who survived them, i.e., their living relatives (*Sidur Hagra*, Shemonei Esrei, Ata Gibor. *Chasam Sofer*, Even HaEzer, 69). Souls enclothed within bodies have the wonderful ability, through thoughts, deeds and actions to bring about a Tikkun for souls that have already left this world.

Embodied souls still existing within the material world have the capability to inspire a spiritual elevation for bodiless souls through the power of their good deeds. So much so that in some instances Olam Habah will not be experienced by one becoming enlivened by one's own unperfected soul, but only through other avenues. Occasionally, souls that are unable to shake off the dust to achieve Olam Habah on their own accord gain entry by receiving sparks from other souls (*Recanti* Ki Sisa. *Rabbeinu Bachya* Vayikra 18:29). These sparks then supplement their own individual light.

A Reality beyond Opposites

Once resurrection occurs bodies will endure in one of two ways: 1) for a very long period of time before finally and fully passing on (*Chovos Haleva-vos*, 4:4. *Igeres Techiyas Hamesim*, 4. *Hilchos Teshuvah*, 8:2. *Kuzari*, 1:115. *Safer Haikkarim*, 4:30–33); or, as others suggest (*Emunos VeDeyos*, 7:5. *Ra'avad* Hilchos Teshuvah, 8:2. *Ramban Sha'ar Hagmul. Recanti*, Bereishis. *Derashos HaRan*, 5), 2) they will, quite literally, live forever. In this state of bodily resurrection mankind will enter a world beyond duality, plurality and separation, existing perennially in absolute oneness.

It will be a time with no desire (*Shabbos*, 151a), as desire reflects an inside and an outside, something that is external to oneself that has not yet been attained. Humanity will return to his/her original conditioning, existing in a state similar to the Garden of Eden (*Ramban* Devarim, 30:6. *Meam Loaz*, Netza-vim 30:6. *Ma'arechs Elokus*, 8). It will be a reality beyond choice, a reality beyond opposites of good and evil, a world of unity and wholeness.

Today, life as we know it is perpetually pushed to a more evolved and developed state of complexity by its constant state of tension and friction. The articulation of human thought, whether in science or philosophy, liter-ature or psychology, is dependent on opposition and contrasting theories. First there is a thesis, then an antithesis, and finally a greater or deeper synthesis that reconciles the first two opposing theorems or calls forth a new paradigm. Later on that too is challenged, which brings forth an even deeper understanding. There are continuous ups and downs, ascents and descents, evolutions and regressions.

In a world of opposites there is nonstop rhythm and fluctuation. Each living body has four basic stages: birth, growth, maturity and eventual death. These stages then give rise to a new life through another process of birth, growth, maturity and then eventual death.

In the world of the living, as well as in the world of abstractions, there is a continuous cycle. Any other reality would seem boring by comparison, being as it would be without desire or striving. And yet in the time of redemption and perfect harmony, when the world will be healed of its fragmentation and splinteredness, life will be defined differently — it will be a life without opposites. In a universe of oneness there can only be one continuous eternal state of perfection.

Life, as hard as it is to fathom within the current paradigm, will be a seamless whole comprised of a paradoxical progression forward and upwards. There will be no need for descents or setbacks, antithetical hypotheses or counter-revolutions to inspire further development. Until, on a most profound level, death as a concept and as a reality will become something of the past. A new world order will thus emerge where life develops, evolves and expands endlessly without any lapses, whether temporal or permanent, partial or complete.

Body as a Reflection of Soul

Speaking of resurrection, some sources contend that to live forever is part of humanity's original lot; it is part of the DNA of the human being (*Ram-*

ban and *Rabbeinu Bachya* Bereishis, 2:17. *Yavatz*, Avos 3:20. Rebbe Shlomo Molcho *Safer Hamefuar*, p. 50. *Avodas Hakodesh*, 2:19). Mortality is a distortion of a higher truth and a foreign invasion to the body's reality. Humans were created to survive perpetually. The original prototypical human beings, Adam and Eve/Chava, were deemed fit to live for eternity. The physical properties of their bodies were 'refined' in such a way that they had the potential to live forever. But apparently, their actions or choices showed that they had other plans. In the time of resurrection, that original distilled version of the human body will be reinstated and mankind will live on everlastingly. Some sources add that in the time of resurrection bodies will be even more refined than the original bodies of Adam and Chava (Rebbe Rashab, *Sefer Hamaamorim Ateres*, p. 415).

Paradoxical as it may appear, in Olam Habah bodies will continue to exist even though they will no longer be needed to properly — or even partially — function. There will come a time when the body will be able to survive, sustain and even nourish itself from within, without the need to consume any external elements. Eating, drinking and all other bodily activities will become something of the past (*Berachos*, 17a). Yet, even though the body will be seemingly superfluous, it will, nevertheless, continue to exist and live on. The reason is twofold (*Toras HaAdam*, Sha'ar Hagmul. *Recanti*, Bereishis. *Magen Avos*, 3:4. *Ohr Hashem*, 3:1:4. *Beis Elokim*, Sha'ar Hayesodos, 53): Since it was the result of the efforts of the body in conjunction with the soul that ushered in this perfect era, the body will get to experience the fruit of its labor. The deeper underlying reason is because the physical structure of the body, as ungraceful and clumsy as it occasionally may appear, has a wonderfully spiritual significance.

The body is not merely a random formation secured simply by the evolution of nature, genetics and other environmental factors. To the contrary, there is a level of deep profundity and meaning to its form. As it states in the book of Iyov/Job: "From my flesh I see G-d" (*Iyov*, 19:26). Taking a deeper look at one's body allows one to catch a glimpse of their soul and a vision of its Creator. The body tells us much about our souls, and much, in fact, about everything else in life, including the purpose of our very being, as well as about the Creator (*Chovos Halevavos*, Sha'ar Habechinah, 5. *Safer Hamevakesh*, Hakdamah. *Igeres HaVikuach*, p. 13).

Outward appearance is a reflection of inward reality. The inner dynamic of the soul expresses itself in the outer manifestations of the body. Body and soul are mirror images of each other. The structure of the body is analogous and representative of the spiritual structure of the soul (*Sha'arei Kedushah*, 1:1). Being that the soul is a spark of the Divine, a part of the All, the soul contains holographic slivers of the totality within itself. The entire reality is contained within the soul. All forces and energies, whether they are physically based or spiritually oriented, are enfolded within it. The body, in turn, which is the vehicle for soul expression, is the physically manifested reflection of the inner-structure of all worlds and all realities.

Having confirmed the body's significance we can now understand why it must endure even when it ceases to function as it does presently. To be sure, especially in that time, the body will achieve a state of maximum potentiality and will self-generate the energy it needs to sustain and nourish itself, so much so that it will actually offer spiritual nourishment to the soul (Rebbe Maharash, *Hemshech Ve'Chacha* 1877, 91–92). As opposed to the hierarchy of created reality as it exists currently, wherein the soul gives life to the body; in the redeemed world of the future the reverse will occur and the body will give life to the soul.

At the time of resurrection mankind will live on under the most favorable conditions possible. Illness, disease and all other maladies will be obliterated and become extinct. It will be a time when body and soul will be completely aligned with each other. Life will be lived harmoniously and holistically. It will be a time when the Infinite will be tangibly felt as present within the finite. The Essence of the Creator, which is transcendent of both physical and spiritual realities, will be apparent in all of reality; from the dimensionless to the dimensional, from the spiritual to the material.

The 'Body' After Death

Aside from the future collective resurrection, which brings about bodily immortality, there are rare situations, even in the present, where a body may be, for better or worse, preserved for an extended period of time, long after their souls have departed. There are also bodies that are less susceptible to decay. One notable example in the Torah is the body of Moshe. Moshe's eyes did not falter and his strength did not leave him even in death (Rashi, *Ohr Hachayim*, Devarim, 34:7). This phenomenon is not an isolated occurrence. Rather, it is something that can happen to anyone who wholeheartedly directs their neutral and amoral bodies toward either the extreme positive or negative realms of existence.

On some level, all souls experience 'bodily' immortality, as there is a body-like continuity in death for each person. As discussed earlier, in addition to the Guf Gas/the coarse tangible body there is a mentally projected body referred to as the Guf Dak/the ethereal body. The ethereal body, which some refer to as the astral body, is commonly known as the Tzelem, one's surrounding aura.

Our internal state is projected outward into our immediate surroundings. This image mirrors the likeness of the material form. This 'body' is a vehicle of consciousness. It can either be mental, emotional or spiritual, depending on the reality we choose to base our lives on. Once the soul/consciousness leaves the material form it initially enters the distilled astral body, which in turn can be projected to one's beloveds even after death. For the living, the appearance of the soul of a departed one in this ethereal 'body' can be observed or felt as a tangible presence, as if that person was in the room for instance. One may also have the experience of 'seeing' something, if not with their physical eyes than with the third eye.

In addition to this afterlife soul projection, there are pious and integrated individuals who are able to project an autocopy of themselves via their Guf Dak into a distant location, even while they are still alive and embodied. Physically they can be in one locality, while spiritually they can project a manifestation of themselves into another place. This phenomenon is referred to as astral projection, or out-of-body traveling. The celebrated Chassidic Rebbe, Rebbe Zusha of Anipoli, once remarked that he saw the face of his revered brother Rebbe Elimelech of Lizhensk in his home, even while Rebbe Elimelech was not physically present.

Those who are full masters in total control of their internal and external reality have the power to detach their Tzurah/substance (their ethereal body) from their Chomer/form (their material body), and to dispatch it at will. The sending of their image to another place allows such a 'person' to be in two different places simultaneously, existing in a non-localized state.

In rare instances, one's own image can be reflected back to oneself. Doppelgangers or autoscopic hallucinations are the preferred terms used to describe a situation where one sees one's own body as an apparition. History is replete with prominent figures that have reputedly experienced an apparition of their own body, a kind of mirror image of themselves.

Chemical imbalance is indeed the root cause for many such cases - found as it is in those who suffer from brain tumors, strokes and migraine head-

aches. However, in some situations the physical symptom is merely the effect, while the cause may be an authentic interaction with the meta-physical and super-natural realms, as in a prophetic experience (*Shoshan Sodos,*
p. 69b. *Ohr Yaakar. Shir HaShirim,* Derisha 2:2. *Toras Ha'olah,* 14. *Dover Tzedek,* p. 96a).
Occasionally, such an image can communicate truth to a person. This can
indicate whether it is indeed a legitimate phenomenon, rather than just
a chemically-induced hallucination. The prophetic experience requires
the prophet's original self to go into a state of suspended animation. The
prophet will often fall to the ground as he apprehends a mirror-like image
of himself that is vibrant, alive and pulsating while transmitting prophetic
insight.

This experience is not reserved for prophets alone, for as the sixteenth century mekubal Rebbe Moshe Cordovero writes, "Some of the pious attain
an observation of their own image" (*Pardes Rimonim,* 31:4). This most extraordinary of phenomena is sometimes viewed as an occurrence that arises
from within the physical workings of the brain; while at other times it is
considered a spiritual occurrence with physical manifestations. In the case
of the former, physicality is the cause; while in the latter, it is the effect.
Although the differences may be difficult to discern, they ought not to be
confused.

CHAPTER 11
And Therefore...

A definitive aspect of the human condition is to continuously query and ask questions. Clearly, what was intellectually or emotionally satisfying at a certain time or age does not always serve to satisfy one's appetite for understanding in the present. There seems to be a constant desire to probe deeper and deeper.

For the empirically minded, the quest to 'know' often leads to science and hard data. For the more mystically minded science is incapable of explaining the totality of their experience. For some people all that they need to know can be found in their immediate surroundings. For others, the vast cosmos calls to them. And yet there are those whose desire to know extends beyond the galaxies and even beyond this realm of existence.

In truth, the deep human desire to peek beyond the grave is as universal as it is ancient. For eons the human race has been trying to figure out what exactly occurs to the soul/consciousness once the body is no longer intact. There appears to be an extensive eschatological tradition in every civilization and culture that has been known to exist.

Aside from the how and what questions, which natural science can answer quite adequately, the question of why is one of the more pronounced questions human beings ask.

Whenever a person encounters death, which is truly the great unknown, the immediate question that arises is why — why does it have to happen? Though one may intellectually or rationally understand that death is an essential part of the cycle of life itself, still, when it occurs the question is always why — why now, why so young, why them, why me?

Being that these weighty existential questions can never truly be 'answered' — either due to a lack of spiritual tools or simply because the 'answers' offered always tend to be intellectually based whereas the questions themselves are, in fact, emotional vexations — a healthier and more empowering approach would be to rephrase the question from why (as in the more despairing why me or why now?) to towards what end, as in, what is the meaning of this? This is taking the same question and redirecting and rephrasing it. In the place of asking Lamah - Hebrew for why, the question ought to be Le-mah - Hebrew for towards what end. Now that one has experienced a tragedy, it is a fact of life, how can one grow from the event?

This perspective does not provide a definitive 'answer' to suffering, and obviously it is not always appropriate to respond to tragedy in such a manner, for at times when one is too close to the pain the immediate experience does not warrant such luxury. On the other hand, without offering an oversimplified and trite justification or excuse for one's suffering, at least by trying to see things in this positive way one can attempt to salvage some spark of redemptive light from their experience of suffering or tragedy. The goal of such an approach is to consider how such a negative experience can help you enhance and even enrich your own life following a painful event or loss. Not that tragedy is a requisite to growth or that there is absolutely no gain without pain, but once tragedy has struck and it is a fact of one's life, the primary issue then becomes to decipher what possible good can emerge from this?

In place of merely absorbing hardship as some kind of punishment, or of obsessively attempting to find out whose fault it is in order to lay blame, a more constructive approach to hardship would be to realize that the only benefit or light that comes out of tragedy and darkness is to be found in how one chooses to respond to it. In this way, everything that life serves up, and occasionally it may appear quite ugly, is seen as an opportunity.

After a person passes on, "the living should take to heart," says the wise king Shlomo (*Koheles*, 7:2). 'Take to heart,' means to attempt to see the experience of loss as an opportunity to grow. True, a person can and must move heaven and earth in order that he should never be faced with such challenges, but once it has occurred, the best way to deal with it is to see the experience as a teacher and a guide, directing the person on their path.

Even the 'what' questions such as — what happens in the afterlife? — contain some virtue. Such a question may in fact be a worthy exploration, and not simply because it satisfies one's inquisitive nature, but because such knowledge can actually assist an individual in becoming a better person in this life right now. The meaning of the afterlife, as well as the belief in it, is only as important as the difference it makes in the actual life of a person who is delving into such a topic.

The validity of this knowledge stems from the wisdom and value it offers a person in the present moment. Even within this rubric there are many levels. For the more spiritually awakened person the awareness of a future transcendent existence presents an ideal to live up to in the present moment so that they aspire to incorporate transcendence into their present day-to-day reality. This is the perspective of bringing heaven down to earth; or, put another way, to experience the world-to-come in the here-and-now. For less spiritually evolved individuals, the knowledge that there are consequences to life, for better or worse, even if not experienced in this life, may lead them to live a more moral and ethical life in the now. This is the perspective of reward and punishment.

As un-empowering as it may sound, there are many people who avoid any immoral or unethical behavior purely out of a sense of fear — either a fear of the law, of other people or of G-d. The Torah's aspiration is to enlighten us to a state of spiritual maturity, where we are able to see each Mitzvah and each moment of life for its intrinsic transformative value. The Torah also recognizes that there are many levels upon which people operate. There are those who act from a place of wholeness and love and those who act from a place of fear and desperation.

For some people the existential equation is this: Let me do or not do this or that because later on I will regret either avoiding or acting on this desire, either in this life or the next. This is a negative, punishment-oriented approach. For others the equation has more to do with reward: Let me do this or not do that so that I will be rewarded, if not in this life than in the next. As inferior a practice or immature a motive as both of these approaches may seem, for some people the path to articulating their highest self is dependent on being able to live properly within the more mundane and material levels of socio-psycho-physical reality, and then to climb from there into the spiritual realms.

Seen from this perspective, knowledge of an afterlife can serve a functional purpose in one's present life. One either incorporates the vision of future transcendence into their experience of the immediate present and thereby melds the two into the eternal now, which is the most desired result; or, the simple awareness that every action taken or not taken has everlasting ramifications may compel one to become more mindful and pay more attention to their behavior. From this vantage point, the belief in an afterlife is the belief in life itself. This is not to insinuate that only by considering the afterlife can life become meaningful; only that there are many people for whom the knowledge of the effects of their actions allows them to see the gravity of their deeds and, as a result, to live life more consciously and compassionately.

One of the revolutionary constructs modern science champions is the interconnectedness of the universe. In the physical world, every time a person waves his arms, there is a ripple effect throughout the entire atmosphere. Indeed, by setting the air in motion with a simple wave of the arm a person causes a continuing reverberation that will never cease. How much more so is this true spiritually, for the idea of the spiritual, by definition, means that which is unhindered and unconfined by space and time. Every thought, emotion and action will continue to exist long after they first occurred, even after the person who perpetuated them physically passes on. Negatively charged actions will ultimately fade away and become obliterated in the afterlife process, whereas positive experiences, thoughts, emotions or deeds live on for eternity.

Keeping in mind the repercussions and ramifications of one's mindset and actions can assist many people and offer them clarity concerning their life decisions. A person may become more aware, mindful, cautious or deliberate with their actions if they are cognizant of their full import and infinite power.

Exploration of the afterlife is therefore not intended as a mere mental or intellectual exercise. Rather, it is a means to acquire practical wisdom and apply it to one's day-to-day reality. Only when we look into the future to assist us in the present is such wisdom deemed meaningful. Too much focus on the future or the past robs a person of their potential to live fully in the moment.

The present is the arena in which life occurs and the present is not a 'bad' place to be. The universe, humanity included, is not a devastating failure; it is not doomed from its very inception nor is it seeping ever deeper into the abyss. One single action, attests the Talmud, can initiate a total, radical and universal transformation from an unredeemed state to one of redemption.

The realization that the future can be lived in the present is most empowering. The intense spiritual truths that will be actualized in the future can be harnessed in the now. According to an eleventh century poet and philosopher, Rebbe Shlomo Ibn Gabirol, we all have the power to return our souls to their Source Above while still being embodied here below (*Mekor Chayim*, 1:2, *Ma'areches Elokus*, 8). Which is another way of saying that it is possible to experience the transcendence of the afterlife in the present moment. The soul, he writes, achieves Deveikus/attachment with its Source through Divine contemplation and ethical behavior. Contemplation brings about action and action inspires further reflection, allowing the soul to reconnect to its deepest nature and very essence.

Olam Habah is not necessarily reserved for a 'next' life, but rather for a 'higher' life, and it can be experienced as a foretaste of what is to come. While living permanently in a condition of Olam Habah is a tall order, the possibility of living for a few moments at this level is more readily accessible. An ancient Medrash relays that when the Torah was about to be given, the Creator of heaven and earth turned to the people of Israel and said, "my children, if you accept my Torah I will give you a beautiful and eternal gift, and that gift is Olam Habah." "Show us an example," the people responded. And the Creator said, "Shabbos." Shabbos is an approximation of Olam Habah. The spiritual elation, rejuvenation, inner peace and tranquility achieved on the holy day of Shabbos is similar to the supernal light that is in store for us in Olam Habah.

Heaven is the spiritual culmination of our work here in this world. For some people this is a glorious end compared to a mediocre middle of life. For others this evolved spiritual condition is attained partially or even fully in this world. Throughout the ages there were, and continue to be, individuals who attain deeper and more expansive states of consciousness than the average person. To them, simply, there is no Galus/exile (*Pelach HaRimon*, Shemos).

Once, the saintly eighteenth century Rebbe, Rebbe Mendel of Vitebsk, was sitting in his study when a young lad rushed in and excitably announced that Moshiach/the redeemer had arrived. Rebbe Mendel stood up, walked over to the window, opened it, took in some air and said sadly, "it's not true." The attending disciple, aware of and impressed by his teacher's spiritual sensitivity and ability to sniff the atmosphere to see if something drastic had occurred remained puzzled as to why the Rebbe needed to open the window. Why could he not just take a whiff from where he was sitting? Later on he mustered the chutzpah to ask. Rebbe Mendel responded matter of factly: "in the room, redemption had already arrived."

The empowering truth is that heightened and expansive states are available to all of us, and at all times. All we need to do is lay claim to what is inherently ours. Each and every one of us can attain such states of consciousness this very moment. The essence of our existence, the quintessential core of our soul is the redemptive, liberated consciousness of Moshiach (*Meor*

Einayim, Pinchas. *Beis Aaron* Bereishis). To operate on this level is our spiritual birthright.

Tellingly, in one traditional prayer we ask for the divine presence to rest within us and for a spirit of wisdom and understating to be bestowed upon us, echoing the verse, which states that "the divine spirit shall rest upon him, the spirit of wisdom and understanding, the spirit of counsel and strength..." (*Yeshayahu* 11:2). Although this verse is clearly referring to the individual Moshiach, still, we ask that the verse should be actualized within us, because this is intrinsically a part of who we are. Our prayer is that this messianic consciousness should become our sole manifest reality.

One way for a person to integrate Olam Haba (a soulful and spiritual existence) on a simple day-to day level is to learn to lessen their desire for worldly power or fame. Additionally, one should attempt to live with less attachment to material possessions. Earthly possessions are hardly what define us. They are merely external paraphernalia that are made-up of what is most transient in our lives. Nothing in the realm of the external can bring us genuine, lasting internal satisfaction. Part of leading a more spiritual and transcendent life is to define ourselves by who we are, as opposed to what we have. We have a body; we are a soul.

If longevity is what we desire, then let us live fuller lives, and the days of our lives will indeed be longer. As younger people we are so impressionable, every new experience is exciting and every newly discovered idea is stimulating. Every day lived as a child brings a host of new experiences and with them our full presence within the day. But as we get older and we become more set in the ways that we think, behave, feel and act in the jobs and relationships we have established, we are gradually less moved, inspired or impressed. Increasingly, our days seem to be somewhat monotonous. When life is habitual, every day is like the other and nothing is memorable. One day comes, the other goes and our presence is scarcely aroused.

Time is measured by its perception. A hot summer day for a child may seem like a year, while a full year in the life of an adult may appear like a day. Even when we get older there are some days or weeks that seem endless while others race by. Scientists have suggested that this is due to the way the brain measures time. Essentially, our perception of time depends on how often a novel or exciting experience is added to the memory, which then affects the way we perceive the quality and quantity of duration. As youngsters, we learn new things every day and the days are more stretched out and filled with many memorable experiences, but as we grow older routine takes over and one day can easily be confused with the next. When nothing memorable is imprinted on the brain time moves on more quickly as each day merges into the next. The key to living 'longer' is to live fuller, to view each day as a unique opportunity to grow and expand. Instead of the colloquial term of 'getting older' we should change our attitude to 'growing older.' Growth can and must be continuous lest you stop living, which is characterized by movement and change.

The greatness of Avraham was that he was able to live life exactly this way. Having reached a ripe old age the Torah says, "now Avraham was old Ba Ba'yamim" – literally meaning "and he came into his days" (Bereishis, 24:1). What does it mean that he 'came into his days?' He entered into each day with his whole self and he therefore lived fully. No two days were alike, and therefore each day was unique. Avraham was totally aware of the preciousness of each and every day and so he was able to be completely present within each moment. A full life is when we see each new day as one that brings new and unexplored possibilities of growth and personal transformation.

Part of being a fully present, integrated and focused human being is to live life without regrets. One of the central themes running throughout the canon of western literature is the author's regret for not living the life they would have wanted to. This ailment is manifest within the protagonist's unfulfilled quest of achievement or unrealized dream. This truth is not reserved for the world of literature. The greatest grief in life is the regret that one could have lived another, better life. More crippling than the fear of death is the fear of not having lived fully.

To a large extent the fear of death is the fear that one's life was meaningless, insignificant or purposeless.

To know whether our lives are being lived fully it is necessary to ask ourselves: What, if anything, would I be doing differently if I had only one day to live? What are the most important values in my life and am I pursuing them?

Let us make sure that we live our lives in such a way that the answer to the first question is a confident and unequivocal, "Nothing!" And to the latter, we should be blessed to answer with a clear and resounding, "Yes!" In doing so, we will find that our lives are that much more inspired, inspiring and overwhelmingly enriched.

NOTE TO THE READER:

The Torah's beauty is such that it glows in a rainbow of colors and a myriad of shades and textures. Clearly, in matters of philosophy and thought there are always many opinions. This is especially true with regard to eschatology. There is no single specific thread of thought passing through all traditional texts regarding the afterlife. Precisely for this reason, the ambition and objective of this text was to cull the various sources and present, as much as possible, a comprehensive understanding as to what the nature of the soul is and by extension, what occurs when a soul departs from the earthly realm of existence. Towards this end the text itself has stayed away, as much is it could, from divergent opinions. These endnotes invite the readers to broaden their horizons and delve deeper into the subject, if they so desire, through the lenses of the various, and often contradictory, sources.

* The entire Torah is called a *Shira*, or "song" *Devarim* 31:19. This reference to "song" possibility refers to the entire Torah. *Shu't Sha'agas Aryeh*, Siman 34. The glory of the Torah as a song, and the essence of its pleasantness, occurs when the various voices differ one from each other and together form a harmonious melody. *Aruch HaShulchan* Hakdamah, Choshen Mishpat. The first word of the Torah, Bereishis contains the letters for Shir (*Tikkunei Zohar*, 24b) and the last word Yisrael is Shir E-l (*Tikkunei Zohar* 3a) so both the beginning and the end is Shir. In fact, the entire Torah is a Shir. *Otzer Chayim* (Kamarna), *Devarim*, 31; 19, a Shir that is Mamtik / sweetens harsh Dinim/ judgements.

* The Torah principle that "the majority rules" is relevant when there is an argument regarding law. This is not the case when the argument entails matters of thought and philosophy. Rebbe Shmuel HaNagid, *Kelalei HaTalmud*. The Rambam, *Pirush HaMishnayos, Sanhedrin*, 10. *Sotah*, 3; *Shevuos*, 1. See however: Rebbe Moshe Sofer, *Chasam Sofer, Yoreh Deah*, Siman 356.

ENDNOTES

Opening

*   The idea of Tzimtzum as contracting emotion. *Likutei Moharan* 1, 49:1. See also *Chesed L'Avraham*, Shoftim, p. 117.

*   The soul is unable to enter the presence of Hashem . . . until the body is buried *Zohar* 3, p. 88a–88b.

*   The Heavenly voice of Sinai never ceases and it can still be heard by the prophets and the sages. Rebbe Meir Ben Gabbai, *Avodas Hakodesh*, 3:23, p. 301–302. All revelations and understandings are rooted in the echo of Sinai. *Sefas Emes*, Shevuos. A revelation by the prophet Eliyahu can also be within human consciousness. *Tikkunei Zohar*, Hakdamah. See also Rebbe Yehudah Loew (The Maharal), *Netzach Yisrael*, Chap. 28. Rebbe Nachum of Chernobyl, *Meor Einayim*, Parshas Vayetze, p. 45. See also Rebbe Klunimus Kalmish (Shapiro) of Peasetzna, *Movo H'Sha'arim*, Chap. 2, p. 202.

*   Regarding the times of Moshiach, no one knows what will happen until it occurs. Rambam, *Hilchos Melachim*, 12:2. See also *Sefer HayaSha'ar,* Sha'ar 5, p. 60.

*   A person should do Teshuvah a day before death. *Shabbos*, 153a. "Return one day before your death" *Avos*, 2:10. Another version adds, "Do Teshuvah today lest you die tomorrow" Rebbe Shimon Ben Tzemach Duran, the Tashbetz, *Magen Avos*, 32b. See also *Meleches Shlomo*, ad loc. For the reason why it says, "one day before death" see Rebbe Yisrael Lipschitz, Derush Ohr HaChayim, *Tiferes Yisrael* at the end of Nezikim. In another location the sages in fact suggest that if all else fails one should remind oneself of the day of death. *Sukkah*, 52b. This is not to be taken literally, thereby becoming a source of depression. Rather, one should aspire to see the transient, fickle nature of physical reality, and thus live a more spiritual life in the present. Rebbe Klunimus Kalman, *Maor Vashemesh*, Parshas Vayigash, p. 127. One may also meditate on how a day wasted is a day that is technically dead. Rebbe Chayim of Tzernovitz, *Be'er Mayim Chayim*, Chaya Sarah, p. 85.

Chapter 1

* The first mitzvah is the counting of time. *Shemos*, 12:2.
* Rebbe Yachanon Ben Zakkai crying. *Berachos*, 28b.
* For the story of the Baal Shem Tov and his share in Gan Eden, see Rebbe Yitzchak Aizik of Komarna, *Notzar Chesed*, Chap. 4, Oys 22. See also *Baal Shem Tov Al HaTorah*, Vaeschanan, Os 17. *Sichos HaRan*, Oys 48.
* Torah is derived from the word Hora'ah. The Maharal, *Nesivos Olam*, Nosiv H'Emuna, Chap. 2. *Tifferes Yisrael*, Chap. 9. See also *Zohar* 3, p. 53b.
* The Torah does not explicitly mention the afterlife because the main point of the Torah is the now. Rebbe Dan Yitzchak Abarbanel, Vayikra, Parshas Bechukosai, Teshuvah 1. The Abarbanel offers seven reasons for this. Among them is the contention that since ancient man believed in a completely transcendent Creator who had no interest in the goings on of the world, the Torah, by speaking of rewards and punishments experience in this world, comes to dispel this notion.
* The logical historical answer is that there was no reason to write about the afterlife, as it was a prevalent belief in the ancient world. Clearly, the lack of mention is not intended as an implicit discrediting of the concept of the afterlife, since such a radical divergence from all other cultures would have been explicitly spelled out in the Torah. Additionally, the phrase "gathered to his people," which is used throughout Torah, – (Bereishis 25:8, 25:17, 35:29, 49:33. Bamidbar 20:24. 27:13, Devarim 32:50) - clearly implies an afterlife, since in many of the above cases it cannot refer to being buried with their ancestors, as

they were being buried alone, or are the first to be buried in that place. Classic Torah commentators suggest various reasons why there is no apparent, unambiguous mention of spiritual reward or afterlife. Rebbe Saddiah Gaon answers: a) spiritual reward is something that the mind understands on its own, so there is no need to mention it; and b) prophetic teachings elaborate on issues that are near, and hint at issues that are distant. Since, for the people entering Israel, the "land" was immediately before them, the blessings are thus about the land. *Emunos Vedeyos*, Ma'amor 9, Chap. 2. Rebbe Hai Gaon answers that there is no need to mention an afterlife, since it is part of the oral tradition (see *Even Ezra*, Devarim, Chap. 32:39). Rebbe Avraham Even Ezra himself answers that because the Torah was given to the masses, and most people will have trouble deciphering the subtleties of bodiless existence, this concept was deemed too deep for most people's understanding. Devarim, Chap. 32:39. Rebbe Avraham Ben HaRambam writes something very similar. *Sefer Hamaspik Leovedei Hashem*, Erech, HaPerishus, p. 127. So does Rabbeinu Bachya, Vayikra, Chap. 26:9. Rebbe Yehudah Halevi answers that the authenticity of Torah can only be proven by guaranteeing physical rewards. Spiritual reward in an afterlife can never be proven or disproven. *Kuzari* Ma'amor 1, Chap. 104–109. See Rebbe Nisan Ben Reuven, the Ran, *Derashos HaRan*, Derush 1, for an elaboration on this theme. There are various answers that arise from the writings of the Rambam. In *Igeres Techiyas Hamesim* ("The Letter regarding the Resurrection of the Dead") Chap. 9, the Rambam explains why there is no explicit mention of resurrection, as it is too far in the distance and will not be a fitting deterrent for unwarranted behavior. In *Hilchos Teshuvah*, Chap. 9, Halacha 1, he writes that the Torah does not speak of physical rewards, rather it implies that material goodness is not a reward in itself, only a means to enable us to do more good. In the *Moreh Nevuchim* ("The Guide to the Perplexed") he suggests that material wellbeing is only offered as a reward to counter the ancient idol worshipers who sought material wellbeing through their pagan practices.

The Ramban, Rebbe Moshe Ben Nachman, answers that there is no need to mention this, as it is obvious, being clear that the soul must return to her source *Ramban*, Shemos, 6:2. Or else it is because the Torah only mentions rewards that apply to the collective, not those that are individually given. Rebbe Yoseph Albo, *Sefer Haikkarim*, Maamor 4, Chap. 39. See also Rebbe Shimon Ben Tzemach Duran, *Magen Avos* (1785), Part 3, p. 87a. Rebbe Meir Eben Aldavia (14th century) *Shivilei Emunah*, Nosiv 9. Others suggest that the Torah does explicitly mention spiritual rewards. See *Abarbanel* ibid, citing Vayikra 26:12. See also Rebbe Menasha ben Yisrael, *Nishmas Chayim*, Ma'amor 1:3.

Rebbe Shlomo Ephraim Lunshitz, offers six answers to this question, one being that the Torah says, "I will be with you and be your G-d, and you will be my nation" (VaYikra, 26:12). If this is possible while one is embodied, how much more so is it true in a bodiless state. *Kli Yakar,* Vayikra, Chap. 26:12. Rebbe Meir Ben Gabbai explains that the Torah's deepest desire is to offer man eternal life, a transcendence of death altogether. In the eyes of Torah we are meant to be immortal, so there is no need to speak of an after-life, as life never ends. *Avodas Hakodesh*, Part 2, Chap. 17–19. Or, because Torah is transmitted through prophecy, and the World to Come/Olam Habah is higher and deeper than prophecy. The Maharal, *Tifferes Yisrael*, Chap. 57. *Gevuras Hashem*, Hakdamah 1. Rebbe Nashan Nate Shapira, the Megalah Amukhos, answers that the blessings of the physical are in addition to the spiritual, as indicated in the word Nasati: "I will give," as in Ve'yiten, of the blessings to Yaakov, "to give and give again". *Megalah Amukhos* Al HaTorah, Parshas Bechukosai, p. 62. The inner essence of creation is Torah. Being in sync with Torah allows for blessings to flow through all levels of existence, beginning in the spiritual sphere, but ultimately permeating the physical. Rebbe Yeshayah Halevi Horowitz, The Shaloh HaKadosh, *Shenei Luchos Habris,* Toldos Adam, Beis Acharon, p. 48–106. Rebbe Tzvi Elimelech of Dinav suggests that while the Torah speaks in the language of man, describing the physical, it is merely a metaphor for the spiritual. Otherwise man would not be able to grasp what it contains. *Bnei Yissochar,* Ma'amorei Ha'Shabbos, Ma'amor 6, 13. The Shaloh explains that, whereas the Torah speaks of Geshem/rain it is hinting at divine energy, which is the "pleasure of the future world of eternity" . *Toldas Adam*, Beis Acharon, ibid.

* The two sages who cried, *Berachos* 5b. Rebbe Akiva cried for the very same reason. *Nedarim*, 50b. See the *Maharsha*, Berachos, 5b. See also *Kesuvos*, 103b, where another sage cried before his death for the lack of Mitzvos in the afterlife.

* The sages speak of wordly experiences that are a taste of the future. *Berachos*, 57b. By doing Mitzvos one enters a state of the World to Come while still in this world. Rebbe Chayim of Volozhin, *Ruach Chayim*, Avos, Mishnah, Kaal Yisrael.

Chapter 2

* The soul is the knower of the known. *Sefer HayaSha'ar*, Sha'ar 5:18, p. 68. The author of this classic work remains unknown. See also the Chidah, *Sheim Hagdalim,* Ma'aeches Seforim, Chof, 72.

* The Rambam calls the Creator "the knower and the known" *Hilchos Yesodei HaTorah*, 2:10. This description also fits the soul as well. S*efer HayaSha'ar*, Sha'ar 5:13.

* Yechidah is a Nitzutz Borah—a spark of the Creator in the form of a Nivrah, creation. The Arizal, *Sha'ar De'Rusei Abyah,* Chap. 1. See also, The Alter Rebbe, *Likutei Torah,* Re'eh, p. 27a. The Miteller Rebbe, Rebbe Dovber, *Biurei HaZohar,* p. 115b. The Rebbe Rashab, *Sefer HaMaamorim Samach Vav,* p. 459. The soul is both infinite and finite, though this is a logical paradox. *Nishmas Chayim,* Ma'amor 2:9. This is a violation of rational thought.

* The bodies of the upright are holy. *Zohar* 3, p. 70b.

* "The body is like the parchment upon which the Torah scroll is written". The Ritvah, *Moed Katan,* 25a. Ramban, *Torahs Ha'adam,* Inyan Keriah.

* Regarding the authenticity of Yosefun, not to be confused with Josephus (see *Shulchan Aruch,* Orach Chayim, 307:16, *Beir Heitiv, Mishnah Berurah*, ad loc. See also Shulchan Aruch Harav, Orach Chayim, 307:30). The Zohar clearly

writes that body and soul should be viewed as friends. *Zohar* 1, p. 134b.

* There is no body without a soul and no soul without a body. *Medrash Tanchumah,* Parshas Vayikra, Chap. 6.

* The metaphor of a blind person. *Sanhedrin*, 91b. *Medrash Rabbah*, Vayikra, Parsha 4:5.

Chapter 3

* Yetzer Tov and Yetzer Hara. See e.g. *Berachos*, 61a. *Sukkah*, 52b.

* Without the Yetzer, man would not get married or get a job. *Medrash Rabbah*, Bereishis, Parshah 9:7. See also *Medrash Rabbah*, Koheles, 3:11.

* Yeast in the dough. *Berachos*, 17a. This Yetzer is our natural instincts. The Talmud speaks of animals possessing a Yetzer Hara. *Berachos*, 61a. Clearly our sages are referring to the animal's survival instincts. The tale of the captured Yetzer, *Yumah*, 69b. See also *Sanhedrin*, 64a. *Medrash Rabbah*, Shir Hashirim, 7:13.

* The animal soul, *Tanya*, Chap. 9. See also, *Shivilei Emunah*, Nosiv 3, p. 107, Nosiv 6, p. 306. The Arizal, *Arba Meos Shekel Kesef,* p. 72b–73. The Gra, Rebbe Eliyohu of Vilna, *Sifra DeZeniuta*, Chap. 4, p. 29a.

* Man makes the Yetzer into Rah/evil. *Tanchumah*, Parshas Bereishis, Chap. 7. See also Rebbe Klunimus Kalmish of Peasetzna, *Derech Hamelech*, Parshas Miketz, p. 63. See also Rebbe Yisrael Salanter, *Ohr Yisrael,* p. 154–155. There is a Talmudic debate. According to one opinion the Yetzer Hara is similar to a fly, while other sages draw a parallel to wheat. *Berachos*, 61a. The argument is about whether this inclination is essentially negative, or is it merely a potential for negative, see *Iyun Yaakov,* ad loc.

* Yetzer Hara enters at birth. *Sanhedrin*, 91b. See however, *Medrash Koheles*, 9:22. *Avos D'Rebbe Nashon*, Chap. 16: 2. *Medrash Talpiyos*, Oys Yud, Yetzirah. Conversely, Yetzer Tov enters at conception (*Iyov*, Chap. 10:12), but it does not fully permeate the body until birth. The Maharal, *Nesivos Olam*. Nesiv H'Tzdakah, Chap. 3. And it only fully integrates with the body at thirteen. *Shulchan Aruch Harav*, Orach Chayim 4. *Menoras Hamaor* 4, Gidul Banim. See also Rebbe Pinchas Eliyohu Ben Meir of Vilna, *Sefer Habris* 2, Ma'amor 1:3. Yetzer Tov enters at thirteen. *Medrash Koheles*, 4:16. *Zohar* 3, p. 165b. *Avos D'Rebbe Nason*, Chap. 16:2. Some sources speak of the Neshamah only being fully absorbed in the body at the age of forty. Thus, the word Neshamah contains the letters N, Sh, and M, which spell out forty years: Mem Shana. *Nitzutuzei Zohar*, Zohar 1, p. 191a.

* Yetzer Tov sees the future. Rebbe Yitzchak Aramah, *Akeidas Yitzchak*, Parshas Naso, Sha'ar 73. See Rebbe Yisrael Salanter, *Igeres HaMusar* (reprinted in the end of Mesilas Yesharim) p. 160–161.

* Yetzer Hara can be sweet and alluring in the beginning, but ultimately it brings bitterness. Yerushalmi *Shabbos*, Chap. 14. *Medrash Rabbah*, Vayikra 16:8.

* Though the Zohar was first published in the year 1290 by Rebbe Moshe DeLeon, the original manuscript/teaching dates back to Rebbe Shimon Bar Yochai of the second century c.e. Some Torah scholars believe that there may have been minor additions throughout the ages. Rebbe Yaakov Emdin, *Matpachas Seforim*. The Radal, *Kadmus HaZohar*. See however Rebbe Chaim Yoseph David Azulay (The Chidah) *Shem Hagdalim*, Ma'areches Seforim, Zayin (8).

* The evil inclination is a divine agent. *Zohar* 2, Parshas Terumah, p. 163a. *Baba Basra*, 16a.

* Evil is a mask. Rebbe Yaakov Yoseph of Polonnye, *Toldos Yaakov Yoseph*, Parshas Vayakhel, p. 252. See also *Baal Shem Tov Al HaTorah*, Parshas Bereishis.

* People with low self-esteem are more inclined towards destructive behavior. Yet there are evil people who do not lack self-esteem and who were loved. In such a case, the cause of their behavior is cultural and philosophical. Being brought up in an environment that preaches hate for one ethnic group or another can also be a source of mass evil, while other possible factors include social pressure or wanting to conform and fit in. Studies show that people who commit hideously evil acts show reduced activity in their prefrontal cortex, the part of the brain

that is associated with judgment and planning. They lack the power of Da'as, which is an intellectual activity that is connected with the brain's frontal lobes. The Miteller Rebbe, *Torahs Chayim*, Shemos, p. 395b. Rebbe Rashab, *Sefer Ha-Ma'amorim 5678*, p. 146.

* According to the Zohar, as explained by its commentators, many Greek pre-Aristotelian ideas are similar to the Torah. *Zohar* 2, p. 236. See Rebbe Yoseph Ergas, *Shomer Emunim*, Part 1, Chap. 37. *Nishmas Chayim*, Ma'amor 4, Chap. 21. See also, *Kuzari*, Ma'amor 2, Chap. 66. The Ramah, *Torahs Ha'olah*, Part 1, Chap. 11. Rebbe Aaron Berechyah of Modena, *Ma'avar Yavak*, Ma'amor 3, Chap. 33. *Shu't MaHaram Merotenberg*, (Teshuvos Ba'alei Tosefos), Siman 19.

* In the West the first philosopher to speak openly about reincarnation was Pythagoras (582–507 bce). Many Jewish and even non-Jewish scholars alike believed that he received his teachings from the Nevi'im /the prophets. Flavius Josephus (37–93 ce) The Complete Works Of Josephus (Michigan: Kergel, 1981), Against Apion, Book One, Chapter 22, p. 614. Rebbe Menasha Ben Yisrael, *Nishmas Chayim*, Ma'amor 4, Chap. 21. Rebbe Yaakov Emdin, *Migdal Oz*, Aliyos HaGilgulim. See also *Shivilei Emunah*, Nosiv 8, p. 352. Many ancient biographers write of the same concepts for example, Hermippus of Smyrna (c. 200 bce) in his book, On Lawgivers, and Iamblichus (250–325 ce). Many scholars believed the same (see David Kaufmann, Mechakrim B'Safrut Ha'Ivrit Shel Yemei Habinayim (Kook, 1965), p. 86). Interestingly, some Kabbalists write that certain gentile sages were Jewish souls reincarnated into non-Jewish bodies. Rebbe Yonashan Eibeschuvetz, Ya'aros D'vash, Part 1, Derush 16, p. 427. Regarding the exchange of souls, see: *Keser Shem Tov*, p. 340. See also *Teshuvas Maharom Me'rotenberg*, (Teshuvas Baalie Ha'Tosfos) Siman 19. p. 286.

* Plato saw the body as a prison cell for the soul. The Last Days of Socrates (Penguin, 1993) The Phaedo, p. 118. See also (LeHavdil), *Tikkunei Zohar*, Tikkun 6. Rebbe Bachya Ibn Pakudah, *Chovos Halevavos*, quoted by the *Sefas Emes*, Parshas Vaeschanan, p. 33. See also Rebbe Eliyahu ben Moshe Di Vidas, *Reshis Chachmah*, Sha'ar Ha'ahvah, Chap. 3. Rebbe Avraham Azulay, *Chesed LeAvraham*, Part 1, Chap. 21.

* The soul is a guest in the body. *Medrash Rabbah*, Vayikra, Parsha 34, Chap. 3. Yet the soul fills and infuses the body. *Berachos*, 10a.

* There are three souls or dimensions of soul, which are called by various names. There is an argument over whether there are three separate souls, or three manifestations of one soul.

* For the argument for three distinct souls, see Rebbe Shlomo Ibn Gabriel, *Mekor Chayim*, Sha'ar 5, Chap. 20. Rebbe Avraham *Even Ezra*, Koheles 7:3. Rebbe Bachya Ibn Pakudah, *Toras HaNefesh* Chap. 4 and Chap. 6.

* For the argument of one soul with three forms of expression, see Rambam *Shemonah Perakim*, Chap. 1. Rebbe Gershon Ben Shlomo (13th century, father of the Ralbag) *Sha'ar HaShamaim*, Ma'amor 11, p. 71; Rebbe Menachem Ben Shlomo Meiri, *Pesicha Beis HaBechira* (1965), p. 15. The Ran, *Derashos HaRan*, Derush 3, p. 45. *Shivilei Emunah*, Nosiv 6, p. 294. *Magen Avos*, Part 2, Chap. 4, p. 35a. Rebbe Moshe Metrani, *Beis Elokim*, Sha'ar Hayesodos, Chap. 62. *Akeidas Yitzchak*, Parshas Bereishis. Sha'ar 6. p. 70b. *Nishmas Chayim*, Ma'amor 2, Chap.1 5. Rebbe Yoseph Shlomo Delmedigo - known as the YaSha'ar of Candi, *Metzareph LeChachmah*. See also Rebbe Moshe Isserles, the Ramah, *Machir Yayin* (1999), p. 19–20, and p. 46.

  Rebbe Saddiah Gaon speaks also of one soul that has three elements: the capacity to decipher, to become angry, and to feel. *Emunos Vedeyos*, Ma'amor 6:3.

* Some of those who argue for three separate souls also propose that these souls are all interlaced and linked. Rebbe Shlomo Eben Gabriel, *Mekor Chayim*, Sha'ar 5, p. 376.

* The lowest part of soul is considered the physical of the spiritual. *Kuzari*, Ma'amor 2, Chap. 26. This is the part that interfaces with the blood of the body see Devarim 12:23. Vayikra 17:11. Ramban and Rabbeinu Bachya, ad loc. Rebbe Menachem Recanti, Parshas Acharei (Levush Malchus (NY.1965), Vol 7, p. 26a). Rebbe Ovadyah Seforno, *Kavanas HaTorah*.

* Chomer and Tzurah. Rambam, *Hilchos Yesodei HaTorah*, Chap. 4: 8–9. *Hilchos Teshuvah*, 8:3.

* The Kabbalists speak of a transcendent, Divine soul. *Ramban*, Bereishis 2:7.

Rabbeinu Bachya, ad loc. See also Ramban, *Kisvei HaRamban,* Derashos Torhas Hashem Temimmah, p. 159. A soul that is part of Hashem. Rebbe Shabtia Sheftel Horowitz, *Shefa Tal* in the Hakdamah. See, *Sefer HayaSha'ar,* Sha'ar 5:15, p. 66–67. See also Rebbe Yoseph Yavatz, *Avos,* Chap. 1 Mishnah 17. Chap. 3 Mishnah 19. The Ramak, *Pardess Rimonim,* Sha'ar 32, Chap. 1. *Ohr Ne'erav* Part 1, Chap. 3, p. 8. Rebbe Menachem Azaryah De Fano, *Ma'amor HaNefesh* Part 3, Chap. 8. Shaloh, *Shenei Luchos Habris* Vol 4; *Ohr Chodash,* p. 23. *Chesed LeAvraham,* Part 2:44. *Ya'aros D'vash,* Part 1, p. 8b. *Da'as Tevunos* in the beginning. Rebbe Menachem Mendel of Vitebsk, *Pri Ha'aretz,* Parshas Vayeshev. *Tanya,* Chap. 2. The Mekubalim and their students are not alarmed by the apparent contradiction in terms — a part of something that is indivisable. See The Rashbah, *Teshuvas HaRashba,* Teshuvah 418.

* Interestingly, Rebbe Chasdai Cresces, (student of the Ran) also speaks of a transcendent soul that is beyond intellect. *Ohr Hashem,* Ma'amor 3, Part 1, 2:2, p. 323. Intellect is an expression of the soul, not the soul itself. *Ohr Hashem,* Ma'amor 2, Klal 6, Chapter 1. See also, *Sefer Haikkarim,* Ma'amor 4, Chap. 29.

* The transcendent part of the soul gives man the ability to transcend to inner/ higher spiritual realms. *Derech Hashem,* Part 3, Chap. 1.

* The transcendent soul inspires one to soar above, as a candle leaping upwards towards its source. *Tanya,* Chap. 19. See also *Nishmas Chayim,* Ma'amor 4:2. Note: *Medrash Shocar Tov,* Tehilim, 62. The highest level of soul is where Creator and creation are one. *Eitz Chayim Sha'ar 42,* Derushei Ab'Ya, Chap. 1.

* The Medrash enumerates the five names of the soul. *Medrash Rabbah,* Bereishis, Parsha 14:9. *Medrash Rabbah* Devarim, Parsha 2:37. See also *Berachos,* 10a. According to Kabbalah, these five names are in fact five separate dimensions of the soul. The level of Yechidah is the essence of soul, as the Medrash in Devarim states, though the Medrash in Bereishis apparently suggests that Chaya is higher than Yechidah. Rebbe Chayim Eliezer (Shapiro) of Munkatsch, *Divrei Torah,* Mahadurah Kama, Chap. 109, p. 53. Each of these five dimensions of soul contains five subdivisions. *Sha'ar HaGilgulim,* Hakdamah 1. *Sefer Sader Gilgulim,* Maasaei Neraim. Some philosophical/mystical texts speak of five levels

of soul as the "vegetative," "animal," "rational," "philosophical," and "prophetic." The latter two refer to intellectual knowledge gained by cognition and intuitive knowledge, containing truth within itself. Rebbe Yitzchak Iban Latif, *Sha'ar HaShamayim*, 1, p. 32a.

* The general metaphor of the soul as a drop of water with the ocean as its source is found in early Chassidic teachings. See the Magid of Mezritch, *Magid Devarav Le'yaakov*, Likutei Amorim, Chap. 53, p. 22 (66). See also Rebbe Meshulam Fievish of Zabriz, *Yosher Divrei Emes*, Shavuos, in the name of the Magid.

* Regarding morphic fields, see Rupert Sheldrake: A New Science of Life (London: Blond & Briggs, 1981). It should be pointed out that there has been great controversy regarding this theory. In the prestigious journal Nature it has been called "a book fit for burning." See: Editorial, Nature 293 (1981), 245–6.

* "And He blew into his nostrils a breath of life," which means a spirit with the ability to speak. Bereishis, Targum *Onkulos* 2:7. See also Rashi and the Ramban, ad loc. *Akeidas Yitzchak*, Parshas Bereishis, Sha'ar 6, p. 70b. *Nishmas Chayim*, Ma'amor 1:1. Others write that "blew into his nostrils" is on the level of Ruach, and "breath of life" is Neshama. Rebbe Shlomo Molcho, *Sefer Hamefuar* (Ben Yishai, 1989), p. 5. Ruach is connected with speech. *Sha'arrei Kedushah*, in the beginning.

* Nefesh is connected with Malchus or "power," Ruach with Tifferes or "beauty," And Neshama with intellect. *Magen Avos*, Part 3, p. 35. *Pardes Rimonim*, Sha'ar 31, Chap. 1. The Yetzer Tov is equated with intellect. See, *Chovos Halevavos*, Sha'ar Avodas Elokim. *Ohr Yisrael*, p. 125.

* Makif Karov—Chaya and Makif Rachok - Yechidah. *Pri Eitz Chayim* 1, Sha'ar Ha'akudim, Sha'ar 6, Chap. 5, p. 84–5; Part 2, Sha'ar Pinimiyus V'Chitzoniyus, Derush 10. *Derush Pinimi Umakif*, Derush 1. Rebbe Yoseph Ergas, *Mavo P'Sachim* (1965), p. 121. See also, the Feriediker Rebbe, *Sefer HaMa'amorim 5703*, p. 43–53. The Rebbe, *Sefer Ha'Ma'amorim Meluket*, Vol. 4, p. 46–47.

* Generally Nefesh, Ruach, and Neshama unfold and reveal themselves in a linear progression. *Sha'ar HaGilgulim*, Hakdamah 3. Rebbe Tzadok HaKohen of Lublin *Tzidkas HaTzadik*, Oys 227. Negative actions only have an effect on the level

of Nefesh. *Zohar* 3, p, 16a. Yet, sometimes people attain higher reaches of soul instantaneously. *Tanya*, Chap. 19. See also, *Nishmas Chayim*, Ma'amor 4, Chap. 2. *Likutei Moharan*, Part 1, Chap. 80.

* Chaya is the source of all thoughts. *Nefesh HaChayim*, Sha'ar 2, Chap. 17.

* Will (Keser) is the underlying foundation of all existence. *Igeres Hakodesh*, 20. See also, the Ramak, *Pardes Rimonim*, Sha'ar 23, Chap. 1, Adam. *Pri Eitz Chayim*, Heichel 1, Anaf 4.

* The five dimensions of soul correspond to the four basic worlds and Adam Kadmon: Nefesh (action) corresponds to the world of Asiyah, "completion;" Ruach (emotion) to the world of Yetzirah, "formation;" Neshama (intellect) to the realm of Beriah, "creation;" Chaya (will) to the world of Atzilus, the world of "emanation;" Yechidah to Adam Kadmon. The Arizal, *Derush Pinimi Umakif,* Derush 1–2. *Mavo P'Sachim,* p.126.

* We can live from the lower levels of soul—from the vegetative or animal soul, or from the higher, Divine soul—and within that itself—from Nefesh, Ruach, or Neshama. *Pardes Rimonim,* Sha'ar 31, Chap. 3.

* All aspects of the soul are one, constituting one totality. *Zohar* 1, p. 142a.

* For the debate between the house of Shammai and Hillel, see *Eiruvin*, 13b.

* Let man reflect upon his actions. *Mesilas YeSha'arim*, Chap. 3.

* "It is Noach (easier) not to have been created". *Nishmas Chayim*, Ma'amor 2, Chap. 6.

* "Against your will you are born…against your will you will die". *Avos* 4:22. The deeper meaning is as follows: before a soul descends into this world the soul observes the temptations and challenges of this world as does not wish to enter a body, as it were. Note, *Reshis Chachmah*, Sha'ar HaTeshuvah, Chap. 1. But then the soul comes to live within a body and realizes the amazing abilities the body and the physical world presents, and thus, "against your will you will die," i.e., the soul, once born, wishes to remain enclothed within the body, the Rebbe Rashab, *Sefer HaMa'amorim Ra'nat,* p. 7–8.

Chapter 4

* There are various degrees of immortality. *Avodas Hakodesh*, Hakdamas Hamech-aber.

* Nothing dies, every death births new life, every fall and death on one side is a rise and birth on the other. *Derush Ohr HaChayim*, Tiferes Yisrael, at the end of Nezikim.

* The individual may die, but not the congregation. *Temurah*, 15b.

* There is Kayamim B'ish, "eternity in its form," such as the stars, sun, moon; and Kayomim B'min, "eternity of the species" Yerushalmi, *Berachos,* 1:1. See also, *Ohr Hashem*, Ma'amor 3:1, Kelal 2:2. *Akeidas Yitzchak*, Sha'ar 38.

* Giving charity in honor of a deceased person. Rabbeinu *Bachya*, Devarim, Chap. 21:8. See also *Beis Yoseph*, Orach Chayim, 284 and 621. Bach, ad loc. By giving charity in the world below, one can assist souls above in reaching their elevation. Medrash *Tanchumah*, Parshas Hazinu. *Koftor U'Perach*, Chap. 44. Ramah, Orach Chayim, 621:4. Yoreh Deah 249:16. *Kav HayaSha'ar,* Chap. 86.

* Building a mausoleum. Yerushalmi, *Shekalim,* 2:5. *Sefer Chassidim*, Chap. 738. This custom dates back to the times of the Avos. Bereishis 35:20. The monument is the seat for the overarching/Makifim levels of soul. *Likutei Torah Arizal*, Parshas Vayechi, p. 118. *Mishnas Chassidim,* Meseches Gemilus Chassadim, 3:13. The Mitteler Rebbe, *Ma'amor Hishtatchus,* Chap. 2. The headstone is referred to as Nefesh, as the soul permeates its space. Rebbe Pinchas of Koritz, *Aimrei Pinchas,* Likutim 41, p. 223.

* Studying Torah. *Yevamos*, 122a. Rashi in the name of the Gaonim.

* Regarding lighting a candle (on Yom Kippur) in honor of and to assist souls above, see *Kalbo,* quoted by the Ramah, in *Darchei Moshe,* Orach Chayim 610:4. The custom is to light a candle every year on the day of a person's passing. *Maharshal*, Siman 46. *Magen Avraham* 261:6. *Nachalas Shiva*, Siman 73. *Mishnah Berurah*, Hilchos Shabbos, 261:16. Note, *Kesuvos*, 103a with regard to Rebbe Yehudah. The reason for the candle is that the soul is likened to the candle of

G-d. Keeping with the metaphor, it would be better to light a flame with an actual fire and not switch on an electric bulb. *Shut Mishana Halachos,* Vol. 5, Siman, 70. See also *Yerushas Pleita,* Siman 6. *Emek Halacha,* Vol. 2, Siman 52. *Chasmal B'Halacha,* Vol.1, Chap. 5. Lighting a candle during the Shiva period creates joy for the soul. *Ma'avar Yavak,* Ma'amor 2, Chap. 15.

*   Souls receive pleasure from the lighting of candles. *Rabbeinu Bachya,* Shemos, 25:31. See also *Teshuvas Torah Leshmah,* Siman. 520.

*   Immortality through deeds. *Nishmas Chayim,* Ma'amor 4, Chap. 3. "We need not to erect monuments for the righteous, for their deeds are their memorials" Yerushalmi, *Shekalim,* 2:5.

*   There is a soul connection between a person and his possessions. *Keser Shem Tov,* Chap. 218 and Chap. 194. *Tzavoas Horivash,* Chap. 109, p. 38. *Baal Shem Tov Al HaTorah,* Parshas Vayechi, p. 286–288. The Magid of Mezritch, *Magid Devarav Leyaakov* 101:d. See also, *Meor Einayim,* Likutim, p. 166. See also *Bear Hagaloa* (Maharal) with regards to "Yiush Shelo MeDa'as" - *Baba Metziah,* 21b, where he suggests that there is no intrinsic bond between a person and his possessions. According to the teachings of the Baal Shem Tov not only is there a connection, but the soul itself expands within a person's possessions. *Ohev Yisrael,* Parshas Matos. Anyone who would hold on to the cane of Rebbe Meir—the brilliant sage who was renowned for his great intellectual capabilities (*Sanhedrin,* 24a. *Eiruvin,* 13b)—would gain wisdom. Yerushalmi, *Nedarim,* 9:1. *Moed Katan* 3:1. The wisdom of Rebbe Meir permeated his entire being, even the most external aspects. Any person or object that came into contact with this great sage was imbued with his wisdom. The Rebbe, *Likutei Sichos,* Vol 4, p. 1096. See also *Divrei Torah,* (Munkatch) Mahadurah Aleph, No. 23. There is a custom of making a sage's casket from the table upon which he studied, or to use the table from which charity was distributed. *Rabbeinu Bachya,* Shemos 25:23. *Shach Al HaTorah,* Parshas Terumah, p. 91. See also, *Likutei Sichos,* Vol. 4, p. 1096. *Kav HaYaSha'ar,* Chap. 46. *Teshuvas MaHaril,* Siman 55. *Shalsheles Hakabalah,* p. 152.

* "A righteous/learned person's words are his memory" Yerushalmi, *Shekalim* 2:5. See *Yefah Marah*, ad loc.
* Regarding the murmur of a person who has passed on. *Yevamos*, 97a. *Sanhedrin*, 90b. Yerushalmi, *Shekalim*, 2:5.
* Biological immortality: Yaakov lives on, "since his children are alive, he is alive" *Ta'anis*, 5a. Dovid HaMelech left an heir equal to himself, thus the word "death" does not appear in reference to Dovid. *Baba Basra*, 116a. When Adam and Chava were first faced with their mortality, they conceived and they called their child Kayin. *Bereishis*, 4:2. They desired to give birth in order to affirm that this child will be dedicated to Hashemafter their death, he will stand in their place. *Ramban* ad loc.
* Death is the rearrangement of the elements, a returning to their source. *Zohar* 1, p. 122b. See also Rebbe Shmuel of Sochatchov, *Sheim Me'Shemuel*, Parshas Emor, p. 311.
* Regarding the Luz bone, see, *Medrash Rabbah*, Bereishis 28:3. *Medrash Rabbah* Vayikra 18:1. *Medrash Rabbah*, Koheles 12:5. *Zohar* 1, p. 69a, 137a. *Zohar* 2, p. 28b. See also *Baba Kama*, 16b, *Tosefos* ad loc. This bone seems to exist as part of the spine, yet some see it as at the back of the skull. Rebbe Nathan Ben Yechiel, *HaAruch*, Erech Luz. See also, *Avodas Hakodesh*, Part 2, Chap. 40, p. 182. Arizal, *Likutei Torah*, Na'ch, Shoftim.
* The Pasuk speaks of a revival of the dead, not a re-creation. Yeshayahu 26:19. *Zohar* 2, p. 28b. See also, *Siddur Beis Yaakov*. Rebbe Yaakov Emdin, Melava Malka, p. 206. And the revival is from the Luz bone, although some opinions view the resurrected form as a completely new body. Medrash *Pirkei D'Rebbe Eliezer*, Chap. 34. *Zohar* 3, p. 169a–b. See also, *Sefer Haikkarim*, Ma'amor 4 Chap. 30. *Derech Hashem*, Part 1:3:9. *Maharsha*, Nidah, 69b. See, however, *Avodas Hakodesh*, Part 2, Chap. 40, where he explains that there is no argument between the Medrashim. There are many Halachic ramifications if the resurrected body is considered new. See e.g., *Teshuvas Rav Poalim*, Part 2, Sod YeSha'arim 2. *Yabia Omer*, 7. Yorah Deah, Siman 37. *Lev Chayim* 1, Siman 31.

* Some scientists would like to prove scientifically that resurrection will eventually and inevitably occur. There are many new discoveries that make the notion of resurrection, especially from the Luz bone, less abstract. For instance, for the purposes of cloning, almost any cell from the body is enough to reproduce the entire human form, even if the cell came from a corpse. Notwithstanding all that can be reproduced by science—which leads us to believe the body is not the house of the memory—what happens if one's entire memory is recorded and then, at a later time, reproduced: is that resurrection? There are many conjectures, some even try to explain this most miraculous of phenomena in rational terms.

One theorist suggests that we can understand the potential final throes of the universe by analyzing current cosmological postulations about its shape. Since it is closed—in the sense that space/time is positively curved by the large mass of mysterious dark matter—the universe will one day stop expanding and reverse on itself, until it reaches what Tipler calls the omega point. At the omega point, the temporal becomes eternal and the entire cosmos is engulfed by the complete information of the universe's history. Furthermore, the omega point could see the resurrection of every person who has ever lived, simply by giving that person's pattern a new transcendent body, or a computer (Frank. J. Tipler "The Omega Point as Eschaton," Zygon (June 1998, vol. 24); see at length, The Physics of Immortality, NY: Doubleday, 1994). At its core, belief in the Resurrection is the belief in a miraculous, otherworldly event (R. Yitzchak Abuhav , *Menoras HaMaor* Ner 4: 2, Part 3, Chap. 1, p. 206. Note 'Rashi', *Sanhedrin*, 90a). The scientific idea that nothing is lost, no memory or information is lost and that there will come a time when all of the past, all memory, all information will become revealed is perhaps an external expression of the inner, Kabbalistic idea that the time of resurrection is the time of Unity, Tree of Life, and thus, everything, all the past will be resurrected.

* Concerning the body being preserved after death. *Medrash Tehilim*, Chap. 119:9. Regarding the righteous, see, *Shabbos*, 152b. *Baba Basra*, 17a. Note *Rashi*, ad loc. See also, *Asarah Ma'amoros*, Ma'amor Olam Kata, Chap. 4. *Reshis Chochmah*,

Sha'ar HaYira, Chap. 11. Rebbe Yaakov Emdin, *Migdal Oz,* Chibut Hakever, Chap. 5, p. 277. Moshe's eyes did not falter, and his strength did not leave him, even in death. Devarim 34:7. *Rashi. Ohr HaChayim,* ad loc. A person is made up of the four (divergent) elements, yet, the source of the elements is Unity. When a person lives in a place of unity his or her body as well attains unification and can "live" on eternally. *Likutei Yekarim,* 290.

* Regarding a person living on the level of Luz. *Maor Vashemesh,* Parshas Vayechi, p. 136. See also *Medrash Talpiyos,* Oys Yud. There is also the level of Luz in space, in terms of a physical space, city, where the people are transcendent of the angel of death. *Sotah,* 46b.

* Regarding the immoral and the preservation of their bodies. Rebbe Yehudah HaChassid, *Sefer Chassidim,* Chap. 1143. See also, *Medrash Talpiyos,* Oys Dalet.

* There is a level of soul that needs body, and a level of soul that does not need body. Rambam, *Hilchos Teshuvah* 8: 3. See also, *Hilchos Yesodei HaTorah* 4:8–9. See also, *Moreh Nevuchim,* Part 1:41.

* The soul that "needs the body" has no prior existence: "It only exists with body" Rambam, *Hilchos Yesodei HaTorah* 4:9. Yet many sources write that it does, in fact, have a prior existence. Rebbe Dan Yitzchak Abarbanel, *Mifalos Elokim* Ma'amor 8, Chap. 6. See also, *Sha'ar HaGilgulim,* Hakdamah 23. One way to reconcile these two opinions, and not widen the argument further is to suggest that the generic soul was created in the beginning of time, while the individualized soul was created with and for the particular body. The Rebbe Maharash, *Igrois Kodesh,* Admur Maharash, p. 94–95.

* The lower parts of the soul do not experience 'personal' immortality. They expire when the body expires. Rambam, *Hilchos Yesodei HaTorah* 4:9. *Hilchos Teshuvah* 8:3. *Orchas Tzadik,* Sha'ar Yiras Shamayim. Yet, it too becomes eternal by becoming one with the heavenly throne. Alter Rebbe, *Likkutei Torah,* Parshas Shelach, p. 40. See also, *HachSha'aras Ha'Avreichim,* Chap. 3.

* The body and soul of an animal are created simultaneously, unlike Adam. Adam's body was first created and only later was he/she given a (extra) soul (Bereishis, 2:7) that comes from a space beyond body or that is in need of a body. As

the soul of an animal is one with its body, when the body dies so does the soul, as it were. Yet, even with animals, while there is no immortality on an individual level, there is still some type of collective immortality. On a level of Chomer - not Tzurah/ form - animals too experience some type of immortality. Rabbeinu Hillel Ben Shmuel, *Tagmulei Ha'Nefesh*, Part 2. p. 31b. In addition, animals that were owned by a human being or had some form of relationship with human beings become part of the memory of the human, and thus, in this way experience immortality as well.

* The highest dimension of soul—which the philosophers believe to be the rational, and the mystics the transcendent—is either a "part of Hashem" (see notes for chapter 3), or at the very least "something from Heaven". Rambam, *Hilchos Yesodei HaTorah* 4:9. Others call the soul "a light from Hashem" Rabbeinu Bachya Ibn Pakudah, *Torahs HaNefesh*, Chap. 19, p. 82. In both cases the soul is a reality from a higher dimension, and thus everlasting. See however, Rambam *Moreh Nevuchim*, Part 2, Chap. 27, where he cites the soul as an example of a creation that is nonetheless eternal. The soul exists prior to the creation of the body. *Yevamos*, 63b, *Nedarim*, 13b. *Avodah Zarah*, 5a. *Medrash Rabbah*, Bereishis, Parsha 24, Chap. 4. See also *Chagigah*, 12b. *Zohar* 1, p. 119a. Note, however, Rebbe Saddiah Gaon, *Emunos Vedeyos,* Ma'amor 6:1.

Chapter 5

* The cessation of breathing is considered in Torah law the definition of death *Yumah*, 85a. Rambam, *Hilchos Shabbos,* Chap. 2, Halacha 19. *Shulchan Aruch*, Orach Chayim 329:4. See also, *Shut Chasam Sofar,* Yoreh Deah 338. Today some argue that brain death is also considered dead according to Halacha. Modern Medicine and Jewish Ethics, p. 263–275. However, most contemporary Halachic authorities do not consider brain death to be de facto death. Rabbi Aaron Soloveichik, "Jewish Law and Time of Death," Journal of the American Medical

Association 240 (1978) p. 109. See also Rabbi J Dovid Bleich, Kevios Z'man HaMaves Leor Halacha (1992), p. 177, in the name of Rebbe Shlomo Zalman Auerbach and Rebbe Yosef Shalom Eliyashav. Although see, *Shut Sheivet Ha-Levi*, 7, Siman 235. 8, Siman 67.

*   Raymond A. Moody divides the near-death experience into 15 phases (Life After Life, p. 21). He also divided it into nine phases. The Light Beyond (1988) p. 6–13. Others write that there are five core features of the near-death experience:

      1) Feelings of peace.

      2) Body separation.

      3) Entering the darkness–tunnel.

      4) Seeing the light.

      5) Entering the light.

Kenneth Ring, Life at Death: A Scientific Investigation of the Near-Death Experience. NY: Quill, 1982. The first serious study of the near-death experience was done by a Swiss geologist, Albert Hein, in the nineteenth century. See Rebbe Noyes and Rebbe Kletti: "The Experience of Dying from Falls," Omega (1972) 3:45.

*   For the idea of shared near-death experience. See Pamela Kircher: Love is the Link: A Hospice Doctor Shares Her Experience of Near-Death and Dying (NY: Larson), p. 141.

*   Moshe declined to offer details. *Sifri*, Devarim 356.

*   The worlds were created in such a way that when standing below, man can tap into worlds above. Rav Hai Gaon, quoted by Rebbe Moshe Botril in his commentary to *Sefer Yetzirah*, Chapter 4, Mishnah 2.

*   Sleep is a sixtieth of death. *Berachos*, 57b. *Medrash Rabbah*, Bereishis, 17:5.

*   The soul journeys upwards during sleep. *Medrash Rabbah*, Bereishis, 14, Chap. 9. See also, *Sha'ar HaGilgulim*, Hakdamah 19.

*   We find in the Torah acts of resurrection. Melachim 1, Chap. 17:22. Melachim 2, Chap. 4:35. See also Yechezkel, Chap. 37:10. Some see these as cases of resuscitation, not resurrection. Rambam, *Moreh Nevuchim*, Part 1, Chap. 42. See however, Rebbe Yitzchak Ben Sheishes, the Rivash, *Teshuvas HaRivash*, Siman 45, with regard to Eliyahu and the child he brought back to life. See also *Radak*, Rebbe Dovid Kimchi, Shmuel 1, Chap. 17:17. Rebbe Dovid Ben Zimra, the Radbaz, *Teshuvas HaRadbaz*, Part 5: 203. Yet most commentaries see this as a case of resurrection. The Medrash says, "Everything that Hashem will bring about in the future He has done already in the present via the prophets . . . the prophets have resurrected the dead as Hashem will in the future." *Medrash Rabbah* Koheles, Parsha 3, 1:16.

* At times the term "death" is employed in reference to a person who is still alive yet very ill. *Moreh Nevuchim*, Part 1, Chap. 42. *Shita Mekubetzes* on Baba Metzia 114b. *Teshuvhas HaRadbaz*, Part 5, Chap. 203. *Tashbetz*, Part 1, Chap. 106. *Tifferes Yisrael*, Ta'anis, Chap. 4, Mishnah 3. See also *Zohar* 1, p. 175a. *Nitzutzei Zohar 9*.

* Regarding the sage who died and returned. *Baba Basra*, 10b. *Kesuvos*, 77b.

* For the story with Rebbe Yosi, see *Zohar* 2, p. 61a–61b.

* The soul hears everything said in front of the lifeless body—until the grave is sealed or the body decomposes. For this reason, one sage told another to be careful what he said at his funeral eulogy, for he will be standing there. *Shabbos* 152b. The Yerushalmi says that, until three days after burial, the soul hovers over its body. *Moed Katan*, 3:5. Still, there is a level of soul that remains connected for all time with the grave. *Ma'avar Yavak*, Ma'amor 2, Chap. 7.

* The soul of the righteous leaves the body, as the withdrawal of a strand of hair from milk. *Berachos*, 8a.

* For the unrighteous, death is similar to trying to pull a tangled rope. *Medrash Tehilim*, 11:6.

* Our sages mention the sounds that are emanated when a soul leaves a body. *Yumah*, 20b, see also 21a. Although this can be a very silent scream, *Sefas Emes*, Ki Tetze. See also, *Medrash Rabbah*, Bereishis, Parsha 6:7. *Medrash Rabbah*, Shemos Parsha 5:9. *Pirkei De'rebbe Eliezer*, Chap. 34. When a person passes away, a loud sound emanates. Medrash *Beis HaMedrash*, Perek Gehenom (Othzor

Medrashim, 1956) Part 1, p. 92.

* Sounds accompany the person to his grave. *Berachos*, 15b. *Zohar* 1, p. 118a, (although these sounds can refer to the wailing of the mourners).

* The refined body is called Guf Dak, whereas the coarse body is called Guf Gas. *Avodas Hakodesh*, Part 2, Chap. 26, p. 144–147. *Nishmas Chayim*, Ma'amor 1, Chap. 13. Others call it a Malbush. Rebbe Ovadyah Seforno, *Kavanas HaTorah*. See also, *Zohar* 2, p. 141b. p. 150a. Others maintain that it is called a Tzelem. *Nishmas Chayim*, 1:13. Others, such as Rebbe Dan Yitzchak Abarbanel, call it Ruach (See ibid). In the Zohar it is often referred to as a Chaluka D'rabanan—"garment of the sages". *Zohar* 1, p. 66a. See also, *Sha'arrei Kedusha*, Part 1, Sha'ar 1. Some sources view the Chaluka D'rabanan as a "borrowed" Levush—garment. *Siach Yitzchak*. See, *Sheivet HaMusar*, Chap. 35, p. 499. Incidentally, Plato calls this body the "heavenly atmosphere." The first (published) reference for this idea of two bodies is found in a text attributed to Rebbe Bachya Ibn Pakudah, *Torahs HaNefesh*, Chap. 4, p. 25.

* The Tzelem exists at the moment of conception, and when a soul enters the world it expands with the Tzelem. *Zohar* 3, p. 13b. See also the Ramak, *Shiur Komah*, Hashgacha (5), p. 119. Conversely, ". . . by the way of the Tzelem the body increases and grows" Rebbe Shem Tov Ben Shem Tov, *Sefer Ha'emunos*, Sha'ar 6, Chap. 4, p. 61b–62a. Other sources speak of the Tzelem as the intermediate medium between the coarse body and refined soul. *Asarah Maamoros*, Ma'amor Chikur Din, Part 4, Chap. 14, p. 278. Indeed, as the Arizal teaches the Tzelem (plurar Tze'lalim) is lower than the soul, even lower than Nefesh. *Sha'ar HaKavanos*, Inyan Sukkos, Derush 7. Since there are many levels of soul thus there are many levels of Tzelem (Tze'lalim). *Eitz Chayim*, Part 2, Sha'ar 26; *Sha'ar Ha'Tzelem*, Chap. 1, p. 48. See also, *Reshis Chochmah*, Sha'ar HaYirah, Chap. 12. According to the Zohar, even before entering a human form, a soul stands above in the very same form in which it will later embody itself. *Zohar* 3, p. 61b. The Malbush is shaped like the Mitzvos. Rebbe Moshe Metrani, *Beis Elokim*, Sha'ar Hayesodos, Chap. 53.

* Regarding Rebbe Yehudah. *Kesuvos*, 104a. He returned in the form of a Guf

Dak. *Rabbeinu Bachya,* Bereishis 49:33. See also, *Avodas Hakodesh,* Part 2, Chap. 26. *Sheivet HaMusar,* Chap. 35. Or his "body" was made up of the basic material of the physical. *Medrash Talpiyos,* Oys Hie, p. 546. It is said that some post-Talmudic sages did the same. *Ma'avar Yavak,* Ma'amor 2, Chap.5, p. 204. There is a "body" for souls even before souls descend. *Yevamos,* 63b. *Avodah Zarah,* 5a. *Nidah,* 13b, *Tosefos* ad loc. Incidentally, it is with some type of "Malbush" that angels at times reveal themselves to man, in some type of distilled form of physicality, in a human shape. *Zohar* 1, p. 101a. *Zohar* 3, p. 152a. See also, *Ramban,* Bereishis 18:1. Rebbe Yitzchak of Acco, *Meiras Einayim,* Parshas Vayechi, p. 87. *Chesed LeAvraham,* Part 1, Chap. 28.

* There is the concept of Shedim, "incomplete creatures," that only exist with two basic elements: fire and wind. *Ramban,* Vayikra 17:7. *Shivilei Emunah,* Nosiv 9, p. 394. *Rabbeinu Bachya,* Vayikra. 17:7. *Nishmas Chayim,* Ma'amor 3:13. *Chesed LeAvraham,* Part 1, Chap. 28. Though see, Rebbe Menachem Recanti, Parshas Acharei Mos, p. 25b. The Rambam is of the opinion that there is no such a thing as Shedim. They are nothing more than figments of the feeble minded imagination. The Rambam interprets some of the Halachos/laws based on "evil spirits" to refer to actual physical danger, for example, *Hilchos Rotzeach,* Chap 12, Halacha 5. The Kotzker Rebbe once quipped that the Rambam is absolutely correct when he dismissed Shedim as nonsense, falsehoods. They are false, fakes, he said. They are nothing but masks concealing the truth of Divine Unity. They exist in our mind as Kelipa perceptions. Another time, when asked how could the Rambam reject a concept that is mentioned by our sages? The Kotzker said, once the Rambam rejected the idea of Shedim, in honor of the Rambam, Shedim became extinct. Either way, the more a person believes in Shedim the more they exist, whether objectively or subjectively.

* Regarding the story of Shaul, the commentaries argue about whether it was a genuine encounter or simply an illusory experience. Samuel 1, 28:14. *Radak, Rashi* and *Ralbag,* ad loc. See also, *Nishmas Chayim,* Ma'amor 1, Chap. 7. According to the Rambam, there is no validity to the concept of speaking to the dead, or ghosts, they are all illusions. Rambam, *Hilchos Avodah Zarah* 11:16. See also *Berachos*, 59a. Regarding mediums and communicating with the dead, even if they were authentic experiences according to those opinions holding this as a possibility, they are nonetheless not allowed. Devarim 18:10–11. This is one of the 365 prohibitions. Rambam, *Sefer Hamitzvos*, negative commandment 38. *Semag*, negative commandment 56. *Chinuch*, Mitzvah 515. Any form of initiation is forbidden. Rambam, *Hilchos Avodah Zarah* 11:13. Interestingly, according to the Medrash, "When a person does in fact summon the dead, the one who summons the soul sees the soul but does not hear anything; whereas the one who asks to speak to the soul hears but does not see" *Medrash Rabbah*, Vayikra, Parsha 26, Chap. 7. *Tanchumah*, Parshas Emor, Chap. 2. This would render mediums incapable of communicating—hearing—the soul, if in fact they can actually see it.

* Reference to going thorough the cave of Machpeila. *Zohar* 1, 127a. Whether this teaching is meant to be taken literally, or meta-physically and metaphorically, and whether it is a reference to the tunnel of the near-death experience or not, remains open for discussion.

* Souls see their relatives and friends, and they accompany them to their place of eternal rest. *Zohar*, Part 1, p. 218b. Note, *Medrash Rabbah* Shemos, Parsha 52. See *Baba Basra*, 75a . The awareness, the sensing of souls from other dimensions of reality, can occur even prior to actual death. *Nishmas Chayim*, Ma'amor 2, Chap. 21.

* The Pasuk says, with regard to King Saul and Yonason, "Those who are beloved and friendly in their lifetime, in death will not be separated" Shamuel 2, 1:23.

* Regarding a man and wife finding each other in the afterlife and being together. *Zohar* 3, Parshas Shelach, p. 167b. The Arizal, *Sha'ar Ta'amei HaMitzvos*, p. 5. See also *Ta'anis*, 25a, with the reference to an "us," as in a husband and wife, though the word Anan/us can mean us, but as two individuals. Not only do husbands and wives find each other in the afterlife, the link between the two is so profound that even after the man's death, his spirit is found within his wife, especially for the first 12 months after his death. The Shaloh HaKadosh, *Shenei Luchos Habris*, Vol 5; Kedushas HaGuf V'Damim, p. 160.

*   Families reunite in Gan Eden. Rebbe Yaakov Tzvi Yallish, *Kehilas Yaakov*, Part 1, Gan Eden 8, p. 324. At the time of resurrection, only souls that share the same primordial root remain connected. *Sha'ar HaGilgulim*, Hakdamah 10. One who remarries after the loss of his first wife will return to his primary first wife. *Zohar* 1, 61b. Ben Ish Chai, *Rav Poalim*, Part 2, Sod YeSha'arim 2. *Matzav HayaSha'ar*, Teshuvah 7. *Ma'avor Yavak*, Maamor 2, Chap. 7. Supposing his "first" wife was his true soulmate, otherwise this situation may be different. *Zera Emes*, Part 2, Siman 146. See *Shut Yabiah Omer* 7, Yorah Deah, Siman 40.

*   Tzadikim in Gan Eden are aware of each other, with complete and open awareness. Medrash, *Beis HaMedrash*, Seder Gan Eden, Part 1. p. 87.

*   When Rebbe Yochanan Ben Zakkai was about to pass on he said, "Prepare a seat for Chezkia the King of Yehudah who has come to welcome me" *Berachos*, 28b. There are many other sources that speak of souls meeting up with illustrious personalities of history, particularly meeting souls that they are connected with. *Zohar* 2, p. 250b. *Baba Kamah*, 111b. *Ramban*, Baba Basrah, 43a (to the Rif). *Recanti*, Parshas Vayera, p. 24a. *Sefer Chassidim*, Chap. 559. *Magid MeSha'arim*, Parshas Vayakhel. *Ma'avar Yavak*, Hakdamah, p. 21; Ma'amor 3, Chap. 25. p. 289. See also *Kesuvos*, 104a. Teacher and student forge an everlasting relationship, and their souls are forever intertwined, in this world and in the next. *Sha'ar HaGilgulim*, Hakdamah 10.

*   According to tradition, a soul that leaves this world first sees Adam. *Zohar* 1, p. 57b. *Medrash Rabbah*, Bamidbar 19:18.

*   The Torah describes someone who has died as one who has gone or is gathered to his ancestors. Bereishis, 15:15; 25:8; 35:29; 29:33. Bamidbar, 27:13. Melachim 1, 11:43.

*   There are various opinions about when angels were created. Rebbe Dan Yitzchak Abarbanel, Bereishis 1:1. *Mifalos Elokim*, Ma'amor 3, Chap. 3–4. Beyond angels that were created in the beginning of time there are angels continually being created anew. *Medrash Rabbah*, Bereishis, Parsha 78: 1. *Medrash Eicha*, 3:23. *Chagigah*, 14a. In addition, man also continuously creates new angels. See notes below.

    *   Angels are messengers, thus every force is viewed as another angelic spirit. *Moreh Nevuchim*, Part 2, Chap. 6. Angels are transmitters of energy. Ramchal, *Ma'amor Haikkarim, B'Ruchnim*.

    *   Angels are identified with light, for lack of any other physical term. *Abarbanel*, Bereishis, Chap. 1:1. *Mifalos Elokim*, Ma'amor 3, Chap. 3. Most opinions view angels as divested of all Chomer, material form. Rambam, *Hilchos Yesodei HaTorah* 2:3. Some opinions write that angels are comprised of a Chomer, albeit a more refined one than mortal man. This is the opinion of Rebbe Shlomo Ibn Gabriel. See *Abarbanel*, Melachim 3:12, where he is quoted. See also Rebbe Yoseph Gikatila, *Sefer HaNikud*, 3:3. Some speak of angels existing as refined fire. See *Pirush* on the Rambam, *Hilchos Teshuvah*, Chapter 8. See also *Meiras Einayim*, Parshas Re'eh, p. 297. *Pardes Rimonim*, Sha'ar 2, Chap. 7. Some speak of angels existing in a refined version of fire and wind. Ramban, *Torahs Ha'adam*, Sha'ar Hagmul, quoted in *Torah Ohr*, Parshas Bereishis, p. 4b. *Siddur Im Dach*, p. 275. Rebbe Eliezer of Worms, *Sodei Razya*, Hilchos Malachim, p. 163. Others speak of angels existing in any one of the four basic elements, a refined version of earth, fire, wind, or water. Rebbe Mattisyohu Delecreta, *Sha'arei Orah*, p. 100–101. See also, *Pardes Rimonim*, Sha'ar 24, Chap. 11. *Kli Yakar*, Bereishis, Chap. 6:16.

    *   The idea of angelic beings comprised of various elements opens the conversation to the possibility of any other living organisms existing outside this planet, on other planets or even comets. Interestingly enough, in the book of Shoftim, Devorah sings a song of praise to Hashem for assisting the general Barak in his battle against Sisera. In chapter 5, she sings, "The stars in their course fought against Sisera . . . . 'curse Meroz,' said the angel of G-d, 'curse bitterly its inhabitants, for they did not come to help...'" (Chap. 5:20–23). Who is Meroz? According to one opinion Meroz is a planet. *Moed Katan*, 16a. Thus the inhabitants of Meroz would seem to indicate that there is life on this other planet *Zohar* 1, p. 40b. 157a; 254a. See also, *Chesed LeAvraham*, Part 2, Chap. 4. *Sefer Habris*, Part 1, Maamor 3, Chap. 3. See also, Rebbe Chasdai Cresces, *Ohr Hashem*, Ma'amor 4, Derush 2, where he writes that this is a possibility. *Pardes Rimonim*, Sha'ar

2, Chap. 7. But, as the Zohar writes, "human life is only found on this planet" *Zohar* 3, Parshas Vayikra, 10:1.

* The Medrash teaches that after a person passes away, angels appear to greet and accompany the soul. *Pesikta Rabasi* 2:3. See also, *Kesuvos*, 104a. Rebbe Bachya Ibn Pakudah, *Torahs HaNefesh*, Chap. 8, p. 41. *Ma'avar Yavak*, Ma'amor 1, Chap. 22, p. 165–166. There are also angels dwelling with the person throughout life. *Pesikta Rabasi* 44:8. The Zohar speaks of one (some say two or three) angels that accompany the soul throughout life. *Hakdamah LeZohar*, p. 12b–13a. *Zohar* 2, p. 199a. See also, *Pardes Rimonim*, Sha'ar 31, Chap. 3.

* Every Mitzvah creates an angel. *Avos*, Chap. 4, Mishnah 11. Rebbe Ovadiah Bartinora, ad loc. See also, the Ramak, *Tomer Devorah* 1:2. *Sha'arei Kedushah*, Part 3, Sha'ar 7. *Sha'ar Ruach Hakodesh*, Derush 1, p. 1. *Chesed LeAvraham*, Part 2, Chap. 19. *Ohr Hachayim*, Devarim, Chap. 13:7. *Maor Vashemesh*, Parshas Yisro, 232.

* These are the angels that accompany man. These angels are "shaped" like the person, and "speak" in his voice. *Tanchumah*, Parshas Vayetze. *Sefer Chassidim*, Chap. 1161. *Ma'avar Yavak*, Ma'amor 1, Chap. 30. In fact, Mitzvos are referred to as angels. Rambam, *Hilchos Mezuzah*, Chap. 6:13. From every action a person does, he creates an angel, and the angel is shaped like the action. *Sheim Me'Shemuel*, Moadim, Shabbos Teshuvah, p. 100.

* Angels go with every person and record his deeds. *Psikta Rabasi* 44:8. See also *Ta'anis*, 11A. *Tana Divei Eliyahu Zuta*, Chap. 1.

* There is also an angel of death that takes the soul from the body. *Avodah Zarah*, 20b. *Baba Metzia*, 86a. *Moed Katan*, 28a. Yet, elsewhere, our sages say that the angel of death is also the evil inclination. *Baba Basra*, 16a. In other words, the ego is the source of death. The name of the angel of death is sam-e'l; Sam is poison of e'l/G-d" *Medrash Rabbah*, Devarim, Parsha 11:10. The ego is thus the conduit that brings the poison of death to the living person.

* "A candle of G-d is the soul of man" Mishlei 20:27. The soul is called a candle of light. *Shabbos*, 32a.

* Each person has an angel that is created in his image. Rebbe Eliezer of Worms

Sodei Razya, Hilchos Malachim, p. 165. *Chachmas Hanefesh,* p. 382.

* The Zohar teaches that no man leaves this world before he sees the Shechinah *Zohar* 3, p. 53a. See also *Zohar* 1, p. 98, 99a, and p. 118b. *Medrash Rabbah* Bamidbar, Parsha 14, Chap. 2, Parsha 19:18. *Chachmas Hanefesh,* p. 350. It should be pointed out that according to many opinions the Shechinah does not refer to Hashem itself, rather to a creation, Kavod Nivrah, as in Hashem's glory. *Emunos Vedeyos,* Ma'amor 2:10. *Kuzari,* Maamor 4:3. *Moreh Nevuchim,* Part 1:19, 1: 25. The Ramban disagrees. He writes that the Shechinah is the Creator's Kavod. *Ramban,* Bereishis, 46:1. In fact there are many levels of Shechinah. *Ohr HaChayim,* Bereishis, Chapter 46:4.

* "After my skin has been destroyed, then from my flesh I shall see G-d". Iyov, 19:26. See also, *Nishmas Chayim,* Ma'amor 2, Chapter 19. The Tzadik before he leaves this world can fathom the level of Keser, the "crown" or Divine transcendence. Rebbe Avraham of Trisk, *Magen Avraham* (1997), p. 260.

* "People do not leave this world until they see Hashem". *Pirkei De'rebbe Eliezer,* Chap. 34. *Torahs Kohanim* end of Chap. 1. *Medrash Rabbah,* Bamidbar, 14:22. Meseches *Chibut Hakever, Reshis Chochmah,* Sha'ar HaYirah, Chap. 12. *Migdal Oz,* Chibut Hakever, Chap. 1, p. 276. This does not mean Hashem's essence, rather a revelation that is otherwise unattainable. *Nishmas Chayim,* Ma'amor 1, Chap. 11.

* Fire is a metaphor for Hashem. Devarim, 4:24. Since it is the most refined of the four elements. Rebbe Yoseph Gikatila, *Ginas Egoz,* Part 2, p. 170. Ohr Ein Sof, "the Infinite Light," is another metaphor (for an early source, see Rebbe Shlomo Eben Gabriel, *Mekor Chayim,* Sha'ar 1, Chap. 4, p. 10). Of course, the metaphor of light is only a metaphor, and the Creator is not light. *Shomer Emunim,* Part 2–5. Rebbe Baruch of Kosav. *Amud Ha'avadah,* Ha'shael U'meishiv 81.

* Everything man does is written down. *Avos* 2:1. See also *Chagigah,* 5b. *Sotah,* 3b. Regarding the postmortem life review. *Ta'anis,* 11a. *Sifri. Zohar* 2, p. 222a. See also *Medrash Rabbah,* Vayikra, Parsha 26, Chap. 7.

* The angels and the soul (some add the limbs) bear witness to one's life. *Ta'anis,* 11A. *Pesikta Rabasi* 44:8. *Tana Divei Eliyahu Zuta,* Chap. 1. The Mishnah says

that Hashem is both the judge and the witness. *Avos*, Chap. 4, Mishnah 22. The person himself is the witness. *Reshis Chaohmah*, Sha'ar HaYirah, Chap. 12, p. 35. *Migdal Oz*, Chibut Hakever, Chap. 1, p. 276. Regarding the angels bearing witness. *Hakdamah LeZohar*, p. 12b. Rebbe Eliezer of Worms writes of the five witnesses that testify: 1) a person's possessions, 2) his accompanying angels, 3) his limbs, 4) his soul, 5) and the Creator. *Sodei Razya*, Chochmas Hanefesh, p. 1328–329. Negative actions become ingrained in one's bones, as it says, "their iniquities have come upon their bones" Yechezkel, Chap 32: 27. While a person's good deeds become inscribed upon his right hand. Medrash, B*eis HaMedrash*, Perek Gehenom, Part 1, p. 92.

* Rebbe Menachem Azaryah De Fano writes that the universal book recording all human actions is the sapphire (colored) ether that surrounds the human being. *Asarah Ma'amoros*, Ma'amor Chikur Din, Part 2, Chap. 12, p. 112. See also by the same author *Ma'amor HaNefesh* (Petrkav: 1903), Part 2, Chap. 10, p. 23. This ethereal material was called by pre-modern physicians the "surrounding ether." See *Yad Yehudah*, on Asarah Ma'amoros: "Nothing is ever lost in this universe" *Zohar* 2, Parshas Mishpatim, p. 100b.

* According to our sages there is a heavenly tribunal. *Rosh Hashanah*, 8b. See also *Sefer Chassidim*, Chap. 1165.

* Cleansing is not revenge, but rather an act of kindness, so that the soul will be able to enter Gan Eden. *Avodas Hakodesh*, Part 2, Chap. 32–33. See also *Ma'avar Yavak*, Ma'amor 3, Chap. 41, p. 316. *Minchas Oni*, Chap. 2, p. 355. The Alter Rebbe, *Ma'amorei Admur Hazoken*, Haktzorim, p. 451. Rebbe Yehudah Petaya, *Minchas Yehudah*, Yechezkel, p. 168. As one Chassidic teacher put it, since the Torah outlaws revenge, certainly the Giver of Torah adheres to this principle. Rebbe Yaakov Leiner of Radzin-Izhbitz, *Beis Yaakov* (1991) Vayikra, p. 4a.

*"Your iniquities have separated you from your G-d" *Yeshayahu* , Chap. 59: 2. See Rambam, *Hilchos Teshuvah*, 7:7. *Tanya*, Igeres HaTeshuvah, Chap. 5.

* First Din, "judgment," and then Cheshban, "accounting". *Avos*, Chapter 4, Mishnah 22. See Rebbe Yoseph Caro, *Ohr Tzaddik*, Avos, p. 126. *Likutei Sichos* Vol 4. p. 1207. *Likutei Maharan*, 113. Every soul is his own judge. *Keser Shem*

Tov, Hosofos, p. 26. *Baal Shem Tov Al HaTorah*, Parshas Kedoshim, p. 427. Thus, "Judge every person favorably". *Avos*, Chapter 1, Mishnah 6.

* The soul sees the missed opportunities. *Medrash Shochar Tov*, Tehilim, Chap. 62. There is a judgment on missed opportunities and actual negativity that was done, this is the difference between Din and Cheshbon. *See, Pirush HaGra*, Avos, 3:1. *Asarah Ma'amoros*, Ma'amor Chikur Din, Part 1, Chap. 22. *Beis Yaakov*, Parshas Emor, p. 116a.

* On the day of a person's death he is granted a vision that is otherwise not available, and he experiences a total life review. *Zohar* 1, p. 79a.

* As righteous people are about to depart this world, Hashem reveals to them their due reward, inspiring within them great joy. *Medrash Rabbah*, Shemos, Parsha 52, Chap. 3. See also *Ta'anis*, 25a. This vision is offered so the soul can leave the physical world in peace. *Ma'avar Yavak*, Ma'amor 1, Chap. 17, p. 155. *Ma'amor HaNefesh*, Part 6, Chap. 7, p. 73. *Nishmas Chayim*, Ma'amor 2, Chap.19. For another reason why this occurs, see *Akeidas Yitzchak*, Sha'ar 22.

* Elements of the near-death experience are similar to drug-induced hallucination. Ron Siegel: "Accounting for 'afterlife' experiences," Psychology Today (Jan. 1981), p. 65–75.

* Some patients have lost light perception for years, yet after NDE they describe what was going on around them, the colors and designs of clothing the people present were wearing. Elisabeth Kübler-Ross On Children and Death (New York: Macmillan, 1983) p. 208. See also Kenneth Ring & Sha'aron Cooper Mindsight: Near-Death and Out-Of-Body Experiences in the Blind. CA. Transpersonal Psychology, 1999.

* When injured, the body produces natural painkillers, endorphins, and pumps them into the bloodstream. Daniel Carr, "Endorphins at the approach of death," The Lancet 14, (Feb. 1981), 390. See also Sherwin Nuland: How We Die (Vintage Books: 1995). Susan Blackmore, Dying To Live (New York: Prometheus Books, 1993) p. 106–110.

* Near-death experience as a reproduction of birth memory, which is a theory put forth by Carl Sagan. Broca's Brain, New York: Random House, 1979, pp.

303–304. This theory has been greatly criticized.

* Depletion of oxygen, causing minor seizures of the temporal lobes, may cause old memories to resurface. Russell Noyes, Jr.: Near-Death Experiences: Their Interpretation and Significance, in Robert Kastenbaum, ed., Between Life and Death, New York: Springer, 1979, p. 76–81.

* The Canadian research was done by Penfield. Wilder Penfield and Phanor Perot: "The brain's record of auditory and visual experience," Brain 86 (1963), p. 635.

* Regarding the notion of revisiting old memories as a way to escape harsh reality. Russell Noyes and Roy Kletti: "Panoramic memory: A response to the threat of death," Omega 8 1977, p. 181–194. Interestingly, in his epic poem The Aeneid, Virgil tells the story of Aeneas the warrior hero who travels to the underworld. Entering paradise, he realizes that reunion with one's loved ones formally separated by death is the greatest and most pleasurable delight of the afterlife.

* Michael White: Weird Science: An Expert Explains Ghosts, Voodoo, The UFO Conspiracy, And Other Paranormal Phenomena, Avon Books, 1999. Where the author explains many of the ideas of NDE according to scientific information. See also, Carl B. Becker: Paranormal Experience and Survival of Death, (NY: State University of New York Press, 1993) for an in-depth analysis of the scientific proofs and contour proofs regarding the afterlife.

* Regarding the research into the posterior superior parietal lobe. Dr. Andrew Newberg and Dr. Eugene d'Aquili: Why God Won't Go Away: Brain Science and the Biology of Belief, Ballantine, 2001.

* Images/metaphors of dogs in the afterlife are found in Sifrei Sod. *Derech Chaim.* Rebbe Naphtali Hirtz Bacharach, *Emek HaMelech*, Sha'ar Tikkunei Ha'Teshuvah, Chap. 6, p. 17b. Rebbe Chayim Yoseph Dovid Azulay, *Chedrei Beten* Al Ha'Torah, Nitzavim, p. 333. *Avodas Hakodesh,* Tziparon Shamir, Oys 212. See also *Sivchei Ha'Baal Shem Tov*, 90.

* Yeshayahu is similar to a city dweller while Yechezkel to a villager. *Chagigah* 13b.

* The world is like a mirror. *Keser Shem Tov,* Hosofos, Chap. 152. *Meor Einayim,* Parshas Chukas, p. 198. Rebbe Avraham of Trisk, *Magen Avraham*, p. 104. See

also, *Toldos Yaakov Yoseph*, Parshas Pikudei. Hashem appears to each person differently. Hashemis likened to man's shadow. Tehilim, Chap. 121:5. *Keser Shem
Tov,* Hosofos, Chap. 60. *Kedushas Levi,* Parshas Nosa. *Nefesh HaChayim*, Sha'ar
1, Chap. 7, p. 26. See also, *Medrash Shemuel,* Avos, Chap.3, Mishnah 17. Rebbe
Yechiel Ben Shmuel of Pisa, *Minchas Kenaos,* p. 84–85.

* Exploring the "NDE" perhaps does not "prove" the afterlife, though it opens the
conversation up to the possibility. Raymond Moody: The Last Laugh, Hampton
Roads Pub Co, 1999; Life After Life, New York: Bantam Books, 1976, p. 5. See
also The Light Beyond, New York: Bantam Books, 1988, in the Foreword.

Chapter 6

* The soul enters the body in stages, see chapter 3.
* The Tzeil is viewed as an aura, a shadow, or a person's double. It is also seen as
the ethereal body. *Zohar* 1, p. 191a; 111, p. 43a. Rebbe Eliezer of Worms, *Choch-
mas Hanefesh,* (Lemberg: 1876), p. 17d–18a. Rebbe Shem Tov Ben Shem Tov,
Sefer Ha'emunos, Sha'ar 6, Chap. 4, p. 61b–62a. See, at length, the Ramak, *Pardes
Rimonim*, Sha'ar 31, Chap. 4.
* The Tzeil leaves before actual death. *Zohar* 1, p. 217b, 220a. See also *Zohar* 3,
p. 13b. Bamidbar, Parshas Shelach, 14:9, *Ramban* and *Rabbeinu Bachya,* ad loc.
Rebbe Yehudah HaChassid, *Sefer Chassidim,* Chap. 547. *Sefer Ha'emunos,* Sha'ar
6:4, p. 62. In fact, every day a person lives another spark of his soul ascends—the
spark connected with that day. *Ohr HaChayim*, Bereishis 47:29.
* Regarding Hargashos Ha'avir, see Rebbe Shem Tov Ibn Gaon, *Keser Shem Tov*
(1997) Parshas Ki Tetze, p. 52a. Rebbe Menachem Recanti, Parshas Ki Tetze, p.
51b. See also Rebbe Yoseph Shlomo Delmedigo, *Metzareph LeChochmah*, p. 15b.
Sheim Hagdalim, Ma'areches Gedalim, Aleph 10.
* A person who will not live to see another year will be without a Tzeil on the

night of Hoshanah Rabbah—the twenty-sixth day from the beginning of creation. Or the image of their eyes and mouths will appear closed. *Zohar* 1, p. 220a. *Zohar* 2, p. 142b. *Ramban*, Parshas Shelach, 14:9. See also Rebbe Menachem Recanti, Parshas Shelach, p. 37b. See also *Maor V'Shemesh*, a compilation of various early kabbalistic teachings, (Ziv, 1997), Parshas Shelach, p. 48a. Rebbe Eliezer of Worms, *Sefer Rokeach*, Chap. 221. *Chochmas Hanefesh*, p. 366. *KalBo*, Chap. 52. *Sefer Chassidim*, Chap. 1143. *Sefer Ha'emunos*, Sha'ar 6, Chap. 4, p. 62. *Tziyoni*, Parshas Shelach. *Medrash Talpiyos*, Anaf Ba'Buah, p. 233.

* Tzadikim are aware of their Tzeil leaving their bodies, and they know when death is imminent. *Ohr HaChayim*, Bereishis, 47:29. See also, *Sheim M'shmuel*, Vayechi, p. 379. In addition, on the day a person passes away, all the sparks of his soul are gathered, including those sparks that have left him over time. A Tzadik, who can sense this accumulation of sparks, knows the day of death itself. *Ohr HaChayim*, ibid.

* One should not pay attention to all of this. The Ramah Orach Chayim 664:1.

* Thirty days before a person will pass on the Makifim, "overarching energies," leave the body. *Zohar* 1, p. 217b and 227a. *Likutei Torah* LeArizal, Parshas Vayechi, p. 117. *Pardes Rimonim*, Sha'ar 31, Chap. 4, p. 73b. *Chesed LeAvraham*, Part 5, Chap. 30, p. 218. Rebbe Menachem Azaryah De Fano, *Ma'amor HaNefesh*, Part 2, Chap. 9, p. 22. *Ohr HaChayim,* Bereishis, Chap. 47:29. For this reason Moshe was mourned thirty days before he died. *Sifri*, end of Vezos Haberachah. This is because they realized that their beloved teacher was about to pass away. Chasam Sofer, *Torahs Moshe*, Parshas Vezos Haberachah, p. 78b–79a. The righteous, those who are more consciously connected with their deeper selves, have a clear knowledge as to when they are about to pass on. *Medrash Rabbah*, Bamidbar, 19:17.

* The Ramak, and later the Arizal, reconcile these two opinions regarding when the Tzeil leaves the body (either the night of Hashanah Rabbah or thirty days before death) by saying that it leaves on the night of Hashanah Rabbah and returns, then leaves again thirty days before death. *Pardes Rimonim*, Sha'ar 31, Chap. 4. *Sha'ar HaKavanos*, Inyan Sukkos, Derush 6. See also, *Ma'avar Yavak*,

Ma'amor 2, Chap. 2.

* All agree that with Teshuvah all decrees can be annulled, even when the Tzeil has already departed. *Sefer Chassidim*, Chap. 452. *Sefer Ha'emunos*, Sha'ar 6, Chap. 4, p. 62. *Ma'avar Yavak*, Ma'amor 3, Chap. 25.

* Concerning not seeing the soul leave the body. *Emunos VeDeyos*, Ma'amor 6:7. According to Rebbe Saddiah the soul is a "substance," albeit a refined and undetectable one.

* Regarding the Nehurah and the sages. *Kesuvos*, 17a and 77b. Torah sources write that before a righteous person passes on a radiant light emanates from above them. *Sefer Chassidim*, Chap. 370. This is connected with the ray of light that streamed from the head of Moshe. *Medrash Rabbah*, Shemos, 47. *Ma'avar Yavak*, Ma'amor 1, Chap. 8.

* Regarding the Nefesh Ha'mekayem and Nefesh Ha'mecahye. The Freiediker Rebbe, *Sefer HaMa'amorim 5694*, p. 29.

* For the first three days the soul hovers above the body thinking it will return. When, after three days it sees that the face has changed, it leaves the body and departs. Yerushalmi, *Moed Katan*, Chap. 3, Halacha 5. *Medrash Rabbah*, Bereishis, Parsha 100, Chap. 7. *Medrash Rabbah*, Vayikra, Parsha 18, Chap. 1.

* The first three days are intended for weeping. *Moed Katan*, 27b. Rambam, *Hilchos Avel*, Chap.13, Halacha 11. *Tur*, Yoreh Deah, 394:1. One who does not weep is Megunah / disgraceful. Ramban, *Torahs Ha'Adam*, Hakdamah. See also *Emek Davar* (Netziv), Vayikra, 10:3. Some have the custom of withholding condolences or not visiting the bereaved for the first three days. *KalBo*, Chap. 4:2. *Gesher Hachayim*, Part 1, Chap. 20:5. *Darchei Chesed*, Chap. 25:5. See also, *Ydei Moshe*, on Medrash Rabbah, Vayikra, Parsha 18:1.

* The period of mourning is meant to console the mourners, as well as to console the soul. Rambam, *Hilchos Avel*, 14:7.

* The first seven days after a person passes on are a time of mourning, known as Shiva. Yerushalmi, *Moed Katan*, Chap. 3, Halacha 5. *Moed Katan*, 20a. Moshe is traditionally held to have instituted this custom of Shiva. Yerushalmi, *Kesuvos* Chapter 1, Halacha 1. Rambam, *Hilchos Avel*, Chap. 1, Halacha 1. Though the

custom was practiced years earlier. See *Rashi*, Bereishis,7:4. Bereishis, 50:10).

* For the first seven days after death, the soul goes to the house where it lived and then to the grave, and from the grave to the house. *Zohar* 1, p. 218b–219a. See also *Pirkei De'rebbe Eliezer*, Chap. 34. The Makif of the Nefesh roams from the grave to the house and then back again for the first seven days. It desires to be in both places. The Arizal, *Likutei Torah LeAriZal*, Parshas Vayechi, p. 118. See also *Zohar* 1, p. 226a–b.

* In the first thirty days, the body and soul are evaluated as one, and for that reason the soul is found below; after that, the soul departs and leaves the body here on earth. *Zohar* 2, p. 199b. The period of Sheloshim mirrors the soul's ascension. *Ma'avar Yavak*, Ma'amor 2, Chap. 20.

* The three periods of mourning—three, seven, and thirty—mirror the soul's ascension. *Nishmas Chayim*, Ma'amor 2, Chapter 29. For an alternate explanation regarding these three periods, see *Akeidas Yitzchak*, Parshas Shemini.

* For twelve months the soul ascends and descends. Afterwards, the body becomes null, and the soul rises and does not descend. *Shabbos*, 152b. The soul stays connected with this earthly realm so long as the body remains. As the body decays the soul slowly rises. *Tziyan Lenefesh Chaya* (The Tzlach), *Berachos*, 18b. See also *Ben Yehoyada* (Ben Ish Chai) *Berachos*, 18b. Some sources speak of a lofty soul ascending to such levels that it completely detaches itself from material reality. Rebbe Yoseph Caro, *Magid MeSha'arim*, Parshas Vaeschanan, p. 128.

* The soul can be informed of what is occurring in the physical realms of existence via the small level of Nefesh that remains connected with the grave. *Zohar* 1, p. 81a. See also *Zohar* 1, p. 225. Others refer to this aspect of soul connected with the body as Hevel. C"H, Tikkun Avonos, p. 237. Our sages mention that souls are aware of this world. *Berachos*, 18b. *Ta'anis*, 16a. See also the Ran, *Derashos HaRan*, Derush 7, p. 113–114. For a lengthy discussion on this issue, see *Nishmas Chayim*, Ma'amor 2, Chap. 22. "The living know they are going to die while the dead do not know anything" Koheles, 9:5. This Pasuk refers to people who are physically alive but lack spiritual awareness. *Medrash Ha'ne'elam*, Ruth. See also, *Nishmas Chayim*, 2:22.

* In the name of the Divrei Chayim (Rebbe Chayim of Tzanz), it is said that after fifty years a person no longer needs to observe the Yartzeit. *Morah Horim*, p. 199. This seems also to be the opinion of the Stiepler Gaon, *Orchas Rabbeinu*, p. 75. Yet, also see ibid., p. 300. Rebbe Chayim Eliezer (Shapira) of Munkatsch, *Minchas Eliezer*, Part 4, Siman 33. The final ruling is based on the AriZal and the Yahrtzeit is always observed. The Ben Ish Chai, *Rav Poalim*, Part 4, Sod Ye-Sha'arim, Chap. 17. See also the Maharil and the Ramah 376:4. Note, *Rashi*, in Yevamos, 122a, expresses another opinion in the name of the Gaonim. Support for this opinion is found in that every year, on the day one passed away, there is a judgment on the soul. *Zohar* 2, Parshas Acharei Mos. *Megalah Amukhos* Al HaTorah, Parshas Emor, p. 24.

* Souls will become disinterested in a world and with a people that is unknown to them. However, they may still be interested in souls that are connected with them. See below, chapter 8.

Chapter 7

* Opinions regarding the notion of reincarnation. The 15th century scholar Rebbe Shem Tov Ben Shem Tov calls reincarnation a fundamental of Jewish belief. *Sefer Ha'emunos*, Sha'ar 7, Chap. 4. The celebrated sage, Rebbe Yom Tov Lipman Heller endorses the work by the Kabbalist Rebbe Naphtali Hertz Bacharach (17th century), entitled Emek HaMelech, since the book elaborates on the topic of reincarnation. While all the Kabbalists elaborate on the notion of reincarnation, some philosophers completely deny it. *Emunos VeDeyos*, Ma'amor 6, Chap. 8. Rebbe Yitzchak Ibn Latif, *Sefer Rav Pe'alim* (1970) Siman 21, p. 9. *Teshuvas HaRashba*, Teshuvah 418. The Ra'avad, *Emunah Ramah*, Ma'amor 1, Chap. 7. *Sefer Haikkarim*, Ma'amor 4, Chap. 29. Perhaps their argument stemmed from the fact that they did not receive these teachings as part of the oral tradition. Had they in fact received this tradition, they too would have agreed, see Rebbe

Chasdai Cresces, *Ohr Hashem*, Ma'amor 4, Derush 7. Rebbe Yitzchak Aramah, *Akeidas Yitzchak*, Megilas Ruth. See also *Avodas Hakodesh*, Part 2:32. The Abarbanel writes that many ancient philosophers prove the idea of reincarnation through logic. *Abarbanel*, Ki Seitzei, 25: 5-10. See also, Rebbe Avraham Abulafia, *Imrei Shefer*, p. 189.

* The question of how reward and punishment, the afterlife, and the concept of resurrection reconciles with the concept of reincarnation was first posed by Rebbe Yedaya Ha'Penini. *Teshuvas HaRashba*, Teshuvah 418. See also *Nishmas Chayim*, Ma'amor 4, Chap. 15. See also Rebbe Yechiel Ben Shmuel of Pisa, *Minchas Kenaos* for an elaborate discussion on these issues.

* "Hashem created man (Adam) . . . . male and female He created them" . Bereishis, 1:27. Later on it says that Chava was created from Adam, 2:18–23. See *Eiruvin*, 18a. Originally, humans fingers were attached as one unit, until Noach. *Paneach Razah*, Bereishis, 5:29. *Seder HaDoros*, Eleph HaSheini, Elef 56.

* All souls are rooted in the collective cosmic soul of Adam, which is comprised of 613 dimensions as the division of the body into 613 parts. *Sha'ar HaGilgulim*, Hakdamah 12. See also *Medrash Rabbah*, Shemos, Parsha 40, Chap. 3. *Tanchumah*, Parshas Ki Sissa, 12. *Tanya*, Igeres HaKodesh, 7. According to our sages, originally Adam's physical body stretched from the earth into the heavens, and from one side of the world to the other. *Sanhedrin*, 38b. *Chagigah*, 12a. *Pirkei D'Rebbe Eliezer*, Chap. 11. After he ate from the tree of knowledge, Adam shrank. Kabbalisticaly, the parts of Adam's soul that paralleled the diminished parts of the body also diminished and became the source of "old souls." The parts of the soul that remained connected to Adam's body are the so-called "new souls." And yet there are some souls who originate from a source beyond Adam, these are "the truly new souls." Most people have new souls. *Sha'ar HaGilgulim*, Hakdamah 3.

* There are 613 general roots of soul. Yet, it is also true that there are "six hundred thousand root souls" as the souls that stood at Sinai. How are both of these true? The Rashash explains (*Nahar Shalom*, p, 10) that every root soul splits into 600,000 personas (Partzufim) and each Partzuf, persona, has within it 613 'body' parts.

* Body is a physical imprint of the soul. *Choker U'Mekubal,* Chap. 1, p. 140.
* Souls tend to incarnate in groups. *Sefer HaGilgulim,* Chap. 12. Souls are grouped into families. The Ramak, *Shiur Komah,* Shit Alfei Shnin, Chap. 3, p. 163. The Shaloh HaKodesh, *Shenei Luchos Habris* vol. 5, Kedushas HaGuf V'Damim, p. 160. Generally, children and parents have a soul-to-soul connection. See Rebbe Yonashan Eibeschuvetz, *Tiferes Yonashan,* Parshas Vayigash. Though at times, because of spiritual confusion, a mix-up can occur and souls will reincarnate into other vessels. *Zohar* 2, p. 95b. See also *Ya'aros D'vash,* Part 1, Derush 16.
* Yet the nucleus of the immediate family can be comprised of various sources, and not all from the same root. *Sha'ar HaGilgulim,* Hakdamah 10. See also *Ohr HaChayim,* Parshas Ki Sissa 32:27.
* The name of the child is given by the parents with divine inspiration, in order for the name to be compatible to the soul reality. *Sha'ar HaGilgulim,* Hakdamah 23. *Emek HaMelech,* Sha'ar 1, Chap. 4, p. 4. *Chesed LeAvraham,* Part 5, Chapter 6, p. 183. *Mishnas Chassidim,* Meseches Chasuna v'Milah, 3:6. *Ohr HaChayim,* Devarim, Chap. 29:17. *Maor Vashemesh,* Pesach. p, 333. Rebbe Tzvi Elimelech of Dinav, *Agrah DeKalah,* p. 107. Rebbe Hillel of Shklav (student of the Gra) *Kol Ha'Tor,* Chap. 3, p. 92.
* A name can affect behavior, for better or worse. *Yumah,* 83b, *Berachos,* 7b. *Tanchumah,* Parshas Ha'azinu. *Zohar* 1, p. 58b. *Zohar* 3, p. 75b. See also *Magid Me-Sha'arim,* Parshas Shemos. Thus it is a custom to name a child after a righteous person. *Sefer Chassidim,* Chap. 244. When a child is named after a righteous person, a spiritual affinity is forged between these two souls. Rebbe Elimelech of Lizhensk, *Noam Elimelech,* Bamidbar.
* Two souls that share the same root will instinctively be averse to each other *Sha'ar HaGilgulim,* Hakdamah 20. Yet, if both these souls reach a more elevated state there will be a beautiful love between the two, *ibid.,* Hakdamah 20. See also *Pri Eitz Chayim,* Vol 1. Sha'ar Hanhagos HaLimud, p. 361. *Kehilas Yaakov,* Erech Mem, Machlokas, p. 53b.
* Our sages attributed 248 body parts to the male body, correlating to the positive Mitzvos. *Bechoros,* 45a. See also, *Makos,* 23b. The 365 negative/abstaining Mitz-

vos correspond to the 365 principal veins and arteries within the body. *Zohar* 1, p. 170b.

* Only the "lower" parts of the soul experience individual incarnations — Nefesh, Ruach, and in other places the text includes Neshamah. *Zohar* 3, p. 178b. *Tikkunei Zohar*, Tikkun 70.

* Every person has a Mitzvah that they are most Zahir. *Shabbos*, 118b.

* To truly tap into the energy of the Mitzvah and the corresponding dimension of the soul, one needs to perform the mitzvah with total involvement and intention. *Sha'ar HaGilgulim*, Hakdamah 11. *Sha'arrei Kedusha*, Part 1, Sha'ar 1, pp. 6–7. See also *Tanya*, Igerres HaKodesh, 29.

*What reincarnates are only the levels of Nefesh, Ruach and Neshamah. The middle letters of these three words, the letters Pei/80, Vav/6, Shin and Mem spells Sheim/name Pei/Vav (numerically) 86. 86 is the number of Elokim.

The outer letters of these three words, Nefesh, Ruach, Neshamah, are Nun/50, Shin/300, Reish/200, Ches/8, Nun/50, Hei/5= 613. Rebbe Yehuda Muscatu, *Nefutzos Yehudah*, Derush 10. This suggests that that we become a true embodiment of the Tzelem Elokim, our Divine image, through the 613 Mitzvos.

* While most people need to work hard to attain the higher levels of soul, there are also some who inherit "a truly new soul," which is above the "general soul of Adam" and can thus access it with more ease. *Sha'ar HaGilgulim*, Hakdamah 6.

* Each individual soul has 613 divisions. *Sha'arei Kedushah*, Part 1, Sha'ar 1. See also, the Shaloh, *Shenei Luchos Habris*, Vol 1. Toldos HaAdam. Beis Irr Chomah, p. 120. *Chesed LeAvraham*, Part 4, Chap. 41.

* There appears to be at least one Mitzvah that every person is connected with, excels in, and radiates with its light. It is this particular Mitzvah through which the Divine light specifically shines. The Freiediker Rebbe, *Sefer Ma'amorim, Tav Shin Ches*, p. 240. This applies to all souls, even totally new souls. *Eitz Chayim*. Sha'ar 150:5. *Sha'ar Hakdomos*. Hakdamah. Hence, there is the purpose of rectifying that which was missed in a past life, and also a soul needs to work on revealing the aspect of soul that is rooted within the primordial soul of Adam (See note 6 to *Sefer Ma'amorim* ibid). It is with this Mitzvah that each person

attains Olam Habah. Rambam, *Pirush HaMishnays,* Sanhedrin, Chap. 10. Rebbe Dovid Ben Yoseph *Avudrham,* Hilchos Shabbos. *Nishmas Chayim,* Ma'amor 1, Chapter 14. Rebbe Mordecai Yoseph of Izhbitz, *Mei Hashiloach,* Part 1, p. 177. See however, *Derashos HaRan,* Derush 5.

* Being that every person embodies a particular Mitzvah, when Rebbe Tarfon was sick and his mother asked the sages to pray for him, saying, what a wonderful son he is that he honors his mother so amazingly, they responded, "He has yet to come to half the level required by the Torah" Yerushalmi, *Kedushin,* Chap 1:7. Their response was a way of prayer. Indicating that he has much to accomplish and his special Mitzvah has not yet been fully fulfilled. *Divrei Torah,* Munkatch, 1:56.

* Infinity cannot be divided: "That which is without end cannot be divided" *Kuzari,* Ma'amor 5:18. "There cannot be a part of that which is endless" *Chovos Halevavos,* Sha'ar HaYichud, Chap. 5. Or, as the Chassidic masters put it, "when you grasp a part of essence, you grasp the whole". *Keser Shem Tov,* Chap. 111, Hosofos 116. *Toldos Yaakov Yoseph,* Parshas Yisro. *Sefer HaMa'amorim 5669,* p. 73. *Yom Tov Shel Rosh Hashanah 5666,* p. 522. For an earlier source see, Rebbe Yoseph Yavatz, *Avos,* Chapter 4, Mishnah 2. See, however, Rebbe Rifael Emanuel Chai Riki, *Mishnas Chassidim* (1998), Seder Nashim, Chapter 2:3, p. 69.

* "... as a pomegranate"— If not literally, at least metaphorically (See chapter 10).

* Though it says that the souls of the unrighteous do not reincarnate after three times. This is only when no elevation occurred in three tries. After three times the soul will cease to re-embody. See *Zohar* 3, p. 72b. *Zohar* 2, p. 91b. *Tikkunei Zohar,* Tikkun 32. *Tikkunei Zohar,* Tikkun 69 and 70. *Kisvei HaRamban,* Parshas Bereishis, 4:1. Rebbe Mayer Eben Aldavia, *Shivilei Emunah,* Nosiv 3, p. 401. Rebbe Yehudah Chayit, *Ma'areches Elokus,* Chap. 10, p. 150b. *Magid MeSha'arim,* Iyov, p. 164. Rebbe Moshe *Alshich* Devarim, Chap. 7:9–10. *Sefer Cheraidim,* Chap. 33. *Sefer Sha'ar HaGilgulim,* Hakdamah 4. *Emek HaMelech,* Hakdamah 2, Chap. 3. *Chesed LeAvraham,* Part 5, Chap. 19. *Avodas Hakodesh,* Part 2, Chap. 32. *Nishmas Chayim,* Ma'amor 4 Chapter 14. *Choker U'Mekubal,* Chap. 10:3, p. 122. *Kehilas Yaakov,* Part 1, p. 309. Maharsha, *Shabbos,* 152b.

Ohev Yisroel, Parshah Ekev. After three times the soul is cut off—though not completely cut off. *Shenei Luchos Habris,* Parshas Ki Tetze. After three times the unrefined human soul can come to inhabit other forms of life. Or else that soul will descend to embody an already existing righteous human being. *Sha'ar HaGilgulim,* Hakdamah 5. See also *Emek HaMelech,* Sha'ar Tikkunei Ha'Te-shuvah, Chap. 1, p. 15. *Nishmas Chayim,* Ma'amor 1, Chap. 4, pp. 18–19. A soul must return to its Source. Rebbe Yoseph Caro, *Ohr Tzadik* (1982), p, 122. Interestingly, the Radbaz writes that the righteous transmigrate three times, while the unrighteous will reincarnate as often as a thousand times. The Radbaz, Rebbe Dovid Ben Zimra, *Magen Dovid,* Oys Nun.

* So long as one activates and articulates even one aspect of the soul that soul will reincarnate, even a thousand times. *Sha'ar HaGilgulim,* Hakdamah 4. *Mishnas Chassidim,* Seder Nashim, Meseches Gilgul, Chap. 2:3, p. 78. Rebbe Yaakov Tzvi Yallish, *Kehilas Yaakov,* Part 1, p. 309.

* "The soul that You have given me is pure" *Berachos,* 60b. No person is rewarded (or for that matter punished) for deeds done in a past or future life. *Pardes Rimonim,* Sha'ar 31:7, p. 75b.

* "The fires of Gehenom have no dominance over Tzadikim". *Chagigah,* 27a. Thus, to amend negative behavior, these beings must reincarnate. *Sha'ar HaGilgulim,* Hakdamah 4 and 22. See however, the Chidah, *Midbar Kadmos,* Ma'areches Gimel, p. 12. In order for souls of the righteous in Gan Eden to attain an even higher level, they may need to reincarnate to achieve their proper elevation. *Medrash Talpiyos,* Oys Gimel, Gilgul, p. 370.

* Occasionally, negative acts cannot be rectified in the afterlife and require reincarnation. *Sha'ar HaGilgulim,* Hakdamah 8 and 11. *Reshis Chochmah,* Sha'ar HaYirah, Chap. 13. *Medrash Talpiyos,* Oys Gimel, Gehenim, p. 356. Rebbe Chayim of Tzernovitz, *Be'er Mayim Chayim,* Parshas Chaya Sara.

* One needs to return to pay back money that was stolen. Rebbe Eliyahu of Vilna, the Vilna Gaon, Mishlei, Chap. 14;25. See also by Gaon, *Even Shelomo,* Chap 3:8).

* For the story of the Maggid and Baal Shem, see *Devarim Areivim,* Mishpatim,

Chap. 18. *Baal Shem Al HaTorah*, Mishpatim, Chap. 1. See also *Degel Machanah Ephrayim*, Mishpatim. Note a similar version of this story is found in an earlier Medrashic source. See *Torah Sheleima*, Parshas Mishpatim.

* One whosesoul needs purification will know which area needs work by examining his nature and finding what negativity he is most inclined to commit. *Shiur Komah*, p. 166. Rebbe Eliyahu of Vilna, *Kol Eliyahu HaShalom*, Yonah, 4:3, p. 5–6. *Sheivet Ha'Musar*, Chap 1, 23. See also Rebbe Tzodok HaKohen of Lublin, *Tzidkas HaTzadik*, Oys 49. Rebbe Yisroel of Modzitz, *Divrei Yisroel*, Parshas Bereishis.

* According to the Arizal in order for a person to do real Teshuvah they need to know the Source of their Neshamah, and to know their previous incarnations. The Ben Ish Chai writes that in today's day and age when we do not have an Arizal to reveal the source of our soul to us, Hashem places within the heart of man the knowledge and ability to do what is necessary for his soul's Tikkun. In other words, each person will be naturally drawn towards that which needs Tikkun. If it is a positive deed, one will be drawn to these actions; and if it is a negative deed, then one will also be drawn to these negative actions, and the purpose is to refrain from them in order to effect the necessary Tikkun. *Da'as V'Tevunah*, Chap. 49. p. 114.

* Rebbe Avraham Azulay writes that the soul has various choices before birth: to be rich or poor, strong or weak, etc. *Chesed LeAvraham*, Part 4, Chap. 11. See also *Midbar Kadmos*, Ma'areches Yud, p. 28. See Nidah 16b.

* A rich person works on kindness while the less fortunate work on being content. The Ramchal, *Derech Hashem*, Part 2, Chap. 3:1.

* "The Master of the Universe does not approach man in trickery" *Avodah Zarah*, 3a. Hashem demands only as much as one is capable. *Medrash Rabbah*, Shemos, Parsha 34, Chap. 1. *Tanchumah*, Parshas Ki Sisa, Chap. 10.

* Having a positive inclination towards certain Mitzvos indicates one's soul purpose, though one may also find that in these areas there is greater inner struggle. *Sheivet HaMusar*, Chap. 1, p. 43; Chap. 23.

* "The Holy One, blessed be He, desired to make the people of Israel meritorious, thus He gave them Torah and Mitzvos in abundant measure". *Makos*, at the end of Chap. 3. There are many Mitzvos, so that each person can find his singular mitzvah to excel in. Rambam, *Pirush HaMishnayos*, ad loc.

* Every person is inclined to at least one mitzvah, and by doing that one special mitzvah he attains a place in the World to Come. Rebbe Moshe Alshich, *Torah's Moshe*, Shemini, 9:5–6.

* It appears that good behavior comes to the person more naturally with each subsequent incarnation. *Magid MeSha'arim*, Parshas Lech Lecha, p. 14. But see *Sha'ar HaGilgulim*, Hakdamah 38 in the beginning.

* The area of a person's deficiency or desire is that with the greatest potential for merit. *Tzidkas HaTzadik*, Oys 70.

* A wealthy person who needs a Tikkun will incarnate as a destitute person, while a poor person will incarnate as a rich one, and his Tikkun is thus enacted through giving charity. *Toldas Yaakov Yoseph*. See *B'urei Hachasidus L'Shas*, Moed Katan, p. 306–307. A person with lots of possessions illustrates his need to elevate more sparks than those with less. *Toldas Yaakov Yoseph*, Parshas Bo, p, 150.

* Some souls come down to this world only to help others (*Sha'ar HaGilgulim*, Hakdamah 8), and thus they can attain high spiritual levels instantaneously and at a young age (Hakdamah 7), and will not sin. Hakdamah 8. See also *Magid MeSha'arim*, Parshas Miketz with regard to Yehoshuah. Children who pass away at a young age may possess souls of holy Tzadikim, and there are Halachic ramifications. *Mishnah Berurah*, Chap. 23:5. Hashem spends time each day, say our holy sages, and teaches the young children who have passed away. *Avodah Zarah*, 3b.

* At times, a person may have completed his task in this world and continues living to assist others in their elevation. Rebbe Yerachmiel Yisrael Yitzchak of Alexander, *Yismach Yisrael*, Hagadah Shel Pesach, p. 45.

* Reincarnation into other forms of life. See *Sefer Hakana* (attributed to Rebbe Nachunya ben Hakana, a first-century sage). Sod Ve'onesh Gilgul Al Ha'arayos, 1973, p. 192. *Magid MeSha'arim*, Parshas Vayikra, p. 87. *Sefer Cheraidim*, Chap. 33. *Avodas Hakodesh*, Part 2, Chap. 34. *Chesed LeAvraham*, Part 2, Chap.

47. *Nishmas Chayim,* Ma'amor 4, Chap. 13. *Sefer Habris,* Part 2, Ma'amor 8, Chap. 2. *Ohr HaChayim,* Bereishis, Chap. 1:26. Some sources assert that human souls transmigrate only into tame animals, not into beasts. *Medrash Talpiyos,* Oys Gimel, Gilgul, p. 365. *Kehilas Yaakov,* Part 1, p. 310.

A human soul that exists in another form of existence experiences memories of past lives. *Sefer Cheraidim,* Chap. 33, p. 141. *Sheivet HaMusar,* Chap. 14, p. 218. C"H, Gehenom V'Gilgulim, Chap. 4, p. 243. However, in the case of reincarnation between one human being and another there is generally no conscious memory of past lives (see ibid). One reason people do not remember past lives is so that old prejudices and grudges should not be carried over from one life to the next. *Shiur Komah,* Shit Alfei, Chap. 4, p. 166. Though ordinarily people cannot recall past lives, there are ways one can in fact recall them, such as through:

Ruach Hakodesh, "Divine intuition," which incidentally is available to all, as the Medrash says. *Tanah Devei Eliyahu,* Chap. 9. See also *Sha'arei Kedushah,* Part 3, Sha'ar 6 and Sha'ar 7. *Sefer Habris,* Part 2, Ma'amor 11, Chap. 3, p. 482.

Deep meditation or hypnosis, which allows the unearthing of levels of soul that existed in previous bodies.

Ibbur, "impregnation," from sparks of the soul that exist in Gan Eden. To be sure, some sources speak of a need to remember past incarnations to help with one's present condition. Rebbe Shlomo of Radomsk, *Tifferes Shlomo* Al Ha-Moadim (1980), Pesach, p. 116a.

Some find past-life regression therapy helpful, and perhaps it is. The flip-side is that people, more often than not, focus not only on the past but become obsessed by it. As a result, the past clouds the present, when the point is to be in the now. What's the point of knowing who you were if you don't know who you are? A person should ask this question before undergoing past-life regression therapy.

There are many skeptics who question hypnosis. Some argue that by entering an hypnotic state, people become incredibly creative and can string together a complete story from bits of information gathered over the years, rather than objectively reporting that which they know to be true. Furthermore, people have a tendency to want to please and perhaps they will fabricate a story when told to go deep into their memory and recall. Additionally, a theory has been circling for many years that posits the existence of what Jung called "the collective unconscious" or general unconscious, and what earlier thinkers called "general mind". Carl G. Jung: Memories, Dreams, Reflections, ed. (NY: Vintage, 1963), 138. In altered states of consciousness one can enter a space where all knowledge and wisdom is found, a place that gives rise to all the similar motifs that appear throughout all world religons and cultures. Indeed, just as there is the individual Guf Dak/astral light body that contains all our impressions, thoughts, words and actions, there is the collective Ohr Makif of the entire world, nothing is lost in the universe. There is also what is called cryptomnesia, hidden memory. Sometimes people see or read things without the concepts or symbols becoming registered consciously. Later on, during hypnosis, these images may come out, and some will then assume it is a past-life memory. How many times do we say, "I was just talking about you, or thinking about you, and here you are." This can be because we noticed the person before, though not consciously. In psychology this is called "backward masking." To be sure, there is validity in many of these arguments, yet these explanations do not explain the strong emotional attachment such people show with regard to the lives they describe. Secret fantasy is not a reasonable way to explain passionate attachment to the uneventful past lives many people describe.

* The transmigrated human soul does not become the soul of the creature or object it embodies. *Sha'ar HaGilgulim*, Hakdamah 22. Rebbe Shimon Agassi, *Bnei Aharon*, ad loc.

* The teaching of Rebbe Pinchas of Koritz is found in *Medrash Pinchas* (1971), p. 81.

* Conceited people reincarnate into bees. *Chesed LeAvraham*, Part 5, Chap. 24). Tzadikim who need to reincarnate into other forms of existence do so in fish. *Sha'ar HaGilgulim*, Hakdamah 4. Fish are more evolved and thus do not need to be ritually slaughtered to be kosher for consumption. For that reason Tzadikim who need to transmigrate do so in fish. *Ya'aros D'vash*, Derush 1, p. 24. See also

Ohr HaChayim, Bereishis, Chap. 1:26. *Bnei Yissochar,* Ma'amorei Chodesh Sivan, Ma'amor 5. The Alter Rebbe, *Meah Sh'arim,* p. 33.

* Tzadikim are analogous to fish. Average people are analogous to birds, while the wicked are likened to land animals. *Kli Yakar.* See the Chidah, *Midbar Kadmos,* Tzadik, 3.

* A human soul existing in another form experiences embarrassment. *Nishmas Chayim,* Ma'amor 4, Chap. 13.

* With regards to the essence of the soul there is no difference in which body it assumes. However, for the lower reaches of the soul there is pain in not being able to express itself. The Alter Rebbe, *Siddur Im Dach* (1965), p. 48. See also, the Rebbe Maharash, *Sefer HaMaamorim 5630* (1980), p. 292.

* The body and soul are mirror images of each other. *Sha'arei Kedushah,* Part 1, Sha'ar 1.

* The numeric value of the Hebrew word for reincarnation, Gilgul, is seventy-two: gimel -3, lamed - 30, gimel - 3, vav - 6, and lamed- 30 = 72. This is the same as the numeric value for the Hebrew word for kindness, Chesed: ches -8, samach -60, dalet -4 = 72. Rebbe Yehudah Chayit commentary to Ma'areches Elokus, Chap. 10, p. 149b. See also *Likutei Torah L'AriZal,* Yisro, p, 149. *Shenei Luchos Habris,* Sefer Bamidbar Devarim, Re'eh, Torah Ohr, 7. *Megalah Amukhos,* Chap. 11. *Emek HaMelech,* Hakdamah 2, Chapter 3. *Nishmas Chayim,* Ma'amor 4, Chap.16.

* When a soul inhabits an animal and that animal passes on, the soul then travels into another animal of that ilk. *Sha'ar HaGilgulim,* Hakdamah 22.

* In order to elevate a soul embodied within another form of life, the person affecting the elevation needs to share a soul root with that entrapped soul. *Sefer Hagilgulim,* Seder Gilgulim, Chap. 4.

* Everything that a person has or is inclined to have is a spark of his own soul. *Keser Shem Tov,* p. 50. *Tzavoas Horivash,* Chap. 109, p. 38. *Baal Shem Tov Al HaTorah,* Parshas Vayechi, p. 286–288. See also *Meor Einayim,* Likutim, p. 166. *Degel Machanah Ephrayim,* Parshas Lech Lecha, p. 14. *Tzidkas HaTzadik,* Oys, 86.

*   Souls that experienced closeness on higher dimensions of reality, in Gan Eden will be attracted to each other in the physical universe as well. *Ohr HaChayim*, Shemos, 32:27. *Noam Elimelech*, Vayechi, p. 79. *Ohr HaGanuz L'Tzadikim*, Bo.

*   An animal that eats a vegetable containing a human soul elevates the soul to the level of the animal kingdom. *Sha'ar HaGilgulim*, Hakdamah 22.

*   Without proper intention the soul contained within the animal or vegetable may cause spiritual damage to the eater. *Shiur Komah*, Shit Alfei, Chap. 4, p. 168. *Sha'ar Hamitzvos*, Parshas Ekev, 43. *Sefer Hagilgulim*, Seder Gilgulim, Chap. 4. *Y'aaros D'vash*, Derush 1, p. 23.

Chapter 8

*   Essence precedes existence. *Avodah Zarah*, 5a. *Yevamos*, 62b. *Nidah*, 13b. See *Ramban*, Iyov, 38:22. Kisvei Ramban, *Torahs Hashem Temimah*, 21. The soul pre-exists the body and is more than simply a potential. *Rabbeinu Bachya*, Vayikra, Chap. 18:29. Rebbe Shem Tov Ben Shem Tov, *Sefer Ha'emunos*, Sha'ar 6, Chap. 1, p. 59; Chapter 5, p. 63. See also, *Magen Avos*, Part 3, Chap. 4, p. 87a. *Sha'ar HaGilgulim*, Hakdamah 2. Some philosophers argue and suggest that the soul is created together with the body. *Emunos VeDeyos*, Ma'amor 6, Chap. 1. And that the soul develops and evolves with the body. Rebbe Levi Ben Gershon, the Ralbag, *Melchemes Hashem*, Ma'amor 1, Chap. 2. Chap. 5. *Akeidas Yitzchak*, Sha'ar 6. See also Rebbe Yitzchak Abuhav, *Menoras HaMaor*, Ner 4, 2, Part 2, Chap. 3, p. 194. See *Moreh Nevuchim*, Part 1, Chap. 70. According to these thinkers, immortality is experienced when potential mind (agent intellect) achieves actuality, and thus lives on. See ibid. See also Rebbe Ovadyah Seforno, *Kavanas HaTorah*, in the beginning of Bereishis. But it is not merely through intellectual pursuit but also thorough good deeds, Iyyun/delving deeply and Ma'asa/actions.

Melchemes Hashem 1, Chap. 2. *Akeidas Yitzchak*, Sha'ar 6.

* The seventeenth-century philosopher, (LeHavdil) John Locke writes that all ideas come from sensation or reflection. And the mind is a white paper, void of all characters, without any ideas. An Essay Concerning Human Understanding, Oxford Press: Oxford, 1947, II.2.

* "At least one being whose existence comes before its essence . . . existence pre-cedes essence" J.P. Sartre, "Existentialism is a Humanism," Existentialism from Dostoevsky to Sartre, Walter Kaufmann, NY: Meridian, 1956, p. 290.

* Research shows that memory is stored throughout the brain. Each brain cell contains the information of the whole. Michael Talbot, The Holographic Uni-verse, NY: Harper Perennial, 1992, p. 11–13.

* For the most part, people do not experience accurate memory. Daniel L. Schacter, The Seven Sins of Memory: How the Mind Forgets and Remembers, Houghton Mifflin Co.: 2002.

* Negativity is not indicative of one's personality, but is seen as an artificial ap-pendage, the Rebbe Rashab, *Sefer HaMa'amorim Ranat*, p. 88. *Likutei Sichos*, Vol. 6, p. 54–55. See also *Bnei Yissochar*, Ma'amorei Chodesh Tishrei, Ma'amor 4, p. 14d.

* Negativity is not Nitzchi, "everlasting" *Ma'avar Yavak*, Ma'amor 3, Chap. 40, p. 314. See also *Tanya*, Chap. 25. *Shenei Luchos Habris*, vol 1, Beis Irr Chomah, p. 122.

* One who embarks on the path of Teshuvah is considered as a new person. *Sifri*, Parshas Vaeschanan, Chap. 30. *Medrash Rabbah*, Vayikra, Parsha 30, Chap. 3. *Medrash Tehilim*, 102:1. See also Rambam, *Hilchos Teshuvah*, Chap. 2, Halacha 4, *Semag*, Mitzvah 16, *Ran*, cited by the Maharsha, *Rosh Hashanah*, 16b. Teshuvah is also equated with the revival of the dead. *Ya'aros D'vash*, Part 1, p. 14–15.

* Teshuvah has the ability to transform past malice into merit. *Yumah*, 86b.

* Memory is a gift from Above. When a person does Teshuvah, Hashem ascer-tains that the incident is no longer remembered and is erased. *Tzidkas HaTza-dik*, Oys. 99.

* Teshuvah does not exist in the afterlife. *Zohar* 3, Parshas Korach, p. 178a. See *Shabbos*, 30a. The reason is because this world is a universe of Chesed, "kindness," with the opportunity for second chances, whereas the next world is a universe of Gevurah, "stringency". The Rebbe the Tzemach Tzedek, *Derech Mitzvosecho,* Viddui Teshuvah, Chap. 4, p. 40. Mitzvas Tefilah, Chap. 45, p. 143. See also, the Alter Rebbe, *Likutei Torah,* Pinchas, 75c.

* Seichel – intellect is the world of Gan Eden. *Akeidas Yitzchak,* Parshas Bereishis, Sha'ar 7. *Magen Avos,* Part 3, Chap. 4, p. 90b. The Ramah, *Machir Yayin,* p. 16. After death, what remains is the highest form of intelligence. *Akeidas Yitzchak,* Sha'ar 6. *Machir Yayin,* p. 46, p. 57. See also, Rambam, *Hilchos Yesodei HaTorah,* Chap. 4, Halacha 9. The individual soul merges with the Seichel Ha'poel, "the active intellect". Rebbe Levi Ben Gershon, *Melchemes Hashem,* Ma'amor 1, Chap. 6 and Chap. 11. Or, as others call it Seichel Ha'kelali/ the General Intelligence. Rebbe Shem Tov Ben Yoseph Ibn Falaquera, *Sefer HaNefesh* (1970), Chap. 20, p. 35.

* Gan Eden is not only for philosophers, the lovers of learning, but "Kaal Yisrael / All of Israel have a portion in the World to Come". *Sanhedrin*, Chap.10, Mishnah 1. In this context, the World to Come refers to Gan Eden, life after life, not the redeemed world of the future, the World to Come. *Kesef Mishnah* on Hilchos Teshuvah, Chap. 3, Halacha 5. It is the love and fear of Hashem that bestows immortality. Rebbe Chasdai Cresces, *Ohr Hashem*, Ma'amor 3. All good people experience immortality. Rambam, *Moreh Nevuchim*, Part 2, Chap. 27. Hilchos Teshuvah, Chap. 3, Halacha 5. See also *Sefer Haikkarim*, Ma'amor 4, Chap. 31.

* We create Olam Ha'bah. Rebbe Chayim Voloshin, *Ruach Chayim*, Avos, Mishnah Kaal Yisrael. *Nefesh HaChayim*, Sha'ar 1, Chap 12. There is the potential Gan Eden that was created in the beginning of time, and through our actions in this world we create Gan Eden, Olam Habah, in actuality. Note, *Zohar* 1, p. 120a. *Medrash Shemuel,* Avos, 5:5.

* Gan Eden exists within the Sefira of Binah. Rebbe Yoseph Gikatala, *Sha'arei Orah*, Sha'ar 8. See also *Rabbeinu Bachya*, Vayikra, Chap. 18:29 at the end. The

Ramak, *Pardes Rimonim*, Sha'ar 8:9. Sha'ar 23:3. Rebbe Avraham Azulay, *Chesed LeAvraham*, Part 5, Chap. 52. The Alter Rebbe, *Likkutei Torah*, 4:88. Rebbe Yaakov Tzvi Yallish, *Kehilas Yaakov*, Gan Eden 10, p. 3a. There is no greater reward for the righteous than when he is given the intelligence to discover how to serve his Creator. *Kedushas Levi*, Likutim, p. 107a–b. There is Gan Eden ha'Tachton/ lower Gan Eden, where souls experience the revelation of G-dliness as an emotional revelation, and there is Gan Eden HaElyon /higher Gan Eden where the experience is felt as a cognitive experience, as profound insights into Divine Truths are revealed.

* Gan Eden is where the soul basks in and is satiated from the ray of the Eternal Light. *Tagmulei Ha'Nefesh*. Part 2. p. 20b.

* Movement and spiritual growth are continuous, even in the afterlife, end of *Berachos*. See also *Tanya*, Igeres Hakodesh, 17. The soul experiences expansion through the study of Torah. *ibid. Medrash Rabbah*, Vayikra 11:8. *Medrash Koheles Rabbah*, 2:1, 5:18. *Yalkut*, Yeshayahu 429. Still, the soul only gains awareness in accordance to the level it attained on earth. *Zohar* 1, p. 185a. Alter Rebbe *Shulchan Aruch*, Hilchos Talmud Torah, Chap. 2, Halacha 13. *Likutei Torah*, Pinchas, 75c. The Rebbe Rashab, *Sefer HaMa'amorim Nun Dalet*, p. 232. *Nun Ches*, p. 115. Thus, unlike drastic movement here on earth, in the world of the soul "movement" is relatively incremental and slow. However, if one inspires others to do good and they continue to do so, even after his demise that soul will ascend with leaps and bounds. *Beis Ha'Levi* (Brisk), Hosofos, Chap. 30, in the name of the Gra. The righteous grieve over death, realizing the wonderful accomplishments that can only be achieved in this world. *Sefer Haikkarim*, Ma'amor 4, Chap. 31. See also *Melchemes Hashem*, Ma'amor 1, Chap. 13.

* The idea that the mind is selective rather than indiscriminate has been developed by the French-Jewish philosopher Henri Bergson. The Creative Mind, An Introduction To Metaphysics (NY: Citadel Press, 1992), p. 135–137. See also William James, On Psychical Research, (NY: Viking Press, 1960), p. 292. Malcolm M. Moncrieff, The Clairvoyant Theory of Perception, (London: Faber & Faber, 1951), p. 7. And a person is capable of remembering everything that has ever happened to him. Aldous Huxley, The Doors of Perception and Heaven and Hell, (HarperCollins, 1990). After life, when the filter is gone, there can be total memory. Henri Bergson, Matter and Memory, (MIT Press: reissue edition, 1990).

* It is estimated that unconscious processing appears to be something around ten billion bits a second, whereas the conscious experience processes something like ten to thirty bits a second. Tor Norretranders, The User Illusion: Cutting Consciousness Down to Size, (New York: Viking, 1998), p. 143–144.

* Aristotle believed that when a person is terminally ill he is able to peer into the future due to the strengthening of his imagination. The latter is no longer distracted by the interference of the sensory powers. Rebbe Shimon Ben Tzemach Duran, explains this idea. *Magen Avos*, Part 3, Chapter 4. During the period of dying, as the body becomes weakened and the senses less pronounced, heightened soul awareness becomes obtainable. Rebbe Menachem Recanti, Parshas Vayera, p. 24a. See also *Ma'avar Yavak*, Ma'amor 1, Chap. 32, p. 185. *Nishmas Chayim*, Ma'amor 3, Chap. 5, p. 196–197. Nearing death, the soul is more aloof. Therefore this is an opportune time to receive blessings from souls in this state. Rebbe Ovadyah *Seforno*, Parshas Toldos, Chap. 27:2.

* The dead are aware of the living. *Berachos*, 18b. See also *Shabbos*, 152b. *Menoras HaMaor*, Ner 4:2, Part 2, Chap. 4, pp. 202–205. Thus they are able to become aware of the pain of mankind. *Zohar* 2, p. 16b, 141b. *Zohar* 3, p. 70b. See also *Teshuvas Maharam Shik*, Orach Chayim, Siman 293.

* The Zohar writes that Nefesh is eternally bound to the grave, and through the Nefesh the soul above can observe what occurs below. *Zohar* 1, p. 81a.

* Bodiless souls can enter a Malbush and thus appear to be dressed in physical form. *Sefer Chassidim*, Chap. 1129. *Ma'avar Yavak*, Ma'amor 3, Chap. 25, p. 289. The righteous have this ability, and they often become apparent as Divine Messengers. *Avodas Hakodesh*, Part 2, Chap. 26.

* Through the Malbush, the spiritually refined garment, souls can become aware and affect physical reality. *Sheivet HaMusar*, Chap. 35, p. 489. Though the soul is continuously aware, only once it enters the malbush does it have the power to influence or alter physicality. Rebbe Menachem Azaryah De Fano, *Ma'amor HaNefesh*, Part 2, Chapter 12, p. 25.

* The dead seem to communicate through dreams to the living. *Meseches Chibut Hakever*. See also *Reshis Chochmah*, Sha'ar HaYirah, Chap. 12, p. 35. Rebbe Yaakov Emdin, *Migdal Oz*, Chibut Hakever, Chap. 5, p. 277. See also, *Tur*, Choshen Mishpat, at the end of 255. *Perisha*, ad loc. And the *Sema* on Shulchan Aruch, ad loc. Though it appears that being visited in dreams is mere imagination, and if someone is told in a dream that in a certain place the food is tithed he does not need to pay attention. *Tosefta*, Ma'aser Shenie, 5:9. *Sanhedrin*, 30a. Yet also see *Chasdei Avos* to Tosefta, where he writes that if the dream appeared without any thoughts regarding tithing foods, it can be a true sign and one should pay attention. Notice the words the Rambam uses: "if in a dream he was told that the tithed food that he was searching for is in a certain place". Rambam, *Hilchos Ma'aser Shenie*, Chap. 6, Halacha 6. This indicates that before the person went to sleep he was involved in tithing But if the person was not searching, perhaps he should consider the dream valid.

* Deceased sages are known to have visited their colleagues in dreams. *Moed Katan*, 28b, *Baba Metzia*, 85b. See at length *Nishmas Chayim*, Ma'amor 2, Chap. 22. This seems to be the case, especially or particularly with the souls of teachers and sages who while sojourning on earth were involved in teaching and inspiring others. *Ohr Ganuz LaTzadikim*, Teitzie. See *Baal Shem Tov Al Ha'Torah*, Parshas Bechukotai, p. 448–449. Though it is no longer the soul's absolute choice whether to come to others in dreams or not. Rebbe Eliezer of Worms, *Sodei Razya*, Chochmas Hanefesh, p. 376.

* "Permission is not granted for the soul . . ." *Sefer Chassidim*, Chap. 1133.

* According to the Zohar, the world receives continuous sustenance via the intercession of the pure souls above. If not for these souls, the world would not survive for a half a day. *Zohar* 2, p. 16b. See also Rebbe Shlomo of Radomsk, *Tifferes Shlomo* Al HaMoadim, Sha'ar Kerias Shema, p. 17. This refers to the souls at the level of Nefesh, the part that remains connected with physicality. *Zohar* 1, p. 81a; see also *Zohar* 1, p. 225; 11, p. 141a, but not the higher elements. *Nitzutei Oros*,

ad loc. Parents, upon receiving their own appropriate refinement, can automatically awaken their children below to do Teshuvah. *Tzidkas HaTzadik*, Oys 112.

* Souls can and do intercede on behalf of their offspring, or simply for the people they loved. *Beis Yoseph*, Orach Chayim, 621. *Magid MeSha'arim*, Parshas Vaeschanan, p. 128. *Sefer Chassidim*, Chap. 710. See also Chap. 170 and 605. Rebbe Eliezer of Worms, *Sefer Rokeach*, Hilchos Yom Kippur, Chap. 217. *Teshuvas HaRashba*, Part 5, Teshuvah 49. *Ma'avar Yavak*, Ma'amor 3, Chap. 23, p. 284; Chap. 24. p. 286. *Sheivet HaMusar*, Chap. 35, p. 487. *Chesed LeAvraham*, Part 4, Chap. 25. Yet some sources write that souls do not intercede for their offspring. *Sifri*, Parshas Hazinu. *Medrash Rabbah*, Vayikra, 4:2. *Koheles Rabbah*, Chap. 6. *Sanhedrin*, 104a. ("The son confers merit upon the father, but the father does not confer merit upon the son"). Yerushalmi, *Sanhedrin*, Chap. 10, Halacha 2. *Avos DeRebbe Nason*, Chap. 12. See also, *Harav M'Liadi Umafleges* Chabad, p. 163.

* Ibbur is similar to a guest: it comes and goes at will. *Sha'ar HaGilgulim*, Hakdamah 5. See also *Chesed LeAvraham*, Part 5, Chap. 20. Ibbur can also be from one's own previously elevated soul. See ibid, Hakdamah 3.

* An appropriate time for impregnation is during sleep. *Pri Eitz Chayim*, Vol. 1, Sha'ar Kerias Shema, Chapter 1, p. 320.

* By doing a Mitzvah that a certain Tzadik excelled in, the soul or a spark of the soul of that Tzadik may impregnate. *Ya'aros D'vash*, Derush 16, p. 424. Ibbur can occur between two people that are alive. *Sha'ar HaGilgulim*, Hakdamah 9. *Chesed LeAvraham*, Part 5, Chap. 20. Regarding whether one can work on receiving an Ibbur, see *Tanya*, end of Chap. 14. See also *Emek HaMelech*, Hakdamah 3, Chap. 4, p. 11.

Chapter 9

*   Gehenom stems from the words Gai Ben Henom. *Yeshayahu*, Chap. 15:8. *Yirmi-yahu*, Chap. 7:31. See also *Emunos VeDeyos,* Ma'amor 9, Chap. 5. *Magen Avos,* Part 3, Chap. 4, p. 89a. Alternatively, Gehenom is from Gei Ha'yashan – 'reward' –or valley- for the one who slept. *Tagmulei Ha'Nefesh.* Part 2. p. 30b.

*   The phrase "going down into Gehenom" is found in *Rosh Hashanah,* 16b see also *Avos*, Chap. 5, Mishnah 19. Yet, as the commentaries explain, this expression is to be taken as metaphor. Tellingly, some traditional sources speak of Gehenom existing somewhere above. *Psikta D'Rav Eliezer,* 191a.

*   The feast is one of the classic Talmudic metaphors regarding a future world *Baba Basra,* 74b.

*   A Tzadik's Gan Eden is a Rasha's Gehenom. Contemplating Torah in Gan Eden is pleasing only to those who have pursued such a lifestyle in the past. For the uninitiated and unaccustomed such spiritual delights may be more confusing than soothing. Rebbe Yaakov Yoseph of Polonnye, *Kesones Posim*, p. 6d. *Toldas Yaakov Yoseph,* Parshas Bo, p. 148. See also, by the same author, *Tzafnas Paneach*, Parshas Beshalach, 59b. The Medrash says "Between Gan Eden and Gehenom there is but a hairbreadth". *Yalkut Shimoni,* Koheles 976. See also *Eiruvin*, 18a.

*   The Shechinah appears to a person who passed away. *Zohar* 3, p. 53.

*   The notion of a hellish NDE is reported in Dr. Maurice S. Rawlings' Beyond Death's Doors, (Nashville: 1978). See also B Grayson and N.E. Bush: "Distressing near-death experience," Psychiatry, 1992, 55 95–110. Dr. Andrew Newberg and Dr. Eugene d'Aquili: The Mystical Mind, Fortress: Minneapolis, 1999, p. 125–126. Though most researchers find no basis for these findings. Kenneth Ring: Life at Death: A Scientific Investigation of the Near-Death Experience.

*   "There is no Gehenom in the time of redemption, for Hashem will take the sun out of its shielded case, the righteous will rejoice and the unrighteous will be blinded" *Nedarim*, 8a. *Medrash Rabbah*, Berieshis, Parsha 6, Chap. 10. See also *Emunos VeDeyos,* Ma'amor 9, Chap. 5.

* Gehenom is darkness. *Tanchumah*, Noach, Chap. 1. See also, *Tanchumah*, Parshas Bo, Chap. 2. *Medrash Rabbah,* Bereishis, Parsha 33, Chap. 1. *Medrash Rabbah,* Shemos, Parsha 14, Chap. 3. *Ohr HaChayim,* Vayikra, Chap. 26:3 (24). *Zohar* 1, p. 185a.

* Gehenom was created on the second day of creation. *Medrash Rabbah,* Bereishis, Parsha 4, Chap. 6, Parsha 21, Chapter 9. *Medrash Rabbah*, Shemos, Parsha 15, Chap. 22. *Pesachim*, 54b. In the realm of numbers, one represents absolute unity, two represents disunity and opposites, three shows a synthesis and marriage of the opposites. In other words, the meaning of two is an incomplete reality. Gehenom as well is an incomplete state; thus it was created on the second day. The Maharal, *Tifferes Yisrael,* Chap. 18.

* "No eye has seen . . ." *Yeshayahu*, Chap. 64:3. See *Berachos*, 34b. See also Rambam, *Hilchos Teshuvah,* Chap. 8, Halacha 7.

* All prophets prophesy regarding what will occur when Moshiach comes, but they do not describe Olam Habah. *Berachos*, 34b. In fact, the Torah does not speak clearly of an afterlife because issues such as these are too ethereal for human comprehension, even for the prophets. *Rabbeinu Bachya*, Vayikra, Chap. 26:9.

* Even Moshe, the greatest of the prophets, declined to offer details of the afterlife. *Sifri*, Devarim, 356.

* The parable of a blind man with colors is offered by the Rambam. *Pirush Ha'Mishnoyos,* Hakdamah L'Parek Hacheilek, *Sanhedrin*, Chap. 10:1.

* Gehenom is experienced for, at most, twelve months. Mishnah, *Ediyos*, 2:10. There are welve mounts of Gehenom so that the entire year passes and no zodiac influence can find merit. *Tagmulei Ha'Nefesh*. Part 2. p. 31a. *Shabbos*, 33b. *Zohar* 1, p. 107b. Though regarding some souls it says they will remain in Gehenom for a loner time. *Rosh Hashanah*, 17a. *Baba Metziah*, 58b. *Zohar* 2, p. 150b. *Zohar* 3, p. 220b. Certainly if one does Teshuvah they can shorten the process. Note, *Baba Metziah*, 58b. *Tosefos* ad loc. *Rosh Hashanah*, 17a. After the period of cleansing they too will enter Gan Eden. *Medrash Talpiyos*, Oys Ches, p. 670. Ultimately, Gehenom (which is a negative) will become null and obsolete, and

the souls therein will also transcend. *Asarah Ma'amoros,* Ma'amor Chikur Din, p. 302. *Emek HaMelech,* Sha'ar Tikkunei Ha'Teshuvah, Chap. 3, p. 17.

* Gehenom is like a sponge. *Emek HaMelech,* Sha'ar Tikkunei Ha'Teshuvah, Chap. 1, p. 15b.

 *After this process, souls will enter Gan Eden. *Medrash Rabbah,* Shemos, Parsha 7, Chap. 4. *Psikta Rabbasi,* 53:2.

* The Rambam writes that the reason there are so many Mitzvos is so that each person can find at least one to latch onto and excel in—and through that Mitzvah attain Olam Habah. See chapter 10.

* Regarding Olam Ha'dimyon. *Keser Shem Tov,* p. 26. In this world of confusion—more broadly viewed as part of Kaf Ha'kela—a soul thinks, speaks, and acts as if still embodied. The Alter Rebbe, *Likutei Torah,* Pinchas, 75c. Note, Rebbe Klunimus of Peasetzna, *Tzav Ve'Ziruz,* 39, p. 380. At the time of death some souls may be in a state of confusion, thus it is better if a person does not pass away in solitude. *KolBo, Ran* on *Moed Katan,* 29a. See *Shulchan Aruch,* Yoreh Deah, 339:3. *Taz* and *Beir HaGolah,* ad loc. *Ma'avar Yavak,* Ma'amor 1, Chap. 24, p. 170. See also *Avodah Zarah,* 20b.

* The Talmud mentions two souls in the afterlife who are fully absorbed and interested in the trivialities of this world. *Berachos,* 18b. See also *Avos De'rebbe Nasan,* 3. Whether souls in the afterlife are naturally aware of physical reality or not depends on their spiritual stature during life. Rebbe Eliyahu Dessler, *Michtav M'Eliyahu* Vol. 2, p. 62. Note *Ya'aros D'vash,* Part 1, Derush 16, p. 409–410.

* It is only recently that the phrase Dybbuk has become the popular way to refer to one who is diabolically possessed. Reb Pinchas Eliyohu Ben Meir of Vilna, *Sefer Habris,* Part 1, Ma'amor 17, Chap. 15, p. 116. Another, older name is Ruach Ra'ah. *Eiruvin,* 41b. Rashi ad loc. The Arizal calls it Choli Ha'Nofel/the illness of falling. *Sha'ar Ruach HaKodesh,* Yichud 15. These are souls that cannot journey onwards into Gan Eden, and are not yet ready for the process of Gehenom. *Emek HaMelech,* Sha'ar Tikkunei Ha'Teshuvah, Chap. 3, p. 16b–17a. This is a form of Gilgul. Rebbe Refael Emanuel Chai Riki, *Mishnas Chassidim,* Seder Nashim, Meseches Gilgul, Chap. 6:4, p. 80. The Arizal refers to such a case of

Choli Ha'nefesh as a sickness of the soul and offers a formula for ridding the body of the possession. *Sha'ar Ruach Hakodesh,* p, 88.

* The Zohar speaks of "wandering souls" who travel to and fro. *Zohar* 3, p. 127a. See also *Zohar* 3, p. 180a. The Zohar calls these souls "naked souls". *Zohar* 2, Parshas Mishpatim.

* The Levush, the garment of the soul after death, can be either comprised of good deeds, or the opposite. *Meseches Chibut Hakever. Reshis Chochmah,* Sha'ar HaYirah, Chap. 7. See also, *Sheivet HaMusar,* Chap. 35, p. 486. The Alter Rebbe, *Ma'amorei Admmur Hazoken,* Haktzorim, p. 450–451. Rebbe Yaakov Emdin, *Migdal Oz,* Chibut Hakever, Chap. 5, p. 277.

* Often, diabolical urges are not Dybbuks, but rather mental/psychological issues that need medicine, not exorcism. *Sefer Habris,* Part 1, Ma'amor 17, Chap. 15. Although, certain Tzadikim have taught that every mental issue is has spiritual undertones, and people who feel and act possessed do in fact have traces of Dybbuks within them. The Rebbe of Lesk, son-in- law of the Sar Shalom of Blez, said that every mental illness is a minor form of Dybbuk.

* The details of exorcism — the prayers, the Yichudim, the order of blowing the Shofar, and so forth — are discussed by Rebbe Shmuel Vital, the son of Rebbe Chayim Vital in the Hakdamah to *Sha'ar Hagilgulim.* One places his hand on the heartbeat of the possessed person, meditates on certain Yichudim, sometimes blows the Shofar near his ear, etc. *Sha'ar Ruach HaKodesh,* Yichud 15, p. 88-89.

* The tale of the Alter was told over by the Rebbe. *Sichos Kodesh,* Vav Tishrei, 1974. Note that it appears these murderers reached their Tikkun in a previous era. *Sha'ar Hakavanos,* Sha'ar 6, Hakdamah.

* Rebbe Yehudah Petaya, a prime student of the Ben Ish Chai, speaks about Dybbuks and their exorcism at length. *Minchas Yehudah* and in *HaNeshamos Me'sopros.*

* For a more detailed discussion on the idea of Ibbur. Reincarnation & Judaism: The Journey of the Soul, p. 108–115.

* "Worms are just as painful to the dead body as needles are in the flesh of the living". *Berachos*, 18b. *Shabbos*, 13b and 152b. This is another way of describing Din Ha'kever, the judgment of the grave and the idea of Chibut Ha'kever, the pounding of the grave. *Emunos VeDeyos*, Ma'amor 6, Chap. 7.

* Nefesh is the part of soul that goes through the process of Chibut Ha'kever. *Zohar* 2, p. 141b–142a. See also *Zohar* 1, p. 226a–b. *Zohar* 2, p. 142b. See, however, *Migdal Oz*, Chibut Hakever, Chap. 2, p. 276. When it speaks of the Guf (body) undergoing this process, it does not mean the actual body, rather it refers to the level of Nefesh, which in comparison to the higher levels of soul is referred to as "body", see *Michtav M'Eliyahu*, Vol. 4, p. 369.

* The anguish of Chibut Ha'kever is psychological, not physical. *Ibid.* See also *Shabbos*, 13b. Rebbe Tzvi Hirsh Chayos, *Maharatz Chayos* ad loc. *Sefer Chassidim*, Chap. 1163. *Sefer Habris*, Part 2, Ma'amor 8:4. See also *Teshuvas HaRashba*, Teshuvah 369. The Medrash says that only the soul experiences pain, while the body lies lifeless. *Medrash Rabbah* Vayikra, 4:5. Several sources write that even after death the body has feelings. *Ma'avar Yavak*, Maa'mor 2, Chap. 1, p. 198. Chap. 7, p. 206. Ma'amor 3, Chap. 41, p. 317, Chap. 42, p. 318. *Chesed LeAvraham*, Part 4, Chap. 52, p. 166. See also, *Menoras HaMaor*, Ner 3:8, Part 3:1, p. 56. *Yumah*, 83b. *Shabbos*, 152b.

* The pain of Chibut Ha'kever is like knowing one's home has been destroyed. *Emunos VeDeyos*, Ma'amor 6, Chap. 7. Or, as others write, like watching a loved one being harmed. *Nishmas Chayim*, Ma'amor 2, Chap. 24.

* Death for the wholly righteous is effortless, like having a hair removed from a glass of milk. *Berachos*, 8a. See also *Moed Katan*, 28a. Thus, it says that the righteous do not experience Chibut Ha'kever. *Sha'ar HaGilgulim*, Hakdamah 23. See however, *Ma'avar Yavak*, Ma'amor 3, Chap. 40, p. 114.

* Regarding Kaf Ha'kela. Shmuel 1, Chap. 25:29. *Shabbos*, 152b, *Maharsha*, ad loc. *Avos De'rebbe Nasan*, Chap 12. *Zohar* 2, p. 59a, 99b, 142b. *Zohar* 3, p. 24b–25a, 186a.

* To forget is a gift. *Chovos Halevavos*, Sha'ar Habechinah, Chap. 5.

* In Kaf Hakela the soul desires to ascend but is unable to forget earthly existence, and is thus torn between the two. *Sefer Haikkarim*, Ma'amor 4, Chap. 33. See

also *Likutei Torah*, Parshas Pinchas, p. 75:3. The negativity weighs the person down. Rabbeinu Yona of Gerondi, *Igeres HaTeshuvah*, Sha'ar 2, Os 18. Rebbe Yitzchak of Acco, *Meiras Einayim*, Parshas Ki Sisa, p. 169. *Magen Avos*, Part 3, Chap. 4, p. 88a. On some level the soul still wants to remain on this earthly realm. *Michtav M'Eliyahu* Vol. 4, p. 169. *Even Shelomo*, Chap. 10, Oys 11.

* Classic sources speak of a Gehenom Shel Aish, "a cleansing of fire", and a Gehenom Shel Sheleg, "cleansing through ice" . *Tanchumah*, Parshas Re'eh, Chap. 13. Yerushalmi, *Sanhedrin*, Chap. 10:3. *Yalkut Shimoni* Tehilim, Chap. 40:37. And the Medrash quoted by *Rabbeinu Bachya*, Bamidbar, 16:33. Reference to the Gehenom of fire is found in many locations. *Berachos*, 57b. *Chagigah*, 13a. *Medrash Rabbah*, Bereishis, Parsha 51, Chap. 3. According to one Medrash, Gehenom was created on the second day of creation, together with the creation of fire. *Medrash Rabbah*, Bereishis, Parsha 4:6. Other Medrashim offer other dates for its creation. *Pesachim*, 54a. *Sifri*, Devarim 37. *Medrash Tehilim*, 90:12.

* Our sages mention seven separate names for the afterlife cleansing process. *Eiruvin*, 19a. There are seven gates of hell. Medrash Ruth HaNelam, *Zohar Chadash*, p. 33. *Ginas Egoz*, Part 2, p. 244. *Reshis Chochmah*, Sha'ar HaYirah, Chap. 13. *Chesed LeAvraham*, Part 5, Chap. 7. *Sefer Ha'emunos*, Sha'ar 6, Chap. 8, p. 67. *Sheivet HaMusar*, Chap. 26, p. 372. *Medrash Talpiyos*, Oys Gimel, Gan Eden, p. 399. *Nishmas Chayim*, Ma'amor 1, Chap. 12. See also *Medrash Tehilim*, 11:6. Others write of thirteen gates. Rebbe Nasan Nate Shapira, *Megalah Amukhos*, Al HaTorah, Parshas Emor, p. 30. Other sources write in the name of the ancient text *Sefer Haplia* that there are 850 gates. *Bnei Yissochar*, Ma'amorei Shabbos, Ma'amor 8, Chap. 17.

* "Everything that comes into the fire (such as cooking utensils), you shall pass through the fire and it will be purified . . . and everything that did not come in contact with fire, (such as drinking cups), you shall pass through the water, (immerse it in a Mikvah, ritual bath)" Bamidbar, 31:23. This is the way Rashi reads this Pasuk. See, however, Ramban, ad loc, for an alternative interpretation.

* Fire erases what was ingrained with fire. *Shulchan Aruch*, Orach Chayim, 451. In the context of Gehenom, see *Reshis Chochmah*, Sha'ar HaYirah, Chap. 12.

Ma'avar Yavak, Ma'amor 1, Chap. 34. *Sheivet HaMusar*, Chap. 26, p. 364–365. Ice takes away coldness. Alter Rebbe, *Ma'amorei Admur Hazoken*, Inyonim, p. 212. See also C"H, Gehenom V'Gilgulim, Chap. 4, p. 241. *Sheim Me'Shemuel*, Sukkos, p. 174.

*   Gehenom is unrelated to the physical. The Maharal, *Be'er Hagolah*, Be'er 5. *Tiffeeres Yisrael*, Chap. 8. See also *Emunos VeDeyos*, Ma'amor 9, Chap. 5. *Kuzari*, end of Ma'amor 1. *Sefer Haikkarim*, Ma'amor 4, Chap. 33. *Tagmulei Ha'Nefesh* (Lyck, 1874) Part 2. p. 20.

*   The Ramban speaks of Gehenom in quite literal terms, affirming that there is a form of distilled fire within Gehenom that consumes the negativity attached to the soul. Ramban, *Torahs Ha'adam*, Sha'ar Hagmul. See also, *Ramban* to Bereishis, 3:22. See also Rebbe Yoseph Gikatala, *Ginas Egoz*, Part 2, p. 197. Rebbe Yoseph Caro, *Ohr Tzadik* (1982), p. 123.

*   There are a number of sources that take the position that Gehenom, as well as Gan Eden, possess physical properties. Rambam, *Sanhedrin*, Chap. 10:1. Rebbe Avraham Ben HaRambam commentary to Bereishis, Chap. 2:8. O*hr Hashem*, Ma'amor 4, Derush 9. *Derashos HaRan*, Derush 7. *Shivilei Emunah*, Nosiv 9, p. 384. See also Rebbe Shem Tov Ben Shem Tov, *Sefer Ha'emunos*, Sha'ar 3, Chap. 3. *Ma'avar Yavak*, Ma'amor 3, Chap. 39. *Nishmas Chayim*, Ma'amor 1, Chap. 10. *Sheivet HaMusar*, Chap. 26. The Ben Ish Chai, *Rav Poalim*, Part 2, Orach Chayim, Chap. 1. See *Shabbos*, 39a. *Eiruvin*, 18a.

*   The "physical" refinement that is experienced in Gehenom is experienced via the Guf Dak. *Avodas Hakodesh*, Part 2, Chap. 33. Or, as others call it, through the Ruach, the Malbush. *Shivilei Emunah*, Nosiv 9, p. 388–391.

*   Shame is one of the experiences that the soul may encounter in the afterlife. *Kiddushin*, 81a. See also *Baba Basra*, 75a. *Zohar* 1, p. 4a. *Tagmulei Ha'Nefesh*, Part 2. p. 31a.

*   The Zohar writes that the fire of Gehenom emanates from within, the soul is aflame with the negative passion of the Yetzer Hara. *Zohar* 2, Parshas Terumah, p. 150b. See also *Ma'avar Yavak*, Ma'amor 3, Chap. 39, p. 313. *Migdal Oz*, Chibut Hakever, p. 278. It is man who inflames the fires of Gehenom. *Yalkut*

Shimonie, Yeshayahu 247, 437, chap 30. The Chidah, *Lev Dovid*. Chap 10. p. 73.

* A human soul in another form of life experiences memory from the time of their existence as a human being, see chapter 5.

* There is a lower and higher Gan Eden and there are levels within Gehenom itself. *Zohar*, p. 141b, 211b. *Zohar* 3, p. 285b, 182b. In Gan Eden there are multiple levels, and souls continuously ascend, from lower emotional Gan Eden, to higher cognitive. *Berachos* at the end. Zohar 2, p. 130a. See also *Sha'ar HaGilgulim*, Hakdamah 22. Souls first enter a lower state, become acclimated, and then enter a higher state. *Recanti*, Bereishis, p. 15a. If souls were to ascend to the higher levels immediately at death, the light would be blinding, much as a person who sits in darkness and becomes blinded when he emerges into the light, see ibid. See also *Shivilei Emunah*, Nosiv 9, p. 389.

* The soul assumes the Guf Dak, the refined body, after physical death, and with it journeys on into the higher and lower realms, until it becomes accustomed to the "light and eternal goodness". Ibid. See also Rebbe Ovadyah Seforno, *Kavanas HaTorah*. The Ramchal, *Ma'amor Haikkarim*, Gan Eden V'Gehenom.

Chapter 10

* Eliyahu's body was transformed. Melachim 2, Chap. 2:11. He entered Gan Eden alive. *Yalkut Shimoni*, Yechezkel, 247:367. See also *Baba Basra*, 121b. Rebbe Dovid Kimchi writes that his "first" body died. *Radak*, Malachi, 3:23.

* "Earth you are and to earth you will return" Bereishis, Chap. 3:19.

* The Baal Shem Tov said that he could have entered paradise with his body, yet he desired to go through the process of returning to earth. The Rebbe Rashab, Sefer Hasichos, *Torahs Sholom*, p. 46. The Rebbe, *Likutei Sichos*, Vol. 4, p. 1031. Although see *Sivchei Ha'Baal Shem Tov*, at the end, and *Baal Shem Tov Al HaTorah*, Hakdamah, p. 34.

* Resurrection as metaphor. Maharsha, *Avodah Zara*, 20b.

*   Resurrection as metaphor of the enlivening of the intellect. *Hayom Yom,* 11th of Sivan.

*   Through transgression one becomes detached from the Source of Life. "Your iniquities have separated you from your G-d". Yeshayahu, Chap. 59:2. Rambam, *Hilchos Teshuvah,* Chap. 7, Halacha 7. See at length *Tanya,* Igeres HaTeshuvah, Chap. 5. By transgressing one disconnects from Hashem, who is the Source of Life and who is the essence of life itself. Devarim, Chap. 30:20.

*   Resurrection as a metaphor for Teshuvah. The Miteller Rebbe, *Derech Chayim,* p. 95.

*   The Rambam places the belief of resurrection as one of his thirteen principles of faith. *Pirush HaMishnayos,* Sanhedrin, Chap. 10. Rebbe Chasdai Cresces argues for different tenets. If the Rambam intended to count fundamentals, he writes, there are no more than seven, and if he meant to include doctrines then there are sixteen. But he too views resurrection as a basic belief. *Ohr Hashem,* Hakdamah. Rebbe Shimon Ben Tzemach Duran, the Tashbetz, formulated three articles of faith: Hashem's existence, revelation, and reward and punishment. *Magen Avos,* Part 1, in the beginning. See also *Sefer Haikkarim,* Ma'amor 1, Chap. 23. Rebbe Yitzchak Aramah speaks of the three foundations as: creation ex nihilo, revelation, and the belief in the World to Come. Simply put, the three are: creation, revelation, and redemption. *Akeidas Yitzchak,* Sha'ar 55. Others sources speak of the whole of Torah as a principle, where nothing is more important than anything else. *Rosh Amanah* by the Abarbanel. See also Rebbe Dovid Ben Zimra, *Teshuvas Radbaz,* Part 1:304. Rebbe Chayim Vital in the name of the Arizal *Sha'ar Ha'Kavanos,* 50.

*   The sages offer many textual proofs to support resurrection. *Sanhedrin,* 90b, 91b, 92a. *Kesuvos,* 111b. There were sages who were able to perform resurrection. *Avodah Zarah,* 10b. See also *Medrash Rabbah,* Vayikra, Parsah 10, Chap. 4. There is a story in the Talmud where one sage performs resurrection on another. *Megilah,* 7b. Though some view the story as a case of resuscitation, not resurrection. *Meiri, Maharsha* and *Ha'Gaos Yavatz,* ad loc. See, *Likutei Sichos,* 31, Purim.

*   According to the Ramban, the time of resurrection is Olam Habah. *Torahs*

HaAdam, Sha'ar Hagmul. See *Targum Yonoson*, Yeshayahu Chap. 58:11.

* Gan Eden is the reward for Torah, resurrection for Mitzvos. The Alter Rebbe, *Torah Ohr*, Parshas Yisro, p 73b. The Tzemach Tzedek, *Derech Mitzvosecho*, p. 15b. The resurrection of the physical body will be the reward for the Mitzvah-action. The Rebbe Rashab, *Sefer HaMa'amorim* 5672, Vol. 3, p. 1212. Note, that the source of resurrection is connected to the Tal, the 'dew' (light) of Torah. *Kesuvos*, 111b. Hakdamah, *Shav Shematasa*. *Shut Beis HaLevi*, Hakdamah.

* "All people of the nation of Israel are satiated with Mitzvos as a pomegranate". *Chagigah*, 27a. Thus "Every Jew has a portion in the World to Come". *Sanhedrin*, Chap. 10, Mishnah 1. The commentaries explain that the World to Come refers to the time of resurrection. *Bartinoro*, ad loc. Even a Nofel/stillborn child, will be resurrected. *Sanhedrin*, 110b. Rashi, ad loc. *Kesuvos*, 111a. Yerushalmi, *Shevi'is*, Chap. 4:5. *Teshuvas Oneg Yom Tov*, Siman 178. *Iggros Moshe*, Vol. 6. Yoreh Deah, Siman 138.

* All good people will rise from the dead. *Medrash Rabbah*, Bereishis, 13:6. *Yefa Toar*, ad loc. See also *Zohar* 1, p. 108a. The righteous of the nations of the world will have a share in the World to Come. Tosefta, *Sanhedrin*, Chap. 13. In the Gemarah, *Sanhedrin*, 105b, there is an argument. See *Rashi*, Sanhedrin, Avol, 110b. See also, *Zohar* 1, p. 181b. *Rabbeinu Bachya*, (Mosad Rav Kook) Bereishis, Chap. 6:12, in the note from the editor.

Since the verse in Daniel (12:2) says, "Many (not all) of those who sleep in the dusty earth shall awaken . . ." Rebbe Saddiah Gaon writes that only the nation of Klal Yisrael will be resurrected, and only those who were righteous. *Emunos VeDeyos*, Ma'amor 7, Chap. 2. See also *Zohar* 1, p. 131a; cf. *Zohar* 2, p. 105b. *Even Ezra*, Daniel 12:2. Rambam, *Sanhedrin*, Chap. 10. Ramban, *Sha'ar Hagmul*, Chap. 11. *Ohr Hashem*, Part 3, 4:4. *Rabbeinu Bachya*, Ve'Zos Habracha, 33: 28. The Arizal writes that only those who belong to Klal Yisrael possess the Luz bone. *Siddur AriZal*, Le'david B'shanosei.

Even those who were not worthy and did not achieve their purpose, they too will be resurrected. *Zohar* 1, p. 131a; cf. *Zohar* 2, p. 105b. Rebbe Dan Yitzchak Abarbanel maintains that all people will be resurrected. *Ma'ayanei HaYeshuya*,

Ma'ayon 11:1. From the commentary ascribed to Rashi on the tractate of Ta'anis it seems that all righteous people will be resurrected. Rashi, *Ta'anis*, 7a. Only the wicked among the gentiles will be excluded from resurrection, although see Ha'gahas Habach, ad loc.

Interestingly, it appears that according to the Rambam, in the future all people will eventually practice Torah, the Da'as HaEmes. Rambam, *Hilchos Melochim*, Chap. 12, Halacha 1. See also *Derashos HaRan*, Derush 7. The Rambam himself, elsehwere, defines what is Da'as HaEmes, and that is the awareness of the true Oneness of Hashem. " One concludes with the Da'as HaEmes/ true faith: how the Omnipresent has drawn us close to Him, separated us from the gentiles, and drawn us near to His Oneness". Rambam, *Hilchos Chametz U'Matzah*, 7:4.

*The sages speak of a future judgment for all people. *Tanchumah*, Parshas Kedoshim, Chap. 1. *Avodah Zarah*, 2a. There is a debate over whether there will be a day of judgment when souls are returned to bodies. The Ramban says there will be such a judgment. *Sha'ar Hagmul*. See also *Rosh Hashanah*, 16b. *Tosefos* L'yom Hadin. The Ramchal, *Ma'amor Haikkarim, B'Geulah*. Rebbe Dan Yitzchak Abarbanel see it differently. *Ma'ayanei HaYeshuya*, Ma'ayon 8:7. See also the Arizal, quoted in *Nishmas Chayim*, Ma'amor 1, Chap. 17. The Medrash speaks of a judgment that occurs each night. *Tanchumah*, Mishpatim, Chap. 9.

* Regarding the concept of reincarnation and how it reconciles with the notion of resurrection, see, *Sha'ar Hagilgulim*, Hakdamah 4. Note: Rebbe Refael Emanuel Chai Riki, *Mishnas Chassidim*, Seder Nashim, Meseches Techiyas Hamesim, Chap. 1, p. 81. See also *Zohar* 1, p. 131a. *Pirush Ramaz*, ad loc. Rebbe Yoseph Caro, *Magid MeSha'arim*, Parshas Miketz, p. 41a. Rebbe Yechezkel Landau, *Tzlach*, Berachos, 58b.

* When someone passes away and is not deserving of Gan Eden, or resurrection, the actions of the family or friends they left behind can assist them in reaching elevation. The Vilna Gaon, *Siddur HaGra*, Shemonei Esrei, Ata Gibor. Regarding parents and children, see *Sanhedrin*, 104a. *Sotah*, 10b, see Tosefos, ad loc. *Ramban*, Bereishis, Chap. 11:32. Regarding friends, see *Chagigah*, 15b. See also *Tanchumah*, Parshas Hazinuh. For this reason, one should say the Kaddish, per-

haps even for the entire year, even in memory of a person upon whom it says will not enter the World to Come. *Shut Chasam Sofer,* Even HaEzer, 69. *Yoreh Deah,* 326. *Maavor Yavak,* Ma'amor 3:21. *Nitei Gavriel,* Chap. 40:4. See also Rebbe Chaim Chizkiah Medini, *Sdei Chemed,* Ma'areces Aveilus, Oys 120. The Ben Ish Chai, *Rav Poalim,* Part 3. Yore Deah, Chap. 29–30. *Chayim BeYad,* Chap. 110.

* Though it says, "There is no Kapara/atonement, for the dead" *Zevachim,* 9b. Rambam, *Hilchos Pesulei Ha'Mukdashin,* Chap. 15:9. This is because the experience of death has already atoned. Tosefta, *Baba Kama,* Chap. 10. *Rashi,* Meila 10b. *Sefer Chassidim,* Chap. 170 and 1171. The Maharal, *Gur Aryeh,* Bereishis, 11:32. Though see *Gevuras Hashem,* Chap. 4. Or, because the burial atones. *Sanhedrin,* 46b. *Tosefos,* Kevurah. Another Medrasic source tells us that even the dead need Kapara. *Sifri,* Parshas Devarim, 21. The living can redeem the dead. *Tanchumah,* Hazinu. See also *Makos,* 11b where it speaks of the death of the high priest, which atones even after the death of the murderer. For the first twelve months, the children of the deceased need to "sign off," declaring that they atone for their parents. *Kedushin,* 31b. Good deeds below can assist a spiritual elevation above. Rebbe, before he passed away said, "I need my children". *Kesuovs,* 103a. Giving charity below can assist departed souls. Medrash quoted by *Rabbeinu Bachya,* Devarim, Chap. 21:8. *Koftor U'Perach,* Chap. 44. *Mordechai,* Yumah, Siman, 726. *Tashbetz,* Siman 440, 8:1171. Ramah, *Orach Chayim* 621:4. *Yore Deah* 249:16. *Choshen Mishpat* 210. *Baal Shem Tov Al HaTorah,* Parshas Vayera, p. 237. So does lighting a candle (on Yom Kippur). *KalBo,* quoted by the Ramah *Darchei Moshe,* Orach Chayim 610:4. See also *Nishmas Chayim,* Ma'amor 2:28. Yom Kippur brings atonement for the living and for the dead. Rabbeinu Yeruchem, quoted by the *Mishnah Berurah,* 621. Rebbe Avraham Ben Chiya of Barcelona writes that one should not think that he will receive benefit from the deeds or prayers of the living that are performed on his behalf. *Higayon HaNefesh* (Leipzig: 1865), Klal 4, p. 32.

* Some souls cannot enter Olam Habah on their own accord, but enter by receiving sparks from other sources. *Recanti,* Parshas Ki Sisa, p. 17b. See also *Rabbeinu Bachya,* Vayikra, Chap. 18:29. Note that the Medrash speaks of "treasures of

unearned gifts," for those who lack their own personal merit. *Medrash Rabba*h Shemos, 45:6.

    *   According to some opinions, even after resurrection (though mankind will live longer), there will still be eventual death. *Chovos Halevavos*, Sha'ar 4:4. Rambam, *Igeres Techiyas Hamesim*, Chap. 4. *Hilchos Teshuvah*, Chap. 8, Halacha 2. *Moreh Nevuchim*, Part 2:27. *Kuzari*, Ma'amor 1:115. *Sefer Haikkarim*, Ma'amor 4: 30–33. See *Medrash Rabbah*, Bereishis, 26:2. See also *Ohr Hashem*, Ma'amor 3, Chap. 4:2. While according to many others the resurrected will live eternally. *Emunos VeDeyos*, Ma'amor 7:5. *Ra'avad* on Hilchos Teshuvah, Chap. 8, Halacha 2. Ramban, *Sha'ar Hagmul*, at the end. *Recanti*, Parshas Bereishis, p. 11a. *Derashos HaRan*, Derush 5, p. 94. Rebbe Moshe Metrani, *Beis Elokim*, Sha'ar Hayesodos, Chap. 55, p. 506. Rebbe Meir Ben Gabbai, *Avodas Hakodesh*, Part 2, Chap. 42–43. The Ramchal, *Derech Hashem*, Part 1, Chap. 3:9. See also *Sanhedrin*, 91a. *Zohar* 1, p. 114a. *Zohar* 3, p. 216a. And when it says, "A lad of one hundred will pass on" (Yeshayahu 65:20), this refers to spiritual descent, not actual death, as it says, "descending a level is called death". *Zohar* 3, p. 135b, as quoted in *Eitz Chayim*, Sha'ar 9. *Sha'ar Sheviras HaKelim*, Chap. 2. See also *Likutei Torah*, Parshas Chukas.

    *   According to many, Olam Habah is Gan Eden—without bodies. *Chovos Halevavos*, Sha'ar 4:4. Rambam, *Hilchos Teshuvah*, Chap. 8:8. *Igeres Techiyas Hamesim*. *Kuzari*, Ma'amor 1:109. *Sefer Haikkarim*, Ma'amor 4, 30–33. While according to others, Olam Habah is the time of resurrection. *Emunos VeDeyos*, Ma'amor 6:4. Ramban, *Torahs HaAdam*, Sha'ar Hagmul, at the end.

    *   According to some opinions in a future time there will be no freedom of choice. It will be a time without desire. *Shabbos*, 151b. See also *Medrash Rabbah*, Koheles, Parsha 12, 1:14. *Yefah Toar*, ad loc. There will no longer be any choices. "The heart will not desire the improper and will have no craving whatever for it . . . Man will return at that time to the way he was before the sin of Adam". *Ramban* Devarim, Chap. 30:6. See also *Meam Loaz*, Devarim, Netzavim 30:6. *Emunos VeDeyos*, Ma'amor 7, Chap. 8. *Ma'arechs Elokus*, (attributed to Rebbe Tordos Halevi Abulafia), Chap. 8, p. 104a. Though the Ramban writes that man

will return to his pre-sin nature, it appears from the Rambam that even within Gan Eden there is choice, not between good and evil but between truth and falsehood. *Moreh Nevuchim*, Part 1, in the beginning.

* Mankind was originally intended to be immortal. Bereishis, Chap. 2:17. *Ramban*, ad loc. His disciple, Rabbeinu Bachya, writes that the opinion of the Mekubalim/ mystics in the name of the prophets is that, originally, mankind was intended to live forever. *Rabbeinu Bachya*, Bereishis, 2:17. See also *Avodah Zarah*, 5a. *Shabbos*, 55b. *Medrash Rabbah*, Bereishis, Parsha 16, Chap. 6. *Yalkut Tehilim*, 846. The Shaloh, *Shenei Luchos Habris*, Vol 1. Toldos Adam, p. 88. Rebbe Yoseph *Yavatz*, Avos, Chap. 3, Mishnah 20. Rebbe Shlomo Molcho, *Sefer Hamefuar*, p. 50. See at length *Avodas Hakodesh*, Part 2, Chap. 19, p. 120–122. "There is no death without sin" *Shabbos*, 55b. See also *Berachos*, 33a. "The nature of their bodies was to live eternally". *Sheim Me'Shemuel*, Parshas Emor, p. 311. The four elements in their natural state are unified, and thus need not fall apart and disintegrate. The Maggid of Mezritch, *Ohr Emes, Imrei Tzadikim*, p. 12. *Ohr Torah*, 391. There are, however, other opinions, see *Tanchumah*, Bereishis, Chap. 4. *Zohar Chadash*, Bereishis, 18:2.

* Adam and Eve had refined bodies, more brilliant than the sun. *Medrash Rabbah*, Vayikra, Parsha 20:2. *Mishlei Rabbah*, at the end. See also *Tukunei Zohar*, Hakdamah. *Baba Basra*, 58a.

* In the time of resurrection, the bodies will be even more refined than the bodies of Adam and Chava. The Rebbe Rashab, *Sefer HaMa'amorim Ateres*, p. 415. The Freiediker Rebbe, *Sefer HaMa'amorim* 5711, p. 209.

* In the World to Come there will be no eating or drinking. *Berachos*, 17a. Some sources write that eating will not be a necessity as it is today. Rebbe Moshe Metrani, *Beis Elokim*, Sha'ar Hayesodos, Chap. 60.

* The Ramban writes that, although the body will no longer need to eat, drink, or sleep, nonetheless olam habah will be a bodily experience:

Because it was the body that got the person to that state.

Since the physical structure of the body has deep spiritual significance. Ramban, *Torahs HaAdam*, Sha'ar Hagmul, p. 305. See also *Recanti*, Parshas Bereishis, p.

15b. *Magen Avos*, Part 3, Chap. 4, p. 91b. In all fairness, the reward needs to be offered to the one who deserves it, which in this case is the body. *Ohr Hashem*, Ma'amor 3, Part 1, Klal 4, Chap. 2. See also *Beis Elokim*, Sha'ar Hayesodos, Chap. 53, p. 487.

* "From my flesh I see G-d". Iyov, 19:26.

* By observing the body, one can gain a greater understating of the Creator *Chovos Halevavos*, Sha'ar Habechinah, Chap. 5. Rebbe Shem Tov Ben Yoseph Ibn Falaquera, *Sefer Hamevakesh*, Hakdamah. By the same author, *Igeres HaVikuach* (1970), p. 13.

* The body is a physical representation of the inner dynamics of soul. *Sha'arei Kedushah*, Part 1, Sha'ar 1. The soul, as the name of Hashem, is divided generally into four elementary compartments. *Tanya*, Igeres Ha'Teshuvah, Chap. 4. The body as well can be divided into four: the head, the torso, the arms, and legs. The Freiediker Rebbe, *Sefer HaMa'amorim* 5708, p. 66.

* The soul contains all forces of reality from the physical and spiritual. *Magen Avos*, Part 2, Chap. 1, p. 8b. Rebbe Yoseph Yavetz, *Avos*, Chap. 4:2. *Shiur Komah*, Torah, Chap. 4, p. 21. *Sha'arei Kedushah*, Chap. 3:2. *Sefer Habris*, Part 2, Ma'amor 1, Chap. 10. *Mei Hashioach*, Part 2, p. 12–13. The *Malbim*, Bereishis, Chap. 1:26.

* The structure of the physical body (as indeed all reality) reflects the ten Sefiros, the basic inner formation of reality. *Ma'areches Elokus*, Chap. 10. Rebbe Yoseph Gikatala, *Sha'arei Orah*, Sha'ar 1, p. 4. *Pardas Rimonim*, Sha'ar 6, Chap. 1–2. Man below is a reflection of "Man" above. *Asarah Ma'amoros*, Ma'amor Aim Kol Chai, Part 2:33. *S'fas Emes*, Adam, p. 26. Rebbe Meir Ben Gabbai, *Tola'as Yaakov* (1967), Sod Birchas Asher Yatzar, p. 12.

* In the time of resurrection, bodies will have become so refined that they will give nourishment to the soul. The Rebbe Maharash, *Hemshech Ve'Chacha* 1877, Chap. 91–92.

* In the time of resurrection there will be a revelation of the Infinite light. *Igeres Hakodesh*, 17. *Torah Ohr*, Parshas Yisro, p. 73b. Until a level of Essence will be 'revealed'. *Derech Mitzvosecho*, p. 28–30. *Ohr HaTorah*, Bereishis, p. 183 and 700.

Shemos, p. 583; Nach, p. 36.

* Moshe's eyes did not falter and his strength did not leave him even in death
Devarim, 34:7. *Rashi, Ohr HaChayim*, ad loc. *Ya'aros D'vash*, Derush 1, p. 17.
Chazal mention various sages who experienced immortality in the body. *Shabbos*, 152b. *Baba Basra*, 58b. *Baba Metzia*, 84b. See above, chapter 4.

* With regard to the Guf Gas and Guf Dak, see above chapter 5. When a soul
from an upper realm embodies, that soul can only be in one location. *Idrah Rabbah*. There are two ways in which the prophet Eliyahu can be revealed:
A) Within a body, and thus present in one location only.
B) As a revelation from a Nitzutz, a spark of his soul, and thus be present in
various locations simultaneously, as in circumcision across the world. Rebbe
Rashab, *Sefer HaMa'amorim Ateres*, p. 209.

* For the story of Rebbe Zusya and his brother., see *Menoras Zahav* (1999), Parshas Miketz, p. 64. There are those who can divest their Tzurah, spiritual form,
from their Chomer, physical form. *Imrei Noam*, Parshas Vayeshev.

* An older text called Sha'arei Tzadek speaks of the prophet transcending body,
through intense meditations, and then seeing an image of his own body speaking to him and revealing future events. *Shushan Sodos* (1784), p. 69b. This text is
attributed to Rebbe Moshe Ben Yaakov of Kiev. See, *Sheim Hagdalim*, Ma'areches Siforim, Shin, 43. See also the Ramak, *Ohr Yakar*, Shir HaShirim, Derisha
2:2. Rebbe Tzodok HaKohen of Lublin, *Dover Tzedek*, p. 96a. It as if he sees his
own image in a glass mirror. The Ramah, *Torahs Ha'olah*, Chap. 14, p. 19b. The
Even Ezra writes that during prophecy, the person who hears is human and the
one who speaks is human. *Even Ezra*, Daniel, Chap. 10:21.

* There are those who can observe their own Tzelem as an objective reality.
Pardes Rimonim, Sha'ar 31, Chap. 4. A student of the Ramban, the Shushan
Sodos (p. 171-172), writes that at the highest level of prophecy, the prophet suddenly sees his own image standing in front of him, and he forgets about himself,
and this image tells him about the future. See also, *Sefer HaGilgulim*, Chap. 64.
Note, *Emek HaMelech*, Hakdamah 3, Chap. 1, p. 10. *Sheivet HaMusar*, Chap. 35, p.
499.

Chapter 11

* Hashem tests the righteous. *Medrash Rabbah*, Shemos, 30:1. *Medrash Rabbah,* Bereishis, 55:2. See also *Keddushin*, 40b. *Yevamos* ,121a. *Medrash Rabbah*, Vayikra, 27:1.

* "And the living should take to heart ". Koheles, Chap. 7: 2.

* At all times one should envision the entire world at an even balance; do one good deed and tip the scale for yourself and the entire world for the better. *Keddushin,* 40b. Ramba, *Hilchos Teshuvah*, Chap. 3, Halacha 1.

* For the quote by Rebbe Shlomo Eben Gabriel, see *Mekor Chayim*, Sha'ar 1, Chap. 2, p. 7. See also, *Ma'areches Elokus,* Chap. 8, p. 98a.

* Chazal tell us that there were three who experienced a taste of Olam Habah in this world. *Baba Basra*, 17a. See also *Baba Basra*, 15b.

* In some areas in life. *Tosefos*, Baba Basra, 17a, Shelosha.

* Regarding Shabbos and Olam Habah, see Medrash, *Osyos D'Rebbe Akiva*, Alef. See also *Otzar HaMedrashim*, p. 439. *Kuzari*, Ma'amor 5, Chap. 10.

* It is said that with regard to Rebbe Shimon Bar Yochai, that he did not experience exile. Rebbe Hillel Paritcher, *Pelach HaRimon*, Parshas Shemos, p. 7.

* The essence of soul is Moshiach consciousness. Rebbe Nachum of Chernobyl,, *Meor Einayim*, Parshas Pincos. See also Rebbe Aaron of Karlin, *Beis Aaron* Bereishis, p. 22a).

* "The Divine spirit shall rest upon him, the spirit of wisdom and understanding, the spirit of counsel and strength . . ." Yeshayahu Chap. 11: 2. Though this speaks of the individual Moshiach, we all recite this Pasuk on Yom Tov.

* "Now Avraham was old, Ba Ba'Yamim," (translated literally as), "and he came into his days". Bereishis, Chap. 24:1.

Other Books by Rav Pinson

———

RAV PINSON ON THE TORAH

———

AWAKENINGS:
Drawing Life from the Weekly Torah Reading

RAV PINSON ON THE LIFE CYCLE

———

A BOND FOR ETERNITY
Understanding the Bris Milah

UPSHERNISH: THE FIRST HAIRCUT
Exploring the Laws, Customs & Meanings
of a Boy's First Haircut

THE JEWISH WEDDING
A Guide to the Rituals and Traditions
of the Wedding Ceremony

THE MYSTERY OF KADDISH
Understanding the Mourner's Kaddish

THE BOOK OF LIFE AFTER LIFE

RAV PINSON ON KABBALAH

———

REINCARNATION AND JUDAISM
The Journey of the Soul

INNER RHYTHMS
The Kabbalah of Music

THIRTY–TWO GATES OF WISDOM
Into the Heart of Kabbalah & Chassidus

PASSPORT TO KABBALAH
A Journey of Inner Transformation

THE GARDEN OF PARADOX
The Essence of Non - Dual Kabbalah

THE POWER OF CHOICE
A Practical Guide to Conscious Living

MYSTIC TALES FROM THE EMEK HAMELECH

NEW!
PROCESS AND PRESENCE
Life in Balance

RAV PINSON ON MEDITATION

MEDITATION AND JUDAISM
Exploring the Jewish Meditative Paths

TOWARD THE INFINITE

BREATHING & QUIETING THE MIND

SOUND AND VIBRATION
Tuning into the Echoes of Creation

VISUALIZATION AND IMAGERY
Harnessing the Power of our Mind's Eye

CONTEPLATING AND TRANSCENDING MIND

RAV PINSON ON THE HOLIDAYS

THE HAGGADAH
Pathways to Pesach and the Haggadah

EIGHT LIGHTS
8 Meditations for Chanukah

THE PURIM READER
The Holiday of Purim Explored

The High Holiday Series:

A CALL TO MAJESTY
The Mysteries of Shofar & Rosh Hashanah

A LIGHTNESS OF BEING
Your Guide to Yom Kippur

THE FOUR SPECIES
The Symbolism of the Lulav & Esrog

RAV PINSON ON PRAYER

INNER WORLDS OF JEWISH PRAYER
A Guide to Develop and Deepen the Prayer Experience

ILLUMINATED SOUND
The Baal Shem Tov on Prayer

RAV PINSON ON JEWISH PRACTICE

RECLAIMING THE SELF
The Way of Teshuvah

WRAPPED IN MAJESTY
Tefillin - Exploring the Mystery

SECRETS OF THE MIKVAH
Waters of Transformation

THE MYSTERY OF SHABBOS
Shabbat Rediscovered

RAV PINSON ON TIME

THE SPIRAL OF TIME
A 12 Part Series on the Months of the Year

VOL 1: THE SPIRAL OF TIME
Unraveling the Yearly Cycle

VOL 2: THE MONTH OF NISAN
Miraculous Awakenings from Above

VOL 3: THE MONTH OF IYYAR EVOLVING THE SELF
& The Holiday of LAG B'OMER

VOL 4: THE MONTH OF SIVAN
The Art of Receiving: Shavuos and Matan Torah

VOL 5: THE MONTHS OF TAMUZ AND AV
Embracing Brokenness -
17th of Tamuz, Tisha B'Av, & Tu B'Av

VOL 6: THE MONTH OF ELUL
Days of Introspection and Transformation

VOL 7: THE MONTH OF TISHREI
A Time of Rebirth & Upward Movement

VOL 8: THE MONTH OF CHESHVAN
Navigating Transitions, Elevating the Fall

VOL 9: THE MONTH OF KISLEV
Rekindling Hope, Dreams and Trust

VOL 10: THE MONTH OF TEVES
Refining Relationships, Elevating the Body

VOL 11: THE MONTH OF SHEVAT
ELEVATING EATING & The Holiday of Tu b'Shevat

VOL 12: THE MONTH OF ADAR
Transformation Through Laughter & Holy Doubt

NEW RELEASE!

THE SEVEN PRINCIPLES
Toward a Life of Meaning and Purpose
A book on the Seven Mitzvos of Noach

www.ingramcontent.com/pod-product-compliance
Lightning Source LLC
Chambersburg PA
CBHW080922100426
42812CB00007B/2346